Learning Spring Application Development

Develop dynamic, feature-rich, and robust Spring-based applications using the Spring Framework

Ravi Kant Soni

open source*
community experience distilled

[PACKT]
PUBLISHING

BIRMINGHAM - MUMBAI

Learning Spring Application Development

First published: April 2015

Production reference: 1240415

Published by Packt Publishing Ltd.
Livery Place
35 Livery Street
Birmingham B3 2PB, UK.

ISBN 978-1-78398-736-8

www.packtpub.com

Credits

Author
Ravi Kant Soni

Reviewers
Wilkołek Damian
Jeff Deskins
Miguel Enriquez
Bala Sundarasamy
Mattia Tommasone

Commissioning Editor
Julian Ursell

Acquisition Editors
Joanne Fitzpatrick
James Jones

Content Development Editor
Pooja Nair

Technical Editors
Vijin Boricha
Shashank Desai

Project Coordinator
Suzanne Coutinho

Copy Editors
Sarang Chari
Tani Kothari
Puja Lalwani
Khushnum Mistry
Aditya Nair
Shambhavi Pai
Sameen Siddiqui
Trishla Singh

Proofreaders
Safis Editing
Paul Hindle

Indexer
Rekha Nair

Graphics
Sheetal Aute
Disha Haria

Production Coordinator
Manu Joseph

Cover Work
Manu Joseph

About the Author

Ravi Kant Soni is a Java Enterprise and Spring Framework specialist with a bachelor's degree in information science and engineering from the Reva Institute of Technology, Bangalore. He has been involved in software development for many years now. Ravi has worn many hats throughout his tenure, ranging from software development, multitenant application design, and the integration of new technology into an existing system, to his current love of writing a Spring Framework book.

Currently, he is a lead engineer at HCL Technologies Limited. Ravi has focused on web and enterprise development using the Spring Framework for most of his career and has been extensively involved in application design and implementation. He has developed applications for core bank, HR and payroll, and e-commerce systems using the Spring Framework.

Ravi has gained extensive experience in all aspects of software engineering, including software design, systems architecture, application programming, and automation testing. He is backed by strong product development experience in Java, Spring, Hibernate, PostgreSQL, and many other enterprise technologies. Ravi is skilled in other techniques such as Bootstrap, jQuery, FreeMarker, Maven, CAS (SSO) Security, Git, Selenium WebDriver, and Agile methodology.

Ravi loves problem statements and really enjoys brainstorming unique solutions. He can be reached at springframeworkbyravi@gmail.com. You can also get in touch with him at in.linkedin.com/in/november03ravikantsoni/.

Acknowledgments

Writing a technical book involves endless research, review, support, and most preciously, my time when I already have a full-time job. Here, I thank all those who helped me with this book.

First of all, I would like to thank the Packt Publishing team for helping me with the utmost professionalism. The one person who has been the roof of this shelter is Joanne Fitzpatrick, the partner relationship manager (at the time of writing this book). My special thanks to James Jones, acquisition editor (level 2), and Suzanne Coutinho, project coordinator, for supporting me in the writing of this book and making me confident to step into this new phase of my life. I feel very privileged to have worked with Pooja Nair, content development editor; her knowledge spans an amazing spectrum. Without her, this book wouldn't have been possible. Also, I would like to express my special gratitude to the technical editor, Shashank Desai, whose vision, commitment, and persistent efforts made the publishing of this book possible in an efficient manner.

My heartfelt thanks go to the reviewers commissioned by Packt Publishing — Wilkołek Damian, Jeff Deskins, Miguel Enriquez, Bala Sundarasamy, and Mattia Tommasone — for their valuable input.

My deepest gratitude and appreciation go to my friend Alok Kumar, software engineer 3 at Juniper Networks, who is even closer to me than my brothers. Alok encourages my knowledge to come out on paper to ignite the imagination of others. My hearty thanks go to Awanish Kumar, Indian Administrative Service (IAS – AGMUT Cadre); Nagendra Kumar, engineering lead at Facebook, Inc., for giving me positive thoughts that work as the fuel to carry on.

Without my family's love, strong support, and understanding, this book would have virtually remained a commodity. My profound thanks go to my family—my mother, Manorma Devi; my father, Ras Bihari Prasad; my uncles, Shyam Bihari Prasad and Arun Kumar Soni; and my aunts, Sushma Devi and Ranju Devi—for their love and support during the writing of this book. Thanks also go to my brothers, Shashi Kant and Shree Kant; my sister, Namrata Soni; my cousins, Anurag Soni, Sonali Soni, Komal Soni, Amrita Soni, Rishi Raj Soni, Anjali Soni, Mohini Soni, Manshi Soni, and Mithu; and my "guruji" Sri Ram Chandra Prasad.

Finally, I would like to thank my colleagues at HCL Technologies Limited. I learn something new every day and enjoy a camaraderie I've never felt in any company before. I am fortunate enough to work with such an experienced team who help me enhance my skills. My hearty thanks to the Deputy General Manager, Gaurav Vrati, for his guidance and strong support.

Last but not least, I am thankful to everyone who supported me in one way or another in writing this book.

About the Reviewers

Wilkołek Damian gained all his experience as a freelancer. After graduation, he started to work on a Polish e-health project. He is an enthusiast of new technologies and is an adrenaline junkie.

He has also reviewed *SoapUI Cookbook, Packt Publishing*.

> I'd like to thank my dear love for providing me with beer and good words!

Jeff Deskins has been building commercial websites since 1995. He loves turning ideas into working solutions. Lately, he has been building most of his web applications in the cloud and is continuously learning best practices for high-performance sites.

Prior to his Internet development career, he worked for 13 years as a television news photographer. He continues to provide Internet solutions for different television stations through his website `http://www.tvstats.com/`.

> I would like to thank my wife for her support and patience with the many hours of my sitting behind my laptop learning new technologies. Love you the most!

Miguel Enriquez is a passionate software engineer with 6 years of experience and is currently working at Accenture as a software engineering senior analyst. Miguel discovered programming when he was 14 years old, and since then he has not stopped for a single day. He studied at the Instituto Tecnologico de Zacatecas and graduated with honors as a systems engineer.

When he is not programming, he takes care of his wife and three daughters. In his spare time, he plays a lot of video games and tabletop RPGs. He also practices kung fu and other martial arts.

> I would like to thank my wife, who is always supportive of my work and has enough patience to watch me code day and night! And now, I am reviewing this third book.

Bala Sundarasamy graduated from the College of Engineering, Guindy. He has an extensive experience of more than 20 years in designing and building applications using the Java and .NET technologies.

He is a founder and director of Ardhika Software Technologies Pvt. Ltd., which specializes in providing quick and efficient solutions to their Indian and overseas customers using iOS, Android, Grails, Node.js, AngularJS, MongoDB, and Elasticsearch.

A certified Grails trainer, he conducts training programs for corporations that want to adopt Grails for application development. He has also taught numerous young developers to write good object-oriented code using Java and C#. He has proven expertise in training fresh engineers to adopt industry-standard best practices and processes in software writing.

Mattia Tommasone is a generalist software engineer focused on the development of web applications, with domain experience ranging from social networking to health and fitness and from data analytics and visualization to automatic deployment management.

He is currently working on the Italian eBay classified ads website as a frontend engineer, exploring ways to test JavaScript code.

www.PacktPub.com

Support files, eBooks, discount offers, and more

For support files and downloads related to your book, please visit www.PacktPub.com.

Did you know that Packt offers eBook versions of every book published, with PDF and ePub files available? You can upgrade to the eBook version at www.PacktPub.com and as a print book customer, you are entitled to a discount on the eBook copy. Get in touch with us at service@packtpub.com for more details.

At www.PacktPub.com, you can also read a collection of free technical articles, sign up for a range of free newsletters and receive exclusive discounts and offers on Packt books and eBooks.

https://www2.packtpub.com/books/subscription/packtlib

Do you need instant solutions to your IT questions? PacktLib is Packt's online digital book library. Here, you can search, access, and read Packt's entire library of books.

Why subscribe?

- Fully searchable across every book published by Packt
- Copy and paste, print, and bookmark content
- On demand and accessible via a web browser

Free access for Packt account holders

If you have an account with Packt at www.PacktPub.com, you can use this to access PacktLib today and view 9 entirely free books. Simply use your login credentials for immediate access.w

To my papa
Ras Bihari Prasad

To my maa
Manorma Devi

It is with your true love and warmest support that the completion of this book has been possible.

Table of Contents

Preface

The Spring Framework is a cutting-edge framework that provides comprehensive infrastructure support for developing Java applications. The Spring Framework handles the infrastructure so that you can focus on your application. It promotes good programming practice by enabling a POJO-based programming model and also provides a good way to structure your application into layers. It is the appropriate time for you to understand how to best leverage the Spring Framework to create high-performing, easily testable, reusable code when architecting, designing, and developing large-scale Java development projects.

Some of you prefer *learning by reading*, while others prefer *learning by coding*. I believe that *learning by coding* results in better learning, which is what I've done in this book. There is plenty of example code and adequate textual description to help you grasp each Spring Framework feature presented. From the very first chapter, you will be able to develop an application using the Spring Framework.

The Spring Framework is an ocean with a number of features. This book covers a lot of commonly used features in applications and has taken care to present code-based examples for every feature. The book is replenished with tons of code and diagrams. Extra effort has been taken to present snapshots of the libraries used in every example and output. For more information about this book, visit http://learningspringapplicationdevelopment.com/

What this book covers

Chapter 1, Introducing the Spring Framework, helps you to understand the architecture of Spring Framework and set up the key components of the Spring application development environment. This chapter serves as a roadmap to the rest of the book.

Chapter 2, Inversion of Control in Spring, configures the Spring Container and manages Spring beans using XML. In this chapter, we take a look at the concepts of Inversion of Control (IoC) and Dependency Injection.

Chapter 3, DAO and JDBC in Spring, grants you access to data using the DAO design pattern and Spring. Implement JDBC support and ORM support in the Spring Framework. This chapter discusses how Spring manages data sources and which data sources you can use in your applications.

Chapter 4, Hibernate with Spring, covers one of the object-relational mapping (ORM) libraries that has wide support in Spring—Hibernate. It covers mapping configurations to map persistent classes and discusses how to configure Hibernate to work in a Spring application.

Chapter 5, Spring Web MVC Framework, lets you leverage the best of Spring web controllers and the Spring form tag library to create a Spring MVC application. It introduces Spring MVC and discusses how we can use the powerful features provided by Spring MVC to develop high-performing web applications.

Chapter 6, Spring Security, allows you to secure your applications against malicious intruders using Spring Security. It introduces Acegi Security System and discusses how to secure web applications using Servlet filters.

Chapter 7, Spring Testing, implements practical testing strategies using JUnit and TestNG. It explains how unit tests work, focusing in particular on the JUnit framework.

Chapter 8, Integrating JavaMail and JMS with Spring, implements the Spring Mail Application programming interface to send and receive e-mails. It introduces Java Messaging Service (JMS) for asynchronous processing.

Chapter 9, Inversion of Control in Spring – Using Annotation, configures Spring beans and Dependency Injection using annotation. It covers annotation-based Dependency Injection and life cycle annotation. It explains how to reference beans using Spring Expression Language (SpEL), invoke methods using SpEL, and work with operators in SpEL. It also covers the text messages and internationalization provided by Spring, which we will learn to implement in our application. This is an online chapter available at `https://www.packtpub.com/sites/default/files/downloads/73680S_Chapter9.pdf`.

Chapter 10, Aspect-oriented Programming with Spring, introduces you to aspect-oriented programming. It shows you how and where to apply your aspects in your application using Spring's powerful pointcut mechanism and discusses proxies in the Spring AOP. This is an online chapter available at `https://www.packtpub.com/sites/default/files/downloads/73680S_Chapter10.pdf`.

Appendix A, Solutions to Exercises, provides solutions to all the exercises from every chapter of this book.

Appendix B, Setting up the Application Database – Apache Derby, teaches you how to set up the Apache Derby Application Database.

Appendix C, Spring Form Tag Library, shows the Spring form tag library provided by the Spring Web MVC framework. The Spring form tag library is a set of tags in the form of a tag library, which is used to construct views (web pages). This is an online appendix available at `https://www.packtpub.com/sites/default/files/downloads/7368OS_AppendixC.pdf`.

What you need for this book

In this book, it is assumed that you have a good understanding of the Java programming language, preferably version 1.6 or later, including the Java basic APIs and syntax. You are also expected to have basic understanding of the JDBC API, relational database, and SQL query language. For *Chapter 5, Spring Web MVC Framework*, you should have a basic understanding of web development with Java, including HTML, JSP, Servlet, and a web container such as Tomcat.

Who this book is for

This book is meant for those who are interested in learning Spring Framework; prior knowledge of the Java programming and web applications is required. No matter what role you play in your team, a developer, an architect, or a manager, this text will help you gain truly applicable Spring skills in the most efficient and relevant manner. It is good to have some XML knowledge, but an XML novice can understand what's happening in this book without much difficulty. It is also good to have enterprise development knowledge, but it is not mandatory. The chapters are based on the core layer, data access layer, and web layer. A step-by-step approach is followed for developing code examples, so it is easy for a beginner to understand the application development.

Conventions

In this book, you will find a number of styles of text that distinguish between different kinds of information. Here are some examples of these styles, and an explanation of their meaning.

Code words in text, database table names, folder names, filenames, file extensions, pathnames, dummy URLs, user input, and Twitter handles are shown as follows: "This `MailHelper` class also contains the `sendMail()` method."

A block of code is set as follows:

```
package org.packt.Spring.chapter10.mail;

import org.springframework.context.ApplicationContext;
import org.springframework.context.support.ClassPathXml
ApplicationContext;

public class MailerTest
{
    public static void main( String[] args )
    {
        //Create the application context
        ApplicationContext context =
            new ClassPathXmlApplicationContext("Spring.xml");
```

When we wish to draw your attention to a particular part of a code block, the relevant lines or items are set in bold:

```
@Configuration
@Import(ConfigA.class)
public class ConfigB {

    @Bean
    public HrService hrService() {
        return new HrService();
    }

}
```

New terms and **important words** are shown in bold. Words that you see on the screen, in menus or dialog boxes for example, appear in the text like this: "Right-click on `MainClass.java` and navigate to **Run As | Java Application**."

 Warnings or important notes appear in a box like this.

 Tips and tricks appear like this.

Reader feedback

Feedback from our readers is always welcome. Let us know what you think about this book—what you liked or may have disliked. Reader feedback is important for us to develop titles that you really get the most out of.

To send us general feedback, simply send an e-mail to feedback@packtpub.com, and mention the book title via the subject of your message.

If there is a topic that you have expertise in and you are interested in either writing or contributing to a book, see our author guide on www.packtpub.com/authors.

Customer support

Now that you are the proud owner of a Packt book, we have a number of things to help you to get the most from your purchase.

Downloading the example code

You can download the example code files for all Packt books you have purchased from your account at http://www.packtpub.com. If you purchased this book elsewhere, you can visit http://www.packtpub.com/support and register to have the files e-mailed directly to you.

Errata

Although we have taken every care to ensure the accuracy of our content, mistakes do happen. If you find a mistake in one of our books—maybe a mistake in the text or the code—we would be grateful if you could report this to us. By doing so, you can save other readers from frustration and help us improve subsequent versions of this book. If you find any errata, please report them by visiting http://www.packtpub.com/submit-errata, selecting your book, clicking on the **Errata Submission Form** link, and entering the details of your errata. Once your errata are verified, your submission will be accepted and the errata will be uploaded to our website or added to any list of existing errata under the Errata section of that title.

To view the previously submitted errata, go to https://www.packtpub.com/books/content/support and enter the name of the book in the search field. The required information will appear under the **Errata** section.

Piracy

Piracy of copyright material on the Internet is an ongoing problem across all media. At Packt, we take the protection of our copyright and licenses very seriously. If you come across any illegal copies of our works, in any form, on the Internet, please provide us with the location address or website name immediately so that we can pursue a remedy.

Please contact us at copyright@packtpub.com with a link to the suspected pirated material.

We appreciate your help in protecting our authors, and our ability to bring you valuable content.

Questions

You can contact us at questions@packtpub.com if you are having a problem with any aspect of the book, and we will do our best to address it.

1
Introducing the Spring Framework

In this chapter, we'll introduce you to the Spring Framework. We'll also summarize some of the other features of Spring. We'll then discuss the Spring Architecture as well as the benefits of the Spring Framework. We will create your first application in Spring and will look into understanding the packaging structure of the Spring Framework. This chapter serves as a road map to the rest of this book.

The following topics will be covered in this chapter:

- Introducing Spring
- Spring Framework Architecture
- Benefits of the Spring Framework
- Creating a first application in Spring

Spring is an open source framework, which was created by Rod Johnson. He addressed the complexity of enterprise application development and described a simpler, alternative approach in his book *Expert One-on-One J2EE Design and Development, Wrox*.

Spring is now a long-time de-facto standard for Java enterprise software development. The framework was designed with developer productivity in mind, and it makes it easier to work with the existing Java and Java EE APIs. Using Spring, we can develop standalone applications, desktop applications, two-tier applications, web applications, distributed applications, enterprise applications, and so on.

As the title implies, we introduce you to the Spring Framework and then explore Spring's core modules. Upon finishing this chapter, you will be able to build a sample Java application using Spring. If you are already familiar with the Spring Framework, then you might want to skip this chapter and proceed straight to *Chapter 2, Inversion of Control in Spring*.

Introducing Spring

Spring is a lightweight **Inversion of Control (IoC)** and aspect-oriented container framework. Historically, it was created to alleviate the complexity of the then J2EE standard, often giving an alternative model. Any Java EE application can benefit from the Spring Framework in terms of simplicity, loose coupling, and testability.

It remains popular due to its simple approach to building applications. It also offers a consistent programming model for different kinds of technologies, be they for data access or messaging infrastructure. The framework allows developers to target discrete problems and build solutions specifically for them.

The Spring Framework provides comprehensive infrastructure support for developing Java EE applications, where the Spring Framework handles the infrastructure and so developers can focus on application development.

Considering a scenario of JDBC application without using the Spring Framework, we have a lot of boilerplate code that needs to be written over and over again to accomplish common tasks. Whereas in Spring JDBC application, which internally uses plain JDBC, the `JdbcTemplate` class eliminates boilerplate code and allows the programmer to just concentrate on application-specific logics development.

- For a plain JDBC application without Spring, follow these steps:
    1. Register driver with the `DriverManager` service.
    2. Establish a connection with the database.
    3. Create a statement object.
    4. Prepare and execute an SQL query.
    5. Gather and process the result.
    6. Perform exception handling.
    7. Perform transaction management.
    8. Close JDBC object.

- For a Spring JDBC application (internally uses plain JDBC), follow these steps:
    1. Get access to `JdbcTemplate`.
    2. Prepare and execute an SQL query.
    3. Gather and process the result.

Spring's main aim is to promote good programming practice such as coding to interfaces and make Java EE easier to use. It does this by enabling a **Plain Old Java Object (POJO)**-based programming model, which can be applicable in a wide range of development environments.

Technically, a POJO is any ordinary object that should not implement pre-specified interface or extend pre-specified class or contains annotation.

The following is the code for the `POJOClass.java` class:

```
package com.packt.spring.chapter1;

/* This is a simple Java Class - POJO */
public class POJOClass {

    private String message;

    public String getMessage() {
        return this.message;
    }

    public void setMessage(String message) {
        this.message = message;
    }
}
```

In the preceding code snippet, we have `POJOClass` containing a field and corresponding `getter` and `setter` methods. This class is a POJO class as it is not extending or implementing any class or predefined interface of Spring API.

Spring is modular, allowing you to use only those parts that you need, without having to bring in extra complexity. The Spring Framework can be used either for all layer implementations or for the development of particular layer of an application.

Features of Spring

The Spring Framework contains the following features:

- **Lightweight**: Spring is described as a lightweight framework when it comes to size and transparency. A lightweight framework helps in reducing complexity in application code. It also helps in avoiding unnecessary complexity in its own functioning. A lightweight framework won't have a high startup time and will run in any environment. A lightweight framework also won't involve huge binary dependencies.

- **Non-intrusive**: This means that your domain logic code has no dependencies on the framework itself. The Spring Framework is designed to be non-intrusive. The object in a Spring-enabled application typically has no dependencies on any predefined interface or class given by Spring API. Thus, Spring can configure application objects that don't import Spring APIs.

- **Inversion of Control (IoC)**: Spring's container is a lightweight container that contains Spring beans and manages their life cycle. The core container of the Spring Framework provides an implementation for IoC supporting injection. IoC is an architectural pattern that describes the Dependency Injection needs to be done by external entity rather than creating the dependencies by the component itself. Objects are passively given their dependencies rather than creating dependent objects for themselves. Here, you describe which components need which service, and you don't directly connect your services and components together in your code. Let's consider an example: we have two classes `Zoo` and `Animal`, where `Zoo` has an object of `Animal`:

    ○ **Without Dependency Injection**: This is a common way to instantiate an object is with a `new` operator. Here, the `Zoo` class contains the object `Animal` that we have instantiated using a `new` operator, as shown in the following screenshot:

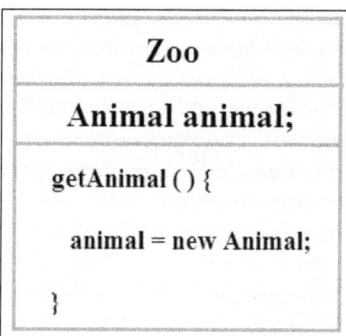

○ **With Dependency Injection**: Here, we supply the job of instantiating to a third party, as shown in following screenshot. zoo needs the object of Animal to operate, but it outsources instantiation job to some third party that decides the moment of instantiation and the type to use in order to create the instance. This process of outsourcing instantiation is called dependency injection.

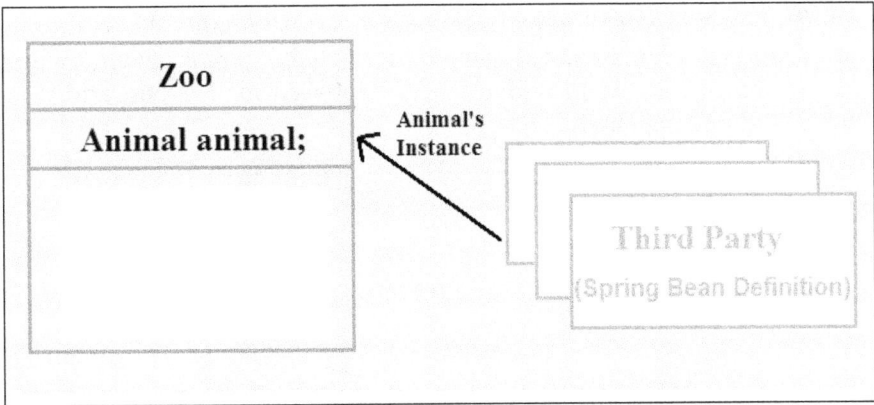

The Spring Framework promotes loose coupling by using the technique known as IoC. We'll talk more about IoC in *Chapter 2, Inversion of Control in Spring*.

• **Aspect-oriented Programming (AOP)**: This refers to the programming paradigm that isolates supporting functions from the main program's business logic. It allows a developer to build the core functionality of a system without being aware of additional requirements.

AOP is used in the Spring Framework to provide declarative aspects such as transactions and security. Here, application objects perform business logic and are not responsible for other system concerns such as logging, security, auditing, locking, and event handling. AOP is a method of applying middleware services such as security service, and transaction management service on Spring's application.

Let's consider a payroll management application where there will be **Employee Service**, **HR Service**, and **Payroll Service**, as shown in the following figure, which will perform some functional requirement to the system such as add/update employee details, remove employee, browse employee details, and much more. While implementing business functionality, this type of application would also require nonfunctional capabilities such as role-based access and logging details. AOP leaves an application component to focus on business functionality. Here, the core application implements the business functionality and is covered with layers of functionality provided by AOP for security, logging, and transaction management.

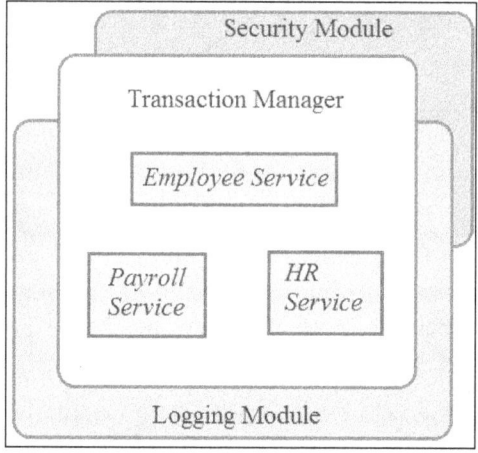

Aspects can be added or removed as needed without changing your code. Spring aspects can be configured using its own IoC container. Spring AOP includes advisors that contain `advice` and `pointcut` filtering.

- **JDBC exception handling**: The JDBC abstraction layer of the Spring Framework provides an exception hierarchy. It shortens the error handling strategy in JDBC. This is one of the areas where Spring really helps in reducing the amount of boilerplate code we need to write in the exception handling. We'll talk more on Spring JDBC in *Chapter 3, DAO and JDBC in Spring*.

- **Spring MVC Framework**: This helps in building robust and maintainable web applications. It uses IoC that provides separation of controller logic. Spring MVC Framework, which is a part of the Spring Framework licensed under the term of Apache license, is an open source web application framework. Spring MVC Framework offers utility classes to handle some of the most common tasks in web application development. We'll discuss more about Spring Web MVC Framework in *Chapter 5, Spring Web MVC Framework*.

- **Spring Security**: This provides a declarative security mechanism for Spring-based applications, which is a critical aspect of many applications. We'll add Spring Security to our web applications in *Chapter 6, Spring Security*.

Other features of Spring

The following are the other features provided by the Spring Framework:

- **Spring Web Services**: This provides a contract-first web services model, whereby service implementations are written to satisfy the service contract. For more information, check out `http://static.springsource.org/spring-ws/sites/2.0`.

- **Spring Batch**: This is useful when it's necessary to perform bulk operations on data. For more information, refer to `http://static.springsource.org/spring-batch`.

- **Spring Social**: Social networking, nowadays, is a rising trend on the Internet, and more and more applications such as Facebook and Twitter are being outfitted with integration into social-networking sites. To know more, have a look at `http://www.springsource.org/spring-social`.

- **Spring Mobile**: Mobile applications are another significant area of software development. Spring Mobile supports development of mobile web applications. More information about Spring Mobile can be found at `http://www.springsource.org/spring-mobile`.

Evolution of the Spring Framework

The Spring Framework is an open source framework that has multiple versions released with the latest one being 4.x. The different versions of the Spring Framework are as follows:

- **Spring Framework 1.0**: This version was released on March 2004, and the first release was Spring Framework 1.0 RC4. The final and stable release was Spring Framework 1.0.5. Spring 1.0 was a complete Java/J2EE application framework, which covered the following functionalities:

  - **Spring Core**: This is a lightweight container with various setter and constructor injection

  - **Spring AOP**: This is an **Aspect-oriented Programming (AOP)** interception framework integrated with the core container

  - **Spring Context**: This is an application context concept to provide resource loading

- **Spring DAO**: This is a generic DAO support that provides access to a generic data exception hierarchy with any data access strategy
- **Spring JDBC**: This is a JDBC abstraction shorten error and resource handling
- **Spring ORM**: This is a hibernate support `SessionFactory` management
- **Spring Web**: This web MVC Framework integrates various view technologies

- **Spring Framework 2.X**: The Spring Framework 2.0 was released in October 2006 and Spring 2.5 was released in November 2007. The Spring Framework 2.x release was based around two themes: simplicity and power. This provides you with the following features:

  - Improvements in the IoC container and AOP, including the `@AspectJ` annotation support for AOP development

  - Introduction of bean configuration dialects

  - XML-based configuration is reduced and XML schema support and custom namespace is introduced

  - Annotation-driven configuration that requires component scanning to auto-detect annotated components in the classpath using annotations such as `@Component` or specialized annotations such as `@Repository`, `@Service`, and `@Controller`

  - Introduces annotations such as `@RequestMapping`, `@RequestParam`, and `@ModelAttribute` for MVC controllers

- **Spring Framework 3.0**: This version was released in December 2009. It makes the entire Spring code base to take advantage of the Java 5.0 technology. This provides you with the following features:

  - Supports REST in Spring MVC, which is one of the beautiful additions to the Spring Framework itself.

  - Introduces new annotations `@CookieValue` and `@RequestHeader` for pulling values from cookies and request headers, respectively. It also supports new XML namespace that makes easier to configure Spring MVC.

  - Task scheduling and asynchronous method execution with annotation support is introduced to this version.

- Spring Framework 3.0.5 is the latest update release, which was released on October 20, 2010. The Hibernate version 3.6 final is supported by this Spring release.

- **Spring Framework 3.1**: This version was released in December 2011. This release introduced many new exciting features that are related to cache abstraction, bean definition profiles, environment abstraction, `PropertySource` abstraction, and a lot more. This provides you with the following features:

  - Introduces Cache Abstraction to add caching concept to any existing application using `@Cacheable` annotation.

  - Introduces annotation called `@Profile`, which is used while applying configuration classes.

  - Introduces `PropertySource` that is an abstraction performed over any different source of the key-value pairs. In `DefaultEnvironment`, there are two configured `PropertySource` objects: `System.getProperties()` and `System.getenv()`.

  - Hibernate 4.x is supported by this release through **Java Persistence API (JPA)**. With this release, the JPA `EntityManagerFactory` can be bootstrapped without `persistence.xml` or other metadata files.

  - Introduces `@RequestPart` annotation to provide access to multipart form-data content on the controller method arguments.

  - Introduces the `c:namespace` to support constructor injection.

- **Spring Framework 3.2.x**: This version was released in November 2013. This release introduced the following new features and enhancements to earlier features:

  - Servlet 3-based asynchronous request processing is supported in this release.

  - Supports Java 7 features.

  - Testing of Spring MVC applications without a Servlet container is supported in this release. Here, `DispatcherServlet` is used for server-side REST tests and `RestTemplate` for client-side REST tests.

  - `ContentNegotiationStrategy` is introduced to resolve the requested media types from an incoming request. It also supports Jackson JSON 2 library.

- ° Method annotated with @ExceptionHandler, @InitBinder, and @ModelAttribute can be added to a class annotated with the @ControllerAdvice annotation.

- ° The @MatrixVariable annotation for extracting matrix variables from the request URI is introduced.

- ° The @DateTimeFormat annotation to remove dependency on the Joda-Time library is introduced.

- **Spring Framework 4.x**: This version supports a few new features. Improvements in Spring 4.X include support for Java SE 8, Groovy 2, and a few aspects of Java EE7. This provides you with the following features:

  - ° Supports external bean configuration using a Groovy DSL

  - ° Auto-wiring is based on generic types

  - ° Introduces the @Description annotation

  - ° Introduces @Conditional that can conditionally filter the beans.

  - ° Introduces the @Jms annotation to support annotation-driven endpoint

  - ° Catching support is revisited, provided CacheResolver to resolve caches at runtime

  - ° Added new testing features such as SQL Script execution, bootstrap strategy, and so on

  - ° Added lightweight messaging and WebSocket-style architectures

Spring Framework Architecture

Spring packaging is modular, allowing you to pick and choose the modules that are applicable to you, without any need to bring in the rest. The following section gives you a detailed explanation about different modules available in the Spring Framework. The following figure shows you a complete overview of the framework and modules supported by the Spring Framework:

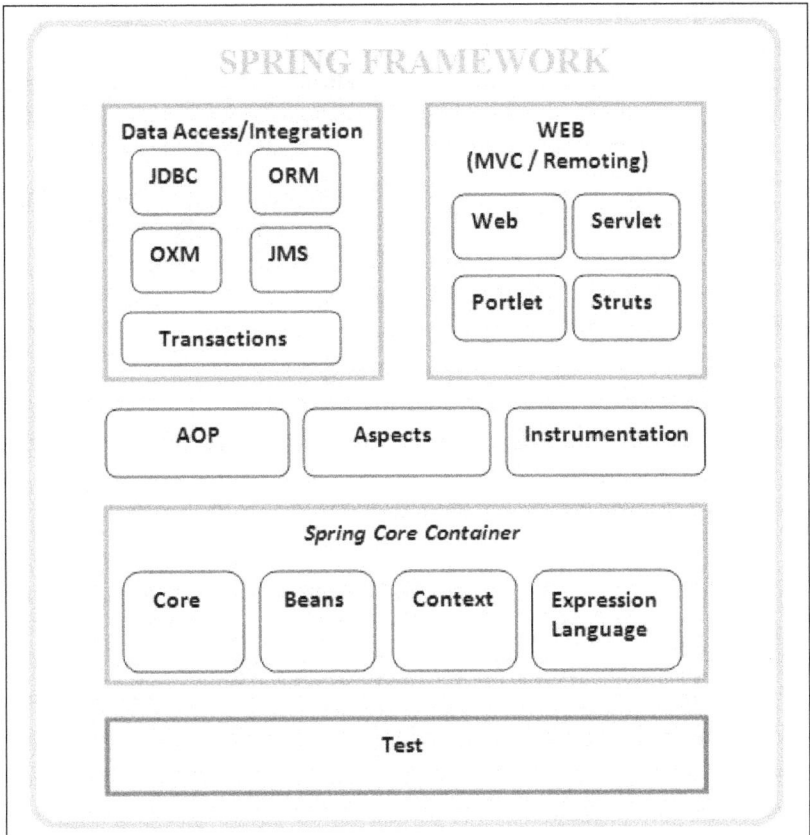

Spring Core Container

Spring Core Container consists of the core, beans, context, and expression language modules, as shown in the preceding figure. Let's discuss these in detail as follows:

- **Core module**: This module of Spring Core Container is the most important component of the Spring Framework. It provides features such as IoC and Dependency Injection. The idea behind IoC is similar to the Hollywood principle: "Don't call me, I'll call you." Dependency Injection is the basic design principle in Spring Core Container that removes explicit dependence on container APIs.

- **Beans module**: The bean module in Spring Core Container provides `BeanFactory`, which is a generic factory pattern that separates the dependencies such as initialization, creation, and access of the objects from your actual program logic. `BeanFactory` in Spring Core Container supports the following two scopes modes of object:

  - **Singleton**: In singleton, only one shared instance of the object with a particular name will be retrieved on lookup. Spring singleton returns a same bean instance per Spring IoC container. Each time you call `getBean()` on `ApplicationContext`, Spring singleton returns the same bean instance.

  - **Prototype or non-singleton**: In prototype, each retrieval results in the creation of a brand new instance. Each time you call `getBean()` on `ApplicationContext`, Spring prototype creates a separate bean instance.

- **Context module**: An `ApplicationContext` container loads Spring bean definitions and wires them together. The `ApplicationContext` container is the focal point of the `Context` module. Hierarchical context is also one of the focal points of this API. `ApplicationContext` supports the `Message` lookup, supporting internationalization (i18N) messages.

- **Expression language**: **Spring Expression Language (SpEL)** is a powerful expression language supporting the features for querying and manipulating an object graph at runtime. SpEL can be used to inject bean or bean property in another bean. SpEL supports method invocation and retrieval of objects by name from IoC container in Spring.

The AOP module

Spring's **Aspect-oriented Programming (AOP)** module is one of the main paradigms that provide an AOP implementation. Spring AOP module is a proxy-based framework implemented in Java. The Spring Framework uses AOP for providing most of the infrastructure logic in it.

AOP is a mechanism that allows us to introduce new functionalities into an existing code without modifying it design. AOP is used to weave cross-cutting aspects into the code. The Spring Framework uses AOP to provide various enterprise services, such as security in an application. The Spring AOP framework is configured at runtime.

Spring integrates with AspectJ, which is an extension of AOP. AspectJ lets programmers define special constructs called Aspects, which contains several entities unavailable to standard classes.

Data access/integration

Spring's data access addresses common difficulties developers face while working with databases in applications.

- **JDBC module**: The Spring Framework provides solution for various problems identified using JDBC as low-level data access. The JDBC abstraction framework provided under the Spring Framework removes the need to do tedious JDBC-related coding. The central class of Spring JDBC abstraction framework is the `JdbcTemplate` class that includes the most common logic in using the JDBC API to access data such as handling the creation of connection, statement creation, statement execution, and release of resource. The `JdbcTemplate` class resides inside the `org.springframework.jdbc.core` package.

- **ORM module**: The **Object-relational mapping (ORM)** module of the Spring Framework provides a high-level abstraction for ORM APIs, including JPA and Hibernate. Spring ORM module reduces the complexity by avoiding the boilerplate code from application.

- **OXM module**: Spring OXM module stands for Spring Object XML Mappers, which supports Object/XML mapping. It also supports integration with Castor, JAXB, XmlBeans, and the XStream framework.

  Most applications need to integrate or provide services to other applications. One common requirement is to exchange data with other systems, either on a regular basis or in real time. In terms of the data format, XML is the most commonly used format. As a result, there exists a common need to transform a JavaBean into XML format and vice versa.

  Spring supports many common Java-to-XML mapping frameworks and, as usual, eliminates the need for directly coupling to any specific implementation. Spring provides common interfaces for marshalling (transforming JavaBeans into XML) and unmarshalling (transforming XML into Java objects) for DI into any Spring beans. Spring also has modules to convert data to and from JSON, in addition to OXM.

- **JMS module**: The **Java Messaging Service (JMS)** module comprises features to produce and consume messages. It is a **Java Message Oriented Middleware (MOM)** API for sending messages between two or more clients. JMS is a specification that describes a common way for Java program to create, send, and read distributed enterprise messages.

  - **Spring Java mail**: The `org.springframework.mail` package is the root package that provides mail support in the Spring Framework. It handles electronic mail.

- **Transaction module**: The Spring transaction module provides abstraction mechanism to supports programmatic and declarative transaction management for classes.

The Web module

The Web module consists of the Web, Servlet, Struts, and Portlet modules.

- **Web module**: The Spring Web module builds on the application context module and includes all the support for developing robust and maintainable web application in a simplified approach. It also supports multipart file-upload functionality.

- **Servlet module**: In Spring, the Servlet module contains **Model-View-Controller (MVC)** implementation that helps to build enterprise web applications. In Spring Framework, the MVC provides clean separation between binding request parameter, business objects, and controller logic.

- **Struts module**: The Web Struts module supports integration of Struts Web tier within a Spring application. It also supports configuration of Struts Actions using Spring Dependency Injection.

- **Portlet module**: Spring Portlet supports for easier development of web application using Spring. Portlet is managed by the Portlet container, similar to the web container. Portlet is used in the UI layer for displaying contents from data source for end user.

The Test module

In the Spring Framework, the Test module helps to test applications developed using the Spring Framework, either using JUnit or TestNG. It also helps in creating mock object to perform unit testing in isolation. It supports running integration tests outside the application server. We'll look at Spring's Test module in *Chapter 7, Spring Testing*.

Benefits of the Spring Framework

The following is the list of a few great benefits of using the Spring Framework:

- Spring is a powerful framework, which address many common problems in Java EE. It includes support for managing business objects and exposing their services to presentation tier component.

- It facilitates good programming practice such as programming using interfaces instead of classes. Spring enables developers to develop enterprise applications using POJO and POJI model programming.

- It is modular, allowing you to use only those parts that you need. It allows us to just choose any part of it in isolation.

- It supports both XML- and annotation-based configuration.

- Spring provides a lightweight container that can be activated without using web server or application server software.

- It gives good support for IoC and Dependency Injection results in loose coupling.

- The Spring Framework supports JDBC framework that improves productivity and reduces the error.

- It provides abstraction on ORM software to develop the ORM persistence logic.

- The Spring Web MVC framework provides powerful and a flexible Web framework as an alternative to Struts and other framework.

- The Spring Test module provides support for an easy-to-test code.

Creating an application in Spring

Before we create an application in Spring, first we need to obtain Spring Library. We can download the Spring distribution ZIP files that are available in the Spring Maven Repository. Else, we can simply add the dependencies for Spring into project's `pom.xml` file whenever we use Maven for application development.

Spring packaging is modular, allowing you to pick and choose the component you want to use in your application. Spring comes with a large selection of sample applications that can be referred while building your application.

Obtaining Spring JAR files

- Downloading Spring distribution ZIP files: The complete Spring Framework library can be downloaded by opening the link `http://repo.spring.io/release/org/springframework/spring/` and selecting the appropriate subfolder for the version needed for your application development. Distribution ZIP files end with `dist.zip`, for example, `spring-framework-4.1.4.RELEASE-dist.zip`.

 While writing this book, the latest version was Spring Framework 4.1.4.

Download the package and extract it. Under the `lib` folder, you will find a list of Spring JAR files that represents each Spring module.

- **Checking Spring out of GitHub**: You can check out the latest version of code from Spring's GitHub repository at `https://github.com/spring-projects/spring-framework`.

  To check out the latest version of the Spring code, first install Git from `http://git-scm.com/`, open the Git Bash tool, and run the following command:

  `git clone https://github.com/spring-projects/spring-framework`

Understanding Spring packaging

After extracting the downloaded Spring Framework ZIP file, you will get the directory structure, as shown in the following screenshot:

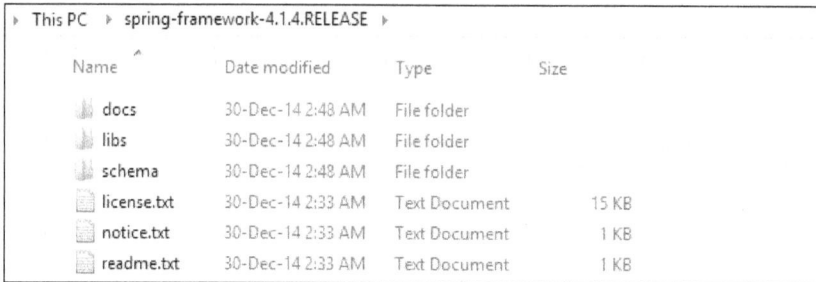

The `spring-framework-4.14.RELEASE` folder, as shown in the preceding screenshot, contains `docs`, `libs`, and `schema` subfolders. The `lib` folder contains the Spring JAR files, as shown in the following screenshot:

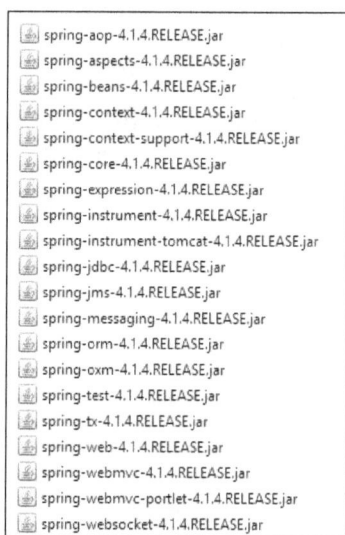

Shown in the preceding screenshot is a list of JAR files required while developing applications using Spring. You can find more details on these JAR files at `http://www.learnr.pro/content/53560-pro-spring/40` and `http://agile-hero.iteye.com/blog/1684338`.

SpringSource Tool Suite

SpringSource Tool Suite (STS) is a powerful Eclipse-based development environment for developing Spring application. The latest version of STS can be downloaded from `http://spring.io/tools/sts`. We will use STS IDE for all our examples in this book. The following screenshot shows a snapshot of an STS dashboard:

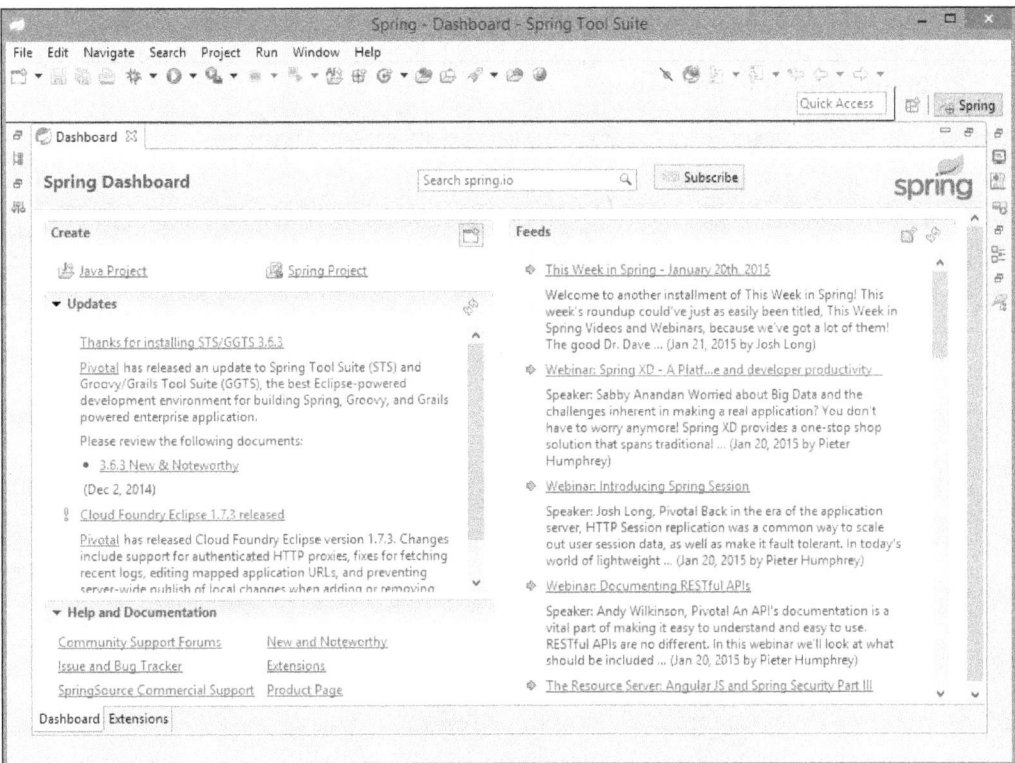

Let's now create a simple Spring application using Spring STS.

The Spring application

With basic understanding of the Spring Framework, we can now create a simple Spring application example. All the examples in this book have been written using the STS IDE.

We will write a simple Spring application that will print greeting message to user. Do not worry if you do not fully understand all the code in this section; we'll go into much more detail on all the topics as we proceed through this book.

Creating a Spring project

The following steps will help you create your Spring project in STS:

1. The first step in creating a Spring application is to create a new Spring project in the STS IDE. Navigate to **File | New | Spring Project**, as shown in the following screenshot:

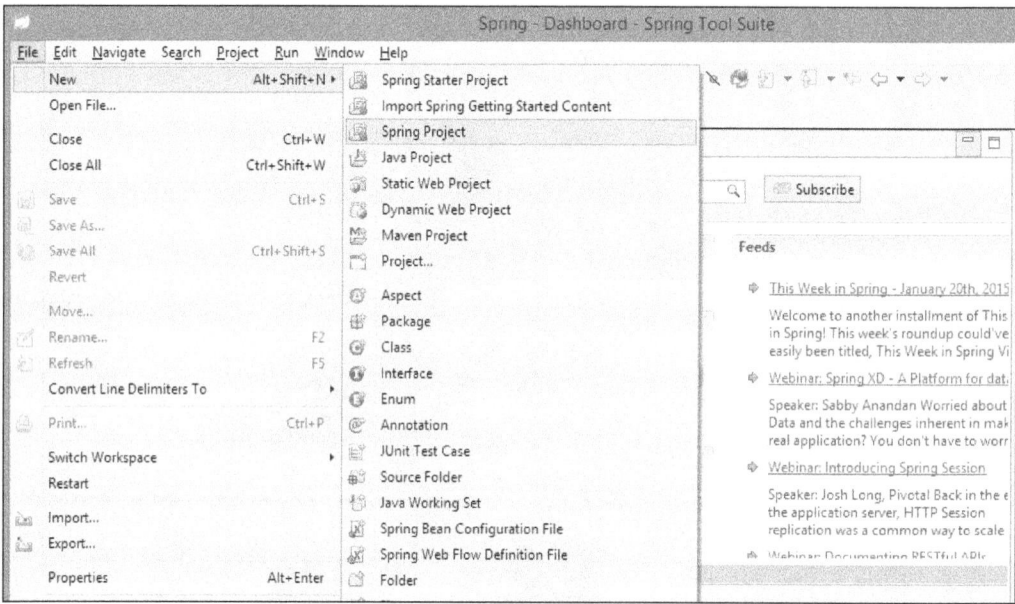

2. Name your Spring project SimpleSpringProject and select the **Simple Java** template, which creates a Simple Spring project using the Java build without a top-level package and with default Spring configuration and project natures, as shown in the following screenshot:

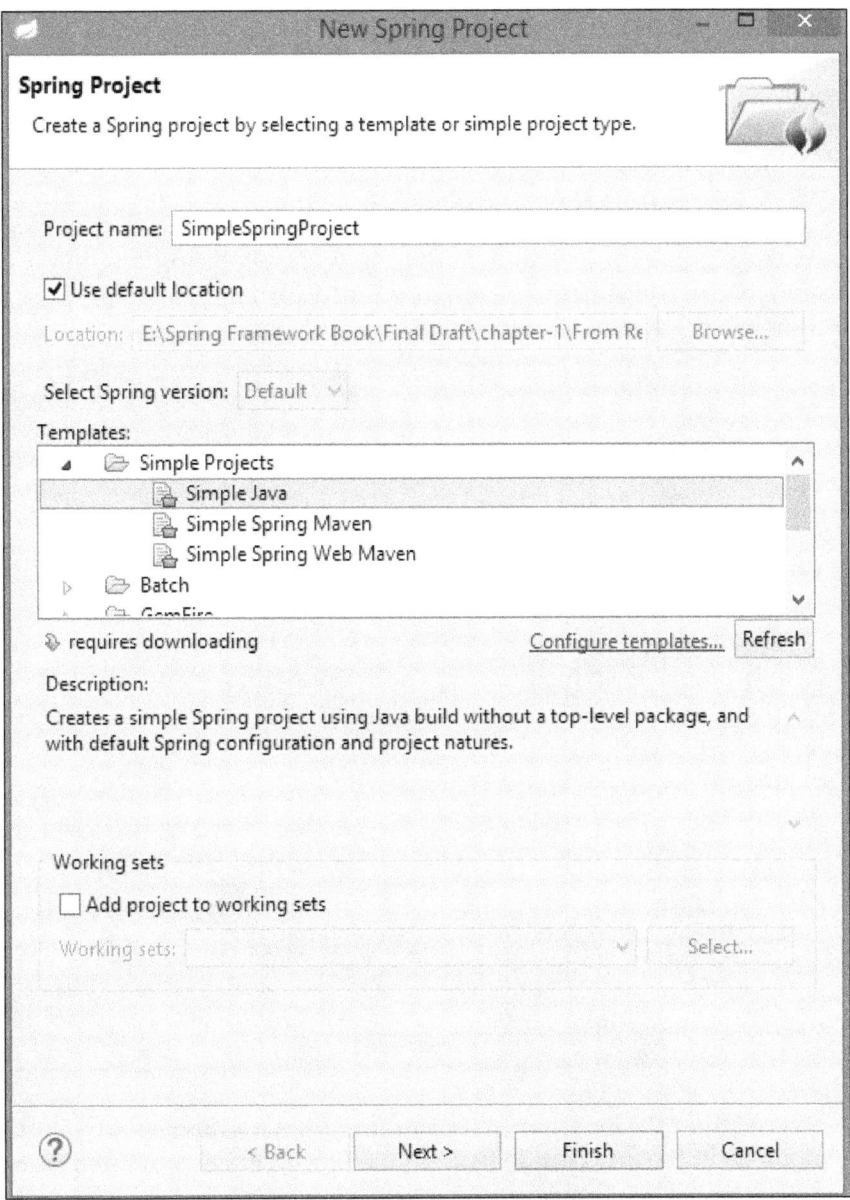

3. Then, click on **Finish**, which will create the project in a workspace.

Adding required libraries

Let's add the basic Spring JAR files to the build path of this Spring project:

1. Add the Spring Framework libraries and common logging API libraries to your project. The common login library can be downloaded from `http://commons.apache.org/proper/commons-logging/download_logging.cgi`. To add required libraries, right-click on the project named `SimpleSpringProject` and then click on the available options in the context menu, that is, **Build Path | Configure Build Path** to display the **Java Build Path** window, as shown in the following screenshot:

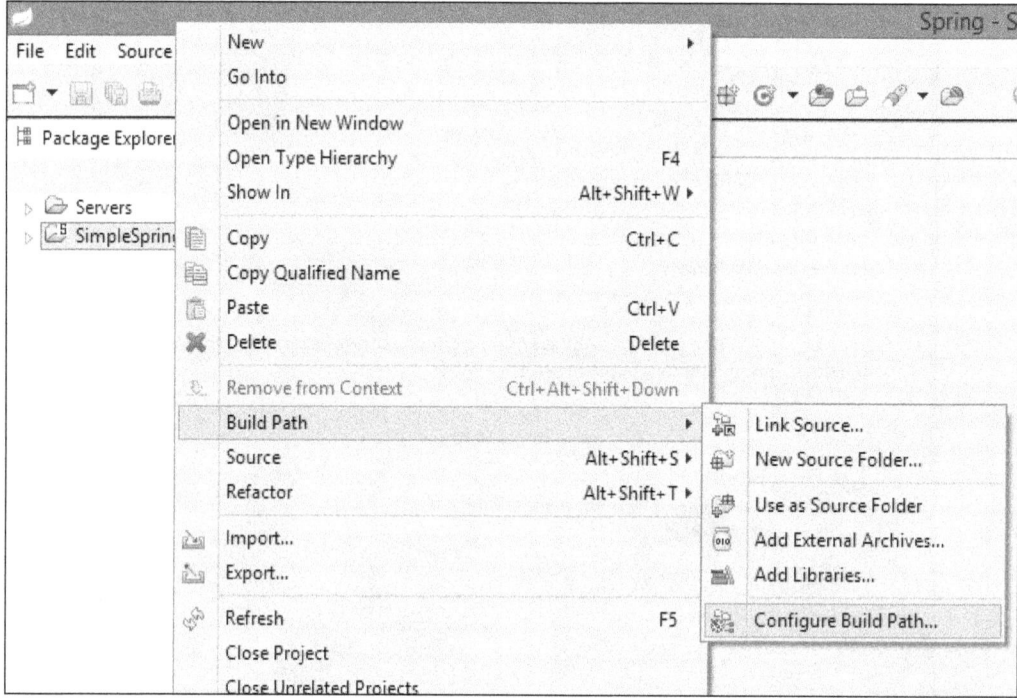

2. Now, use the **Add External JARs** button from the **Libraries** tab in order to include the following core JARs from the Spring Framework and common logging installation directories:

   ° `spring-aop-4.1.4.RELEASE`

   ° `spring-aspects-4.1.4.RELEASE`

   ° `spring-beans-4.1.4.RELEASE`

   ° `spring-context-4.1.4.RELEASE`

- ○ spring-context-support-4.1.4.RELEASE
- ○ spring-core-4.1.4.RELEASE
- ○ spring-expression-4.1.4.RELEASE
- ○ commons-logging-1.2

The **Libraries** tab is as shown in the following screenshot:

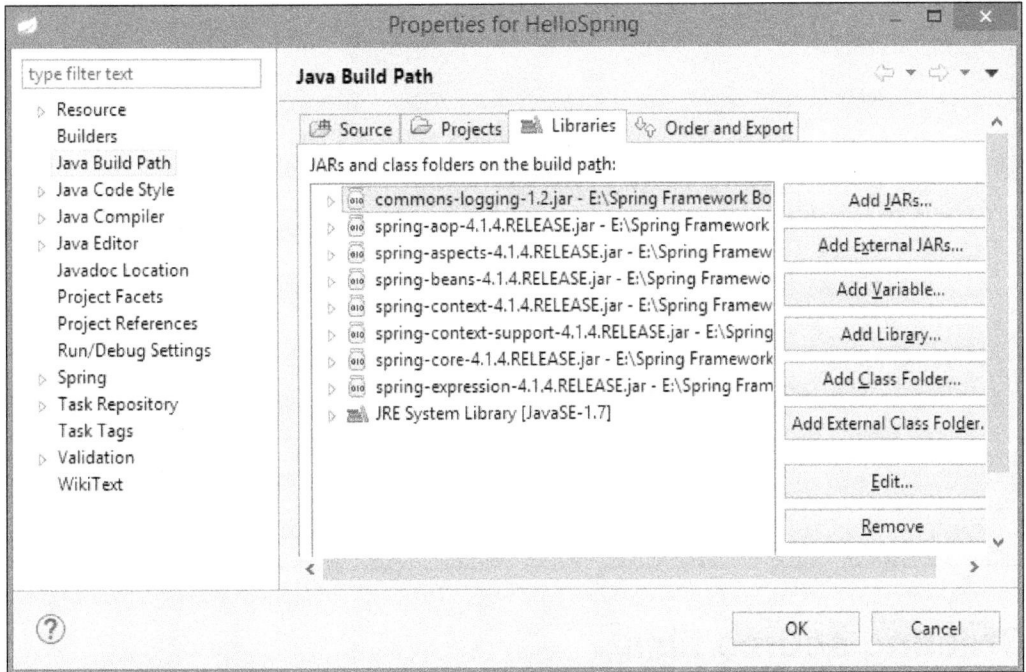

Now, you will have the content in your Project Explorer, as shown in the following screenshot:

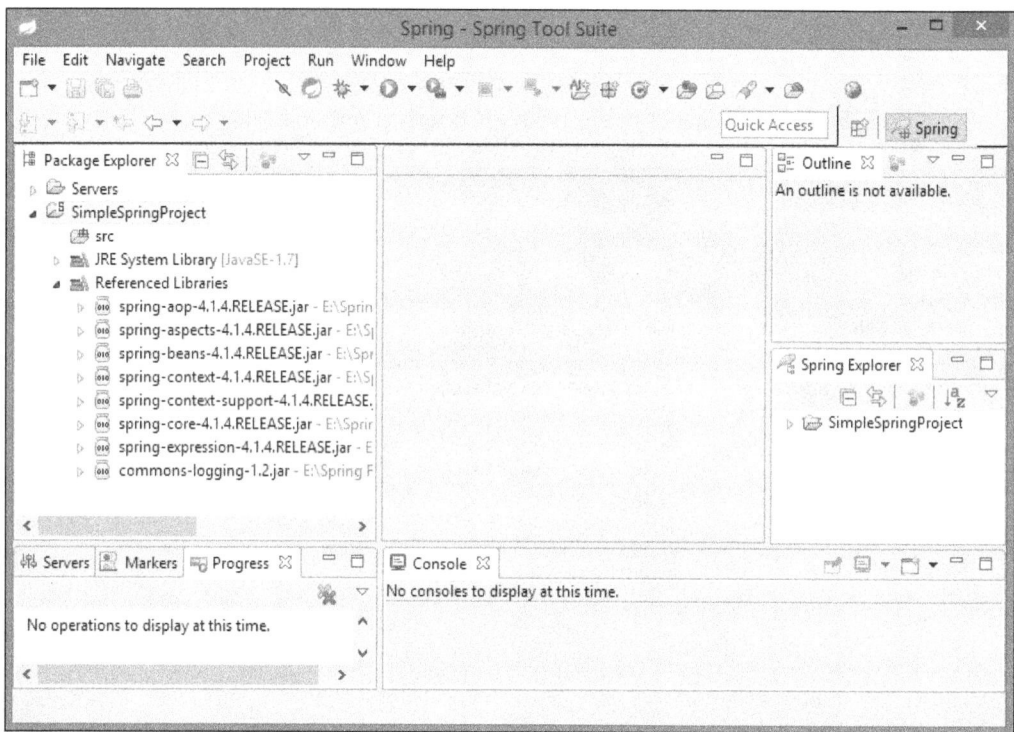

Creating source files

Now let's create the actual source files under the SimpleSpringProject project:

1. First, create the packages named org.springframework.chapter1.service and org.springframework.chapter1.main, as shown in the following screenshot. To do this, right-click on src in package explorer section and navigate to **New** | **Package**.

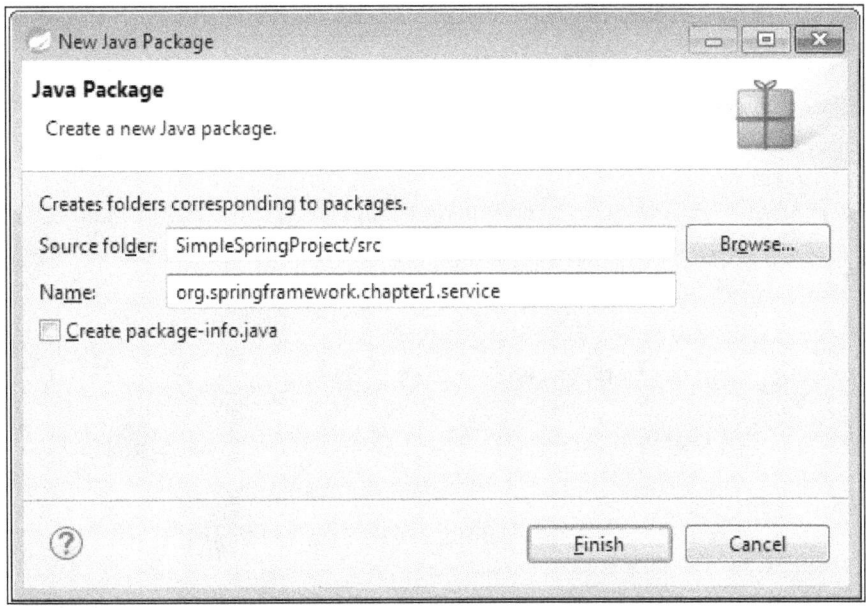

2. Create a class called `MainClass.java` inside the `org.springframework.chapter1.main` package. Then, create an interface named `GreetingMessageService.java` and its implementation class `GreetingMessageServiceImpl.java` inside the package `org.springframework.chapter1.service`, as shown in the following screenshot:

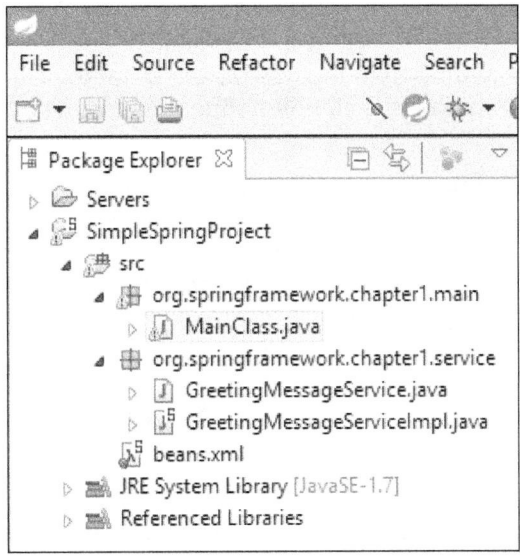

The following is the content of interface `GreetingMessageService.java` and its implementation `GreetingMessageServiceImpl.java`:

- `GreetingMessageService.java`:

```
package org.springframework.chapter1.service;

public interface GreetingMessageService {
   public String greetUser();
}
```

- `GreetingMessageServiceImpl.java`:

```
package org.springframework.chapter1.service;

import org.springframework.stereotype.Service;

@Service
public class GreetingMessageServiceImpl implements
GreetingMessageService {

   public String greetUser() {
        return "Welcome to Chapter-1 of book Learning
Spring Application Development";
   }

}
```

The `GreetingMessageService` interface has a `greetUser()` method. The `GreetingMessageServiceImpl` class implements the `GreetingMessageService` interface and provides definition to the `greetuser()` method. This class is annotated with the `@Service` annotation, which will define this class as service class.

Downloading the example code

You can download the example code files from your account at `http://www.packtpub.com` for all the Packt Publishing books you have purchased. If you purchased this book elsewhere, you can visit `http://www.packtpub.com/support` and register to have the files e-mailed directly to you.

The following is the content of the file `MainClass.java`:

```
package org.springframework.chapter1.main;

import org.springframework.chapter1.service.
GreetingMessageService;
```

```
import org.springframework.context.ApplicationContext;
import org.springframework.context.support.
ClassPathXmlApplicationContext;

public class MainClass {
    public static void main(String[] args) {
            ApplicationContext context = new
ClassPathXmlApplicationContext(
                    "beans.xml");
            GreetingMessageService greetingMessageService =
context.getBean(
                    "greetingMessageServiceImpl",
GreetingMessageService.class);
            System.out.println(greetingMessageService.greetuser());
    }
}
```

In `MainClass.java`, we are creating `ApplicationContext` using framework API, as shown in the following:

```
ApplicationContext context = new ClassPathXmlApplicationContext(
                    "beans.xml");
```

This API loads Spring beans configuration file named `beans.xml`, which takes care of creating and initializing all the bean objects. We use the `getBean()` method of the created `ApplicationContext` to retrieve required Spring bean from the application context, as shown in the following:

```
GreetingMessageService greetingMessageService = context.getBean(
    "greetingMessageServiceImpl", GreetingMessageService.class);
```

The `getBean()` method uses bean ID and bean class to return a bean object.

Creating the Spring bean configuration file

The Spring bean configuration file is used to configure the Spring beans in the Spring IoC container. As we have annotated the `GreetingMessageServiceImpl` class with `@Service` annotation, the next step is to add `<context:component-scan>` in the bean configuration file. To do this, follow these steps:

1. Create a Spring Bean Configuration file under the `src` directory. To do this, right-click on `src` in package explorer section and then navigate to **New | Spring Bean Configuration File**.

2. Enter the bean name beans and click on **Next**, as shown in the following screenshot:

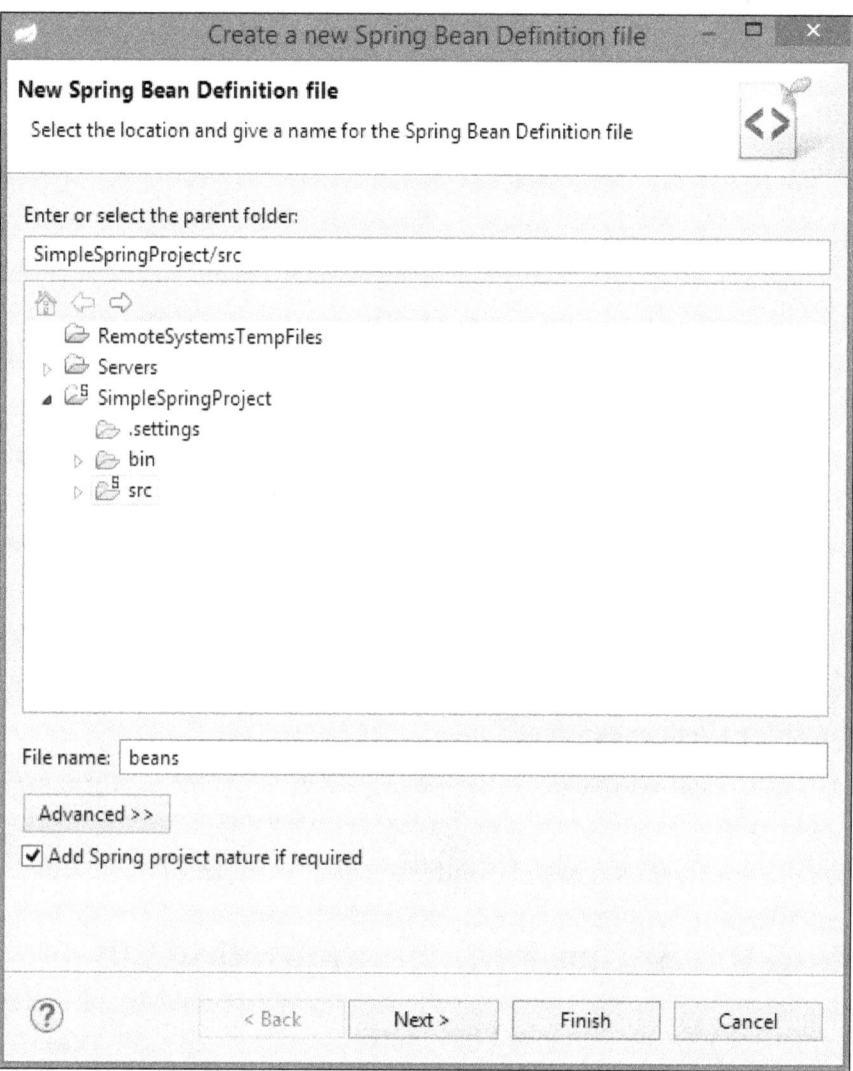

3. Select the context option and click on **Finish**, as shown in the following screenshot:

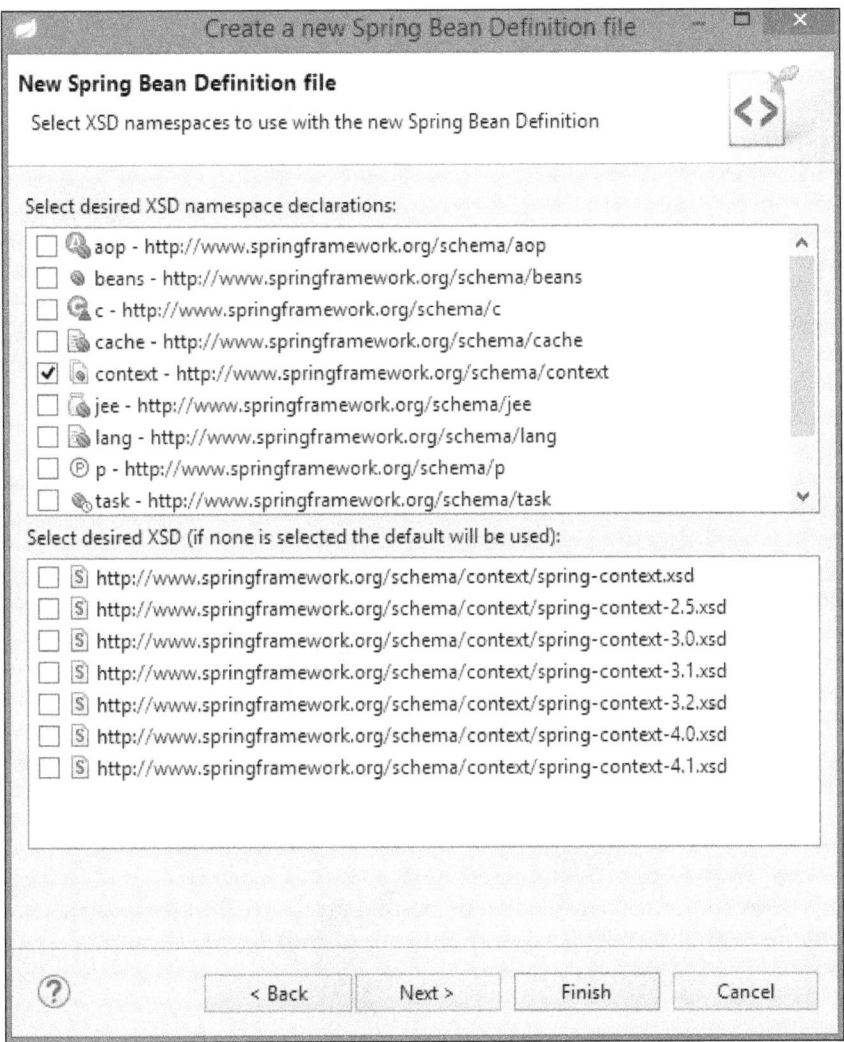

4. Now the Spring bean configuration file is created. Add the following code to create an entry. The contents of the beans.xml file are as follows:

```
<?xml version="1.0" encoding="UTF-8"?>
<beans xmlns="http://www.springframework.org/schema/beans"
    xmlns:xsi="http://www.w3.org/2001/XMLSchema-instance"
```

```
    xmlns:context="http://www.springframework.org/schema/
context"
    xsi:schemaLocation="http://www.springframework.org/
schema/beans
    http://www.springframework.org/schema/beans/spring-
beans.xsd
        http://www.springframework.org/schema/context
    http://www.springframework.org/schema/context/spring-
context-4.1.xsd">

    <context:component-scan base-
package="org.springframework.chapter1.service"/>

</beans>
```

When the Spring application gets loaded into the memory, in order to create all the beans, the framework uses the preceding configuration file, as shown in the following screenshot:

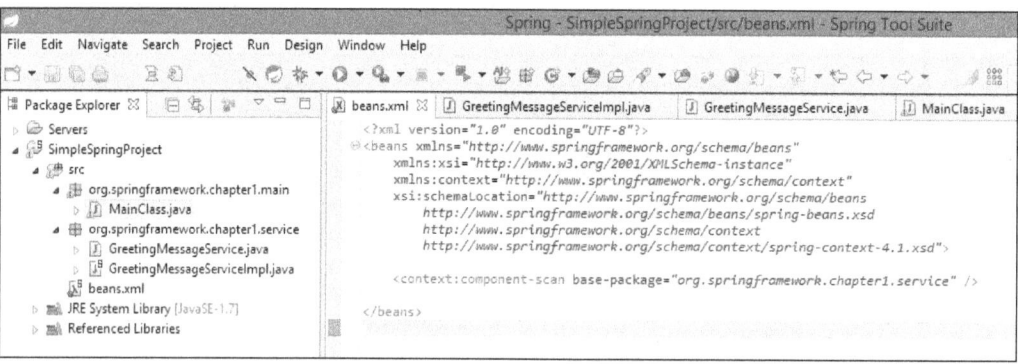

The Spring bean configuration file can be named anything, but developers usually keep the name beans.xml. This Spring bean configuration file should be available in classpath.

The S in the upper-right corner of the project icon indicates it is a Spring Project.

Running the program

Once you are done with creating source files and beans configuration files, you are ready for the next step, that is, compiling and running your program.

To execute the example, run the `MainClass.java` file. Right-click on `MainClass.java` and navigate to **Run As | Java Application**. If everything goes fine, then it will print the following message in STS IDE's console, as shown in the following screenshot:

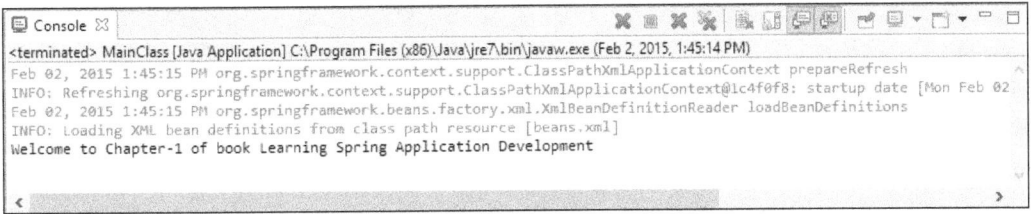

We have successfully created our first Spring application, where you learned how to create the Spring project and executed it successfully. We will see detailed examples in the next chapter.

Exercise

Q1. What is Spring?

Q2. List some of the features of Spring.

Q3. Explain different modules in the Spring Framework.

 The answers to these are provided in *Appendix A, Solution to Exercises.*

Summary

In this chapter, you were introduced the Spring Framework and acquainted with its features. You took a look at the versions of Spring. Then, you studied the architecture, and different modules in the Spring Framework such as the Spring Core Container, Spring AOP, Spring data access/integration, and the Spring Web module and Test module. You also understood the benefits of the Spring Framework. Finally, you created an application in Spring and took a look on package structure of Spring.

In the next chapter, we'll explore IoC, Dependency Injection, and Spring Core Container service. We'll also see bean's life cycle and bean's scope.

2
Inversion of Control in Spring

In this chapter, we'll explore the concept of **Inversion of Control (IoC)**. We'll then explore Spring Core Container, `BeanFactory`, and `ApplicationContext`, and you will learn how to implement them. We will take a look at **Dependency Injection (DI)** in Spring and their types: setter and constructor. We will wire beans using setter- and constructor-based Dependency Injection for different data types. We will also go through bean definition inheritance in Spring. We will then see autowiring in Spring and their modes. We will also see Spring bean's scope and its implementation. Then, we will move on to the life cycle of Spring bean.

The following is a list of topics that will be covered in this chapter:

- Understanding IoC
- Spring Container
- `BeanFactory`
- `ApplicationContext`
- Dependency Injection
- Constructor-based Dependency Injection
- Setter-based Dependency Injection
- Bean definition inheritance
- Autowiring in Spring
- Bean's scope
- Singleton
- Prototype
- Request
- Session
- Global-session

- Spring bean life cycle
- Initialization callback
- Destruction callback

Let's understand Inversion of Control.

Understanding Inversion of Control

In software engineering, IoC is a programming technique in which object coupling is bound at runtime by an assembler object and is usually not known at compile time using static analysis.

IoC is a more general concept, whereas DI is a concrete design pattern.

IoC is a way of thinking; a mechanism is required to activate components that provide specific functionality, due to which IoC depends on DI. The IoC pattern inverts responsibility of the managing the life cycle from the application to the framework, which makes writing Java applications even easier. IoC makes your code more manageable, more testable, and more portable. IoC also keeps component dependencies, life cycle events, and configuration outside of the components.

Consider the following example: we have a Car class and a Vehicle class object. The biggest issue with the code is tight coupling between classes. In other words, the Car class depends on the vehicle object. So, for any reason, changes in the Vehicle class will lead to the changes in, and compilation of, the Car class too.

So let's put down the problems with this approach:

- The biggest problem is that the Car class controls the creation of the vehicle object
- The Vehicle class is directly referenced in the Car class, which leads to tight coupling between the car and vehicle objects

The following figure illustrates this:

```
public class Car {

        private Vehicle vehicle;  ──────▶Problem 1: References

        public Car() {
            vehicle = new Vehicle();
        }                         ──────▶ Problem 2: Aware of concrete classes
}
```

If, for any reason, the `vehicle` object is not created, the whole `Car` class will fail in the constructor initialization stage. The basic principle of IoC stands on the base of the Hollywood principle: Do not call us; we'll call you.

In other words, it's like the `Vehicle` class saying to the `Car` class, "don't create me, I'll create myself using someone else".

The IoC framework can be a class, client, or some kind of IoC container. The IoC container creates the `vehicle` object and passes this reference to the `Car` class, as shown here:

```
public class Car {

    private Vehicle vehicle;

    public Car(Vehicle vehicle) {
        this.vehicle = vehicle;
    }
}
```

Step 2: Passes the vehicle object to the Car class

IoC container

```
public class Vehicle {

    // ...

}
```

Step 1: Creates the vehicle object

What is a container

In software development terminology, the word "container" is used to describe any component that can contain other components inside it. For example, Tomcat is a web container to contain deployed WAR files. JBoss is an application server/ container; it contains an EJB container, web container, and so on.

The container first creates the objects and then wires them together, after which it moves on to configure them, and finally manage their complete life cycle. It identifies the object dependencies, creates them, and then injects them into the appropriate objects.

So, we can think about a container as an intermediate who'll register `vehicle` and `car` objects as separate entities, create the `vehicle` and `car` objects, and inject the `vehicle` object into `car`.

Spring Container

Spring Container is the central component of the Spring Framework. Spring Container manages the life cycle of an application's bean, which will live within Spring Container. Spring Container is responsible for wiring an application's beans by associating different beans together. Spring Container manages the components of applications using DI. The configuration metadata, which can be represented in XML, Java annotations, or Java code, helps Spring Container to decide the object to initiate, configure, and assemble.

Let's take an example of Tomcat, which is a Servlet container. Tomcat creates the Servlet objects, which are required in order to run an application. While deploying an application, we configure all Servlets in an XML file. Tomcat reads this XML file, identifies the Servlet to be instantiated, and then creates the identified Servlet.

Spring is a container but not a container of Servlet. It is a container of beans and behaves as a factory of beans. So, we can have Spring Container and we can have as many objects as we want, as shown in the following diagram. Also, all these objects are managed by Spring Container. The container handles the instantiation of object, their whole life cycle, and finally their destruction too:

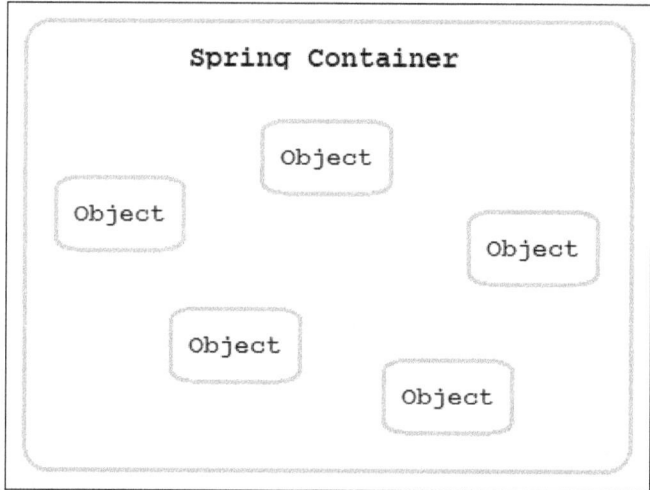

Beans

Beans are reusable software components that are managed by the Spring IoC container. It contains the properties, setter, and getter methods of a class.

The Spring IoC container is represented by the interface `org.springframework.context.ApplicationContext`, which is responsible for instantiating, configuring, and assembling beans. Beans are reflected in the configuration metadata used by a container. The configuration metadata defines the instruction for the container and the objects to instantiate, configure, and assemble. This configuration metadata can be represented in XML, Java annotations, or Java code. In this chapter, we will configure using XML, which has been the traditional format to define configuration metadata. Refer to *Chapter 9, Inversion of Control in Spring – Using Annotation*, which is available online, on instructing the container to use Java annotations by providing a small amount of the XML configuration.

XML-based bean configuration

The bean configuration information is stored in an XML file, which is used to create a bean definition using the `<bean>...</bean>` element. The bean definition contains the following metadata, which represents the configuration information of a bean:

- A fully qualified class name that represents bean name
- The behavioral configuration elements, such as scope, life cycle, and so on, describe the bean's behavior in the Spring IoC container.

The following code snippet shows the basic structure of the XML configuration of the metadata:

```xml
<?xml version="1.0" encoding="UTF-8"?>
<beans xmlns="http://www.springframework.org/schema/beans"
    xmlns:xsi="http://www.w3.org/2001/XMLSchema-instance"
    xsi:schemaLocation="http://www.springframework.org/schema/beans
    http://www.springframework.org/schema/beans/spring-beans.xsd">

    <bean id="..." class="...">
        <!-- configuration for this bean here -->
    </bean>
    <!-- more bean definitions here -->

</beans>
```

The configuration files have <beans> as the root element. The beans element has all other individual beans configured using the <bean> tag. Every <bean> tag needs to specify a class attribute and can have an optional ID or name attribute. The ID attributes enforce uniqueness in naming the beans. The class attribute has the fully classified class name; for example, the src.org.packt.Spring.chapter2.Employee class can be configured as follows:

```
...
<bean id="employeeBean"
        class="src.org.packt.Spring.chapter2.Employee">
    </bean>
    ...
```

A reference of the Employee class instance is returned when the configuration file is loaded using the BeanFactory or ApplicationContext container, and employeeBean is accessed using the getBean (employeeBean) method. The Spring IoC container is responsible for instantiating, configuring, and retrieving your Spring beans. The Spring IoC container enforces DI in its various forms and employs a number of established design patterns to achieve this.

Spring provides the following two interfaces that act as containers:

- BeanFactory: This is a basic container, and all other containers implement BeanFactory.

- ApplicationContext: This refers to the subinterface of BeanFactory and is mostly used as a container in enterprise applications.

To instantiate Spring Container, create an object of any of the BeanFactory or ApplicationContext implementation classes that supply the Spring bean configuration. The basic packages in the Spring IoC container of the Spring Framework are org.springframework.beans and org.springframework.context. An advanced configuration mechanism is provided by the BeanFactory interface to manage any type of object. The ApplicationContext interface implements the BeanFactory interface, which provides enterprise-specific functionality and supports message-resource handling, Spring's AOP features, event publication, and WebApplicationContext for use in web applications.

Both the containers, `BeanFactory` and `ApplicationContext`, are responsible for providing DI. For all the configured beans, these containers act as a repository. These containers initiate a registered bean, populate the bean's properties, and call the `init()` method to make the bean ready for use. The `destroy()` method of bean is invoked during the shutdown of the application. The `init()` and `destroy()` methods reflect the Servlet life cycle, where initialization can be performed during the `init()` method and cleanup during the `destroy()` method.

BeanFactory

Spring creates all the instances, along with the references to the objects you require. This is different from when you create an instance yourself with the help of the `new` method. This is called a factory pattern.

What is a factory pattern?

In a factory pattern, we have an object that behaves as the object factory. Basically, if you need an instance of any object, you don't have to create the instance yourself. Instead, you call a method of this factory, which then returns the instance you wanted. This factory reads from a configuration file, which acts as a blueprint that contains guidelines on how we can create the object.

Assume that we have an object `Foo` and instead of creating a new object `Bar`, we make a call to another Java object, which is a `Factory` object. The job of the `Factory` object is to create and hand over a new object `Bar` to the object `Foo`, as shown in the following figure. The whole purpose of this factory is to produce objects.

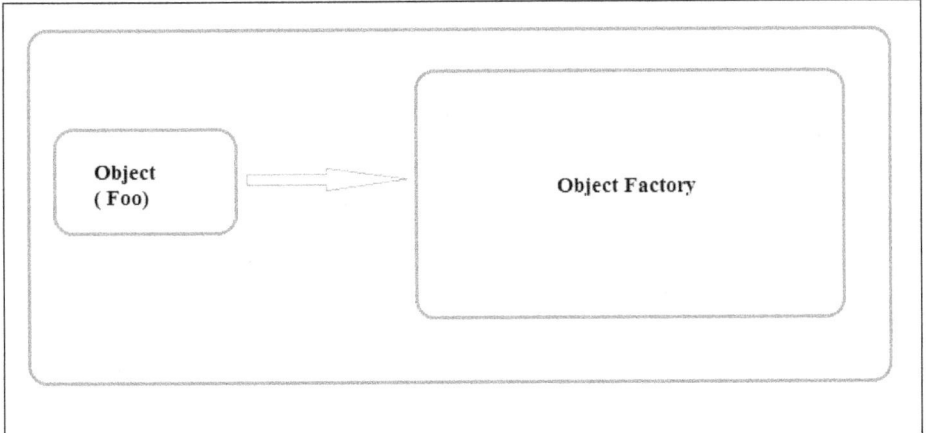

The Factory object reads from the configuration, which has metadata with details about the object that needs to be created. Configuration is a blueprint of all those objects that Factory creates. The Factory object reads from this configuration file, as shown here:

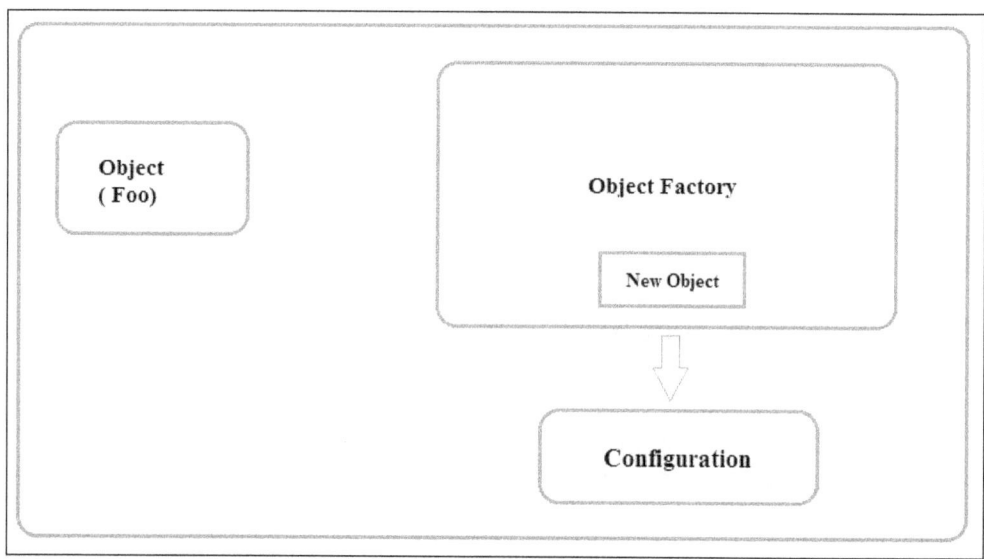

The Foo object interacts with the Factory object to get an object with a certain specification. Then the Factory object finds out what the blueprint for that particular object specification is and then creates a new object, as shown in the following figure:

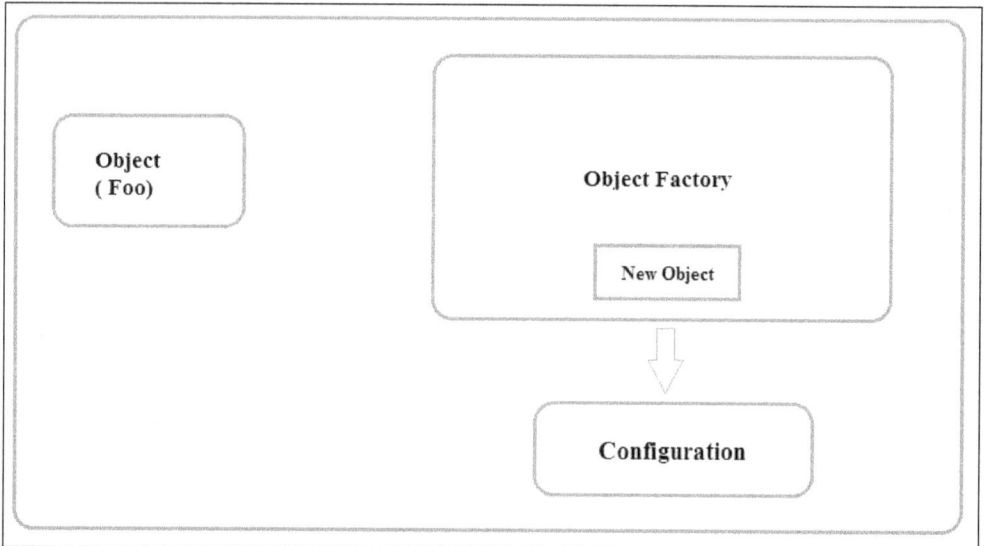

Once the object has been created, `Factory` hands back the requesting `Bar` object to the `Foo` object. So, now `Foo` will have a new object it wants not using `new()` but using `Factory`, as shown in the following figure. This is something that Spring does.

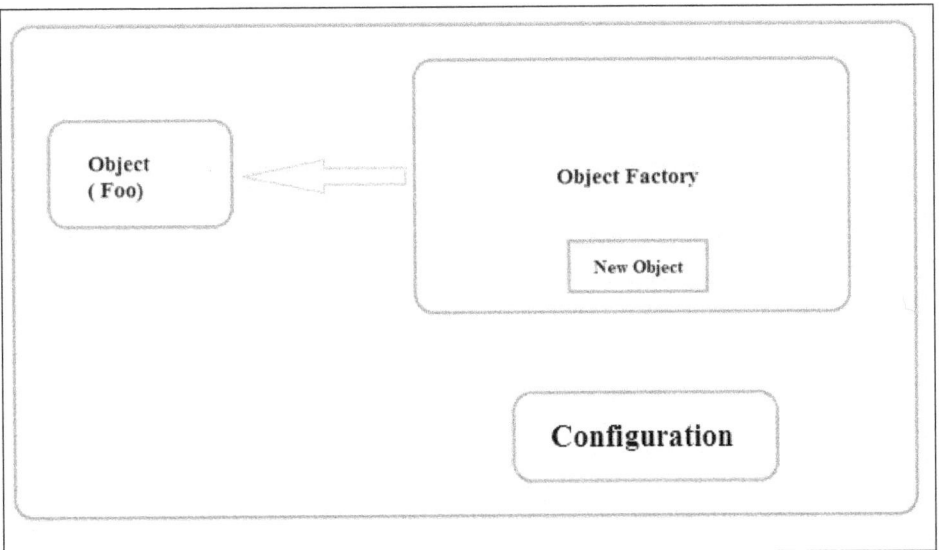

Spring BeanFactory

Spring has objects of the `BeanFactory` type that behave like the `Factory` object. You specify the `blueprints` object in a configuration file, which is an XML file, and then supply it to `BeanFactory`. Later, if you need the instance of any object, you can ask `BeanFactory` for it, which then refers to the XML file and constructs the bean as specified. This bean is now a Spring bean as it has been created by Spring Container and is returned to you. Let's now summarize this:

1. Spring has `BeanFactory`, which creates new objects for us. So, the `Foo` object will call `BeanFactory`.

2. `BeanFactory` would read from Spring XML, which contains all the bean definitions. Bean definitions are the blueprints here. `BeanFactory` will create beans from this blueprint and then make a new Spring bean.

3. Finally, this new Spring bean is handed back to `Foo`, as shown here:

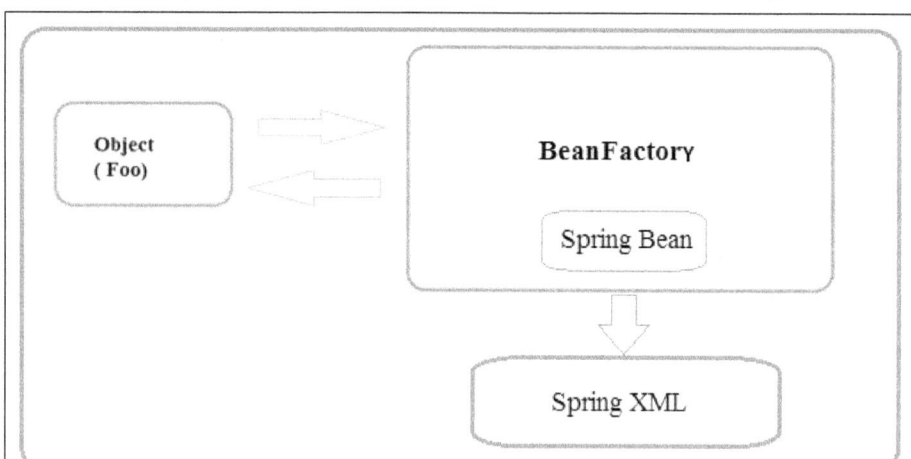

The advantage here is that this new bean has been created in this `BeanFactory`, which is known by Spring. Spring handles the creation and the entire life cycle of this bean. So, in this case, Spring acts as container for this newly created Spring bean.

`BeanFactory` is defined by the `org.springframework.beans.factory.BeanFactory` interface. The `BeanFactory` interface is the central IoC container interface in Spring and provides the basic end point for Spring Core Container towards the application to access the core container service.

It is responsible for containing and managing the beans. It is a factory class that contains a collection of beans. It holds multiple bean definitions within itself and then instantiates that bean as per the client's demands.

`BeanFactory` creates associations between collaborating objects as they're instantiated. This removes the burden of configuration from the bean itself along with the bean's client. It also takes part in the life cycle of a bean and makes calls to custom initialization and destruction methods.

Implementation of BeanFactory

There are many implementations of the `BeanFactory` interface, with the `org.springframework.beans.factory.xml.XmlBeanFactory` class being the most popularly used one, which reads the bean definition and initiates them based on the definitions contained in the XML file. Depending on the bean definition, the factory will return either an independent instance or a single shared instance of a contained object.

This class has been deprecated in favor of `DefaultListableBeanFactory` and `XmlBeanDefinitionReader`, and the purpose of this implementation is just to explain `BeanFactory`. The constructor for `XmlBeanFactory` takes an implementation of the `Resource` interface as an argument, as shown in the following line of code:

```
XmlBeanFactory (Resource resource)
```

The `Resource` interface has many implementations. The two commonly used implementations are shown in the following table:

The `Resource` **interfaces**	Description
`org.springframework.core.io.FileSystemResource`	This loads the configuration file from the underlying filesystem
`org.springframework.core.io.ClassPathResource`	This loads the configuration file from the classpath

Let's assume that beans are configured in the `beans.xml` file located in the C drive:

```
...
<bean id="mybean" class="...">
  ...
</bean>
...
```

The code snippet to load the configuration file using `BeanFactory` is given as follows:

```
BeanFactory bfObj = new XmlBeanFactory (new FileSystemResource
("c:/beans.xml"));

MyBean beanObj= (MyBean) bfObj.getBean ("mybean");
```

Here, we've used `FileSystemResource`, which is one of the `Resource` interface implementations. The `bfObj` object corresponds to Spring Container, one that has loaded the bean definitions from the `beans.xml` file. `BeanFactory` is a lazy container, so at this point, only bean definitions get loaded, but beans themselves are not instantiated yet. At the second line, we call the `getBean()` method of the `BeanFactory` object created by passing the bean ID `"mybean"` as an argument to this method.

`BeanFactory` reads the bean definition of a bean with the ID `"mybean"` from Spring's `beans.xml` file, instantiates it, and then returns a reference.

The `BeanFactory` interface has different methods, such as `getBean`, `containBean`, and so on, for client code to call. You can get the complete list of these methods from `http://docs.spring.io/spring/docs/2.0.x/reference/beans.html`.

The `BeanFactory` container is usually used in very simple applications; however, in real-time projects, the `ApplicationContext` container is used.

ApplicationContext

Like `BeanFactory`, `ApplicationContext` is also used to represent Spring Container, built upon the `BeanFactory` interface. `ApplicationContext` is suitable for Java EE applications, and it is always preferred over `BeanFactory`. All functionality of `BeanFactory` is included in `ApplicationContext`.

The `org.springframework.context.ApplicationContext` interface defines `ApplicationContext`. `ApplicationContext` and provides advanced features to our Spring applications that make them enterprise-level applications, whereas `BeanFactory` provides a few basic functionalities. Let's discuss them:

- Apart from providing a means of resolving text messages, `ApplicationContext` also includes support for i18n of those messages.

- A generic way to load file resources, such as images, is provided by `ApplicationContext`.

- The events to beans that are registered as listeners can also be published by `ApplicationContext`.

- `ApplicationContext` handles certain operations on the container or beans in the container declaratively, which have to be handled with `BeanFactory` in a programmatic way.

- It provides `ResourceLoader` support. This is used to handle low-level resources, Spring's `Resource` interface, and a flexible generic abstraction. `ApplicationContext` itself is `ResourceLoader`. Hence, access to deployment-specific `Resource` instances is provided to an application.

- It provides `MessageSource` support. `MessageSource`, an interface used to obtain localized messages with the actual implementation being pluggable, is implemented by `ApplicationContext`.

Implementation of ApplicationContext

The most commonly used `ApplicationContext` implementations are as follows:

- `ClassPathXmlApplicationContext`: This bean definition is loaded by the container from the XML file that is present in the classpath by treating context definition files as classpath resources. `ApplicationContext` can be loaded from within the application's classpath using `ClassPathXmlApplicationContext`:

```
ApplicationContext context =
new ClassPathXmlApplicationContext("spring-beans.xml");
```

- `FileSystemXmlApplicationContext`: This bean definition is loaded by the container from an XML file. Here, the full path of the XML bean configuration file should be provided to the constructor:

```
ApplicationContext context =
new FileSystemXmlApplicationContext("classpath:beans.xml");
```

In the preceding code snippet, the `ApplicationContext` instance is created using the `FileSystemXmlApplicationContext` class and `beans.xml` is specified as a parameter.

The `getBean()` method can be used to access a particular bean by specifying its ID, as shown in following code snippet:

```
MyBean beanObj= (MyBean) context.getBean ("mybean");
```

In the preceding code snippet, the `getBean()` method accepts the ID of the bean and returns the object of the bean.

`ApplicationContext` is an active container that initiates all the configured beans as soon as the `ApplicationContext` instance is created and before the user calls the `getBean()` method. The advantage of this active creation of beans by `ApplicationContext` is the handling of exceptions during the startup of the application itself.

- `XmlWebApplicationContext`: This is used to create the context in web application by loading configuration the XML file with definitions of all beans from standard locations within a web application directory. The default location of the configuration XML file is `/WEB-INF/applicationContext.xml`.

- `AnnotationConfigApplicationContext`: This is used to create the context by loading Java classes annotated with the `@Configuration` annotation instead of XML files. The `AnnotationConfigApplicationContext` class is used when we define Java-based Spring bean configuration for the bean definition instead of XML files.

- `AnnotationConfigWebApplicationContext`: This is used to create the web application context by loading the Java classes annotated with the `@Configuration` annotation instead of XML files in the web application.

To demonstrate an implementation of `ApplicationContext`, an example of `PayrollSystem` can be considered. It will have the `EmployeeService` interface, `EmployeeServiceImpl` class, and `PayrollSystem` class with the main method.

In the `EmployeeService.java` interface, you'll find the following code:

```
package org.packt.Spring.chapter2.ApplicationContext;

public interface EmployeeService {

    public Long generateEmployeeId();

}
```

The `EmployeeService.java` interface is a plain old Java interface that has a method named `generateEmployeeId()` to generate a unique employee ID on each call.

In the `EmployeeServiceImpl.java` class, you'll find the following code:

```
package org.packt.Spring.chapter2.ApplicationContext;

public class EmployeeServiceImpl implements EmployeeService {

    @Override
    public Long generateEmployeeId() {
            return System.currentTimeMillis();
    }
}
```

The `EmployeeServiceImpl.java` class implements the `EmployeeService` interface. This `generateEmployeeId()` class-implemented method is used to generate a unique employee ID on each part of this method based on the system's current time.

In the `PayrollSystem.java` class, you'll find the following code:

```
package org.packt.Spring.chapter2.ApplicationContext;

import org.springframework.context.ApplicationContext;
import org.springframework.context.support.ClassPathXmlApplication
Context;

public class PayrollSystem {
```

```
    public static void main(String[] args) {

        ApplicationContext context = new
ClassPathXmlApplicationContext(
                    "beans.xml");

        EmployeeService empService = (EmployeeServiceImpl)
context
                    .getBean("empServiceBean");
        System.out.println("Unique Employee Id: " +
empService.generateEmployeeId());
    }

}
```

The `PayrollSystem.java` class is a main class that contains the `main()` method. This method creates an instance of `ApplicationContext`, calls the `getBean()` method to get the bean of `EmployeeService`, and then prints the generated unique employee ID by calling the method from this bean.

The `beans.xml` file contains the bean definition for `EmployeeServiceImpl`, as shown in the following code snippet:

```
...
<bean id="empServiceBean"
class="org.packt.Spring.chapter2.ApplicationContext.
EmployeeServiceImp">
</bean>
...
```

When you successfully run `PayrollSystem.java`, the output will be printed on the console as follows:

```
Unique Employee Id: 1401215855074
```

The generated `Employee Id` value will be different for you when you run the preceding code in your local system as it is based on the current time.

A Spring application requires several beans or objects to work together in order to develop a loosely coupled application. Objects depend on each other to carry out their respective functions and this applies to beans too. Now let's understand DI.

Dependency Injection

Dependency Injection (DI) is a design pattern in which an object's dependency is injected by the framework rather than by the object itself. It reduces coupling between multiple objects as it is dynamically injected by the framework. In DI, the framework is completely responsible for reading configuration.

The advantages of DI are as follows:

- Loosely coupled architecture.
- Separation of responsibility.
- Configuration and code are separate.
- A different implementation can be supplied using configuration without changing the code dependent.
- Improves testability.
- DI allows you to replace actual objects with mock objects. This improves testability by writing simple JUnit tests that use mock objects.

Dependency Injection in Spring

In the Spring Framework, DI is used to satisfy the dependencies between objects. It exits in only two types:

- **Constructor Injection**: By invoking a constructor containing a number of arguments, constructor-based DI can be accomplished. These arguments are injected at the time of instance instantiation.
- **Setter Injection**: Setter-based DI is attained by calling setter methods on your beans. Using setter methods defined in a Spring configuration file, the dependencies are "set" in the objects.

The following figure gives us a better picture:

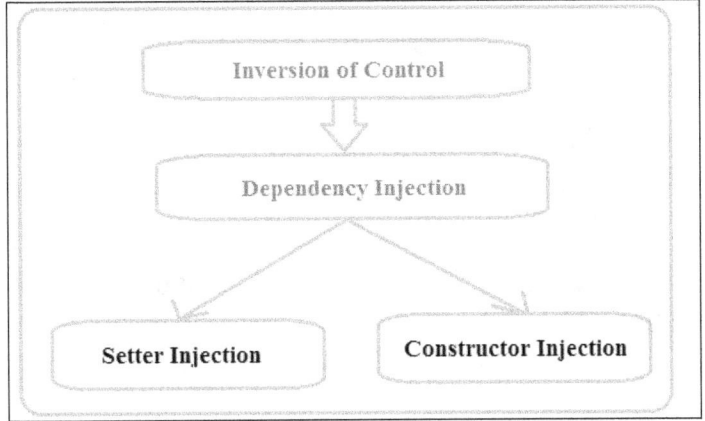

Let's consider an example where the EmployeeServiceImpl class has an instance field employeeDao of the EmployeeDao type, a constructor with an argument, and a setEmployeeDao method.

In the EmployeeServiceImpl.java class, you'll find the following code:

```
public class EmployeeServiceImpl implements EmployeeService {

    private EmployeeDao employeeDao;

    public EmployeeServiceImpl(EmployeeDao employeeDao) {
        this.employeeDao = employeeDao;
    }

    public void setEmployeeDao(EmployeeDao employeeDao) {
        this.employeeDao = employeeDao;
    }
}
```

In the EmployeeDaoImpl.java class, you'll find the following code:

```
public class EmployeeDaoImpl implements EmployeeDao {

    // ...

}
```

Here, an instance of EmployeeDao can be provided by the configuration file by either the constructor method or the setter method. Before we understand what these are in more detail, let's understand how generally two objects interact with each other to make an even more meaningful object.

The Has-A relationship

When a class contains another class as instance field; for example, the EmployeeServiceImpl class contains EmployeeDao as its field. This is called a Has-A relationship since we say, "EmployeeServiceImpl has an EmployeeDao". So, without employeeDao, EmployeeServiceImpl cannot perform. The following code illustrates this:

```
public class EmployeeServiceImpl implements EmployeeService {

    private EmployeeDao employeeDao = null;

}
```

So, employeeDao is the dependency that needs to be resolved in order to make EmployeeServiceImpl fully functional. The way to create an object of the EmployeeDao type or, in other words, satisfy the dependency of EmployeeServiceImpl in Java is shown here:

```
public class EmployeeServiceImpl implements EmployeeService {

    private EmployeeDao employeeDao = null;

    public EmployeeServiceImpl() {
            this.employeeDao = new EmployeeDaoImpl();
    }

    public void setEmployeeDao() {
            this.employeeDao = new EmployeeDaoImpl();
    }
}
```

It is not a very good option as once the EmployeeServiceImpl object is created, you don't have any way to have the object of the employeeDao type swapped with a subclass implementation.

Constructor-based Dependency Injection

Constructor Injection is the process of injecting the dependencies of an object through its constructor argument at the time of instantiating it. In other words, we can say that dependencies are supplied as an object through the object's own constructor. The bean definition can use a constructor with zero or more arguments to initiate the bean, as shown here:

```java
public class EmployeeServiceImpl implements EmployeeService {

    private EmployeeDao employeeDao = null;

    public EmployeeServiceImpl(EmployeeDao employeeDao) {
        this.employeeDao = employeeDao;
    }
}
```

In the preceding code, the object of the `EmployeeDao employeeDao` type is injected as a constructor argument to the `EmployeeServiceImpl` class. We need to configure bean definition in the configuration file that will perform Constructor Injection.

The Spring bean XML configuration tag `<constructor-arg>` is used for Constructor Injection:

```xml
. . .
    <bean id="employeeService"
    class="org.packt.Spring.chapter2.dependencyinjection.
EmployeeServiceImpl">
            <constructor-arg ref="employeeDao" />
    </bean>

    <bean id="employeeDao"
    class="org.packt.Spring.chapter2.dependencyinjection.
EmployeeDaoImpl">
    </bean>
. . .
```

In the preceding code snippet, there is a Has-A relationship between the classes, which is `EmployeeServiceImpl HAS-A EmployeeDao`. Here, we inject a user-defined object as the source bean into a target bean using Constructor Injection. Once we have the `employeeDao` bean to inject it into the target `employeeService` bean, we need another attribute called `ref`—its value is the name of the ID attribute of the source bean, which in our case is `"employeeDao"`.

The <constructor-arg> element

The <constructor-arg> subelement of the <bean> element is used for Constructor Injection. The <constructor-arg> element supports four attributes. They are explained in the following table:

Attributes	Description	Occurrence
index	It takes the exact index in the constructor argument list. It is used to avoid ambiguity such as when two arguments are of the same type.	Optional
type	It takes the type of this constructor argument.	Optional
value	It describes the content in a simple string representation, which is converted into the argument type using the PropertyEditors Java beans.	Optional
ref	It refers to another bean in this factory.	Optional

Constructor Injection – injecting simple Java types

Here, we inject simple Java types into a target bean using Constructor Injection.

The Employee class has employeeName as String, employeeAge as int, and married as boolean. The constructor initializes all these three fields.

In the Employee.java class, you'll find the following code:

```
package org.packt.Spring.chapter2.constructioninjection.
simplejavatype;

public class Employee {

    private String employeeName;
    private int employeeAge;
    private boolean married;

    public Employee(String employeeName, int employeeAge, boolean
married) {
        this.employeeName = employeeName;
        this.employeeAge = employeeAge;
        this.married = married;

    }
    @Override
    public String toString() {
```

```
            return "Employee Name: " + this.employeeName + " , Age:"
                    + this.employeeAge + ", IsMarried: " +
    married;
        }
    }
```

In the `beans.xml` file, you'll find the following code:

```
    ...
        <bean id="employee"
        class="org.packt.Spring.chapter2.constructioninjection
    .simplejavatype.Employee">
                <constructor-arg value="Ravi Kant Soni" />
                <constructor-arg value="28" />
                <constructor-arg value="False" />

        </bean>
    ...
```

Constructor Injection – resolving ambiguity

In the Spring Framework, whenever we create a Spring bean definition file and provide values to the constructor, Spring decides implicitly and assigns the bean's value in the constructor by means of following key factors:

- Matching the number of arguments
- Matching the argument's type
- Matching the argument's order

Whenever Spring tries to create the bean using Construction Injection by following the aforementioned rules, it tries to resolve the constructor to be chosen while creating Spring bean and hence results in the following situations.

No ambiguity

If no matching constructor is found when Spring tries to create a Spring bean using the preceding rule, it throws the `BeanCreationException` exception with the message: `Could not resolve matching constructor`.

Let's understand this scenario in more detail by taking the `Employee` class from earlier, which has three instance variables and a constructor to set the value of this instance variable.

The `Employee` class has a constructor in the order of `String`, `int`, and `boolean` to be passed while defining the bean in the definition file.

In the `beans.xml` file, you'll find the following code:

```
. . .
    <bean id="employee"
    class="org.packt.Spring.chapter2.constructioninjection
.simplejavatype.Employee">
            <constructor-arg value="Ravi Kant Soni" />
            <constructor-arg value="False" />
             <constructor-arg value="28" />
    </bean>
. . .
```

If the orders in which `constructor-arg` is defined are not matching, then you will get the following error:

```
Exception in thread "main" org.springframework.beans.factory.
UnsatisfiedDependencyException:
Error creating bean with name employee defined in the classpath
resource [beans.xml]: Unsatisfied dependency expressed through
constructor argument with index 1 of type [int]: Could not convert
constructor argument value of type [java.lang.String] to required
type [int]: Failed to convert value of type 'java.lang.String' to
required type 'int'; nested exception is
java.lang.NumberFormatException: For input string: "False"
```

Solution – use index attribute

The solution to this problem is to fix the order. Either we modify the `constructor-arg` order of the bean definition file or we use the `index` attribute of `constructor-arg` as follows:

```
. . .
    <bean id="employee"
    class="org.packt.Spring.chapter2.constructioninjection
.simplejavatype.Employee">
            <constructor-arg value="Ravi Kant Soni" index="0" />
            <constructor-arg value="False" index="2" />
            <constructor-arg value="28" index="1" />
    </bean>
. . .
```

Remember that the `index` attribute always starts with `0`.

Parameter ambiguity

Sometimes, there is no problem in resolving the constructor, but the constructor chosen is leading to inconvertible data. In this case, `org.springframework.beans.factory.UnsatisfiedDependencyException` is thrown just before the data is converted to the actual type.

Let's understand this scenario in more depth; the `Employee` class contains two constructor methods and both accept three arguments with different data types.

The following code snippet is also present in `Employee.java`:

```java
package
org.packt.Spring.chapter2.constructioninjection.simplejavatype;

public class Employee {

    private String employeeName;
    private int employeeAge;
    private String employeeId;

    Employee(String employeeName, int employeeAge, String
employeeId) {
        this.employeeName = employeeName;
        this.employeeAge = employeeAge;
        this.employeeId = employeeId;
    }

    Employee(String employeeName, String employeeId, int
employeeAge) {
        this.employeeName = employeeName;
        this.employeeId = employeeId;
        this.employeeAge = employeeAge;
    }

    @Override
    public String toString() {
        return "Employee Name: " + employeeName + ", Employee
Age: "
                        + employeeAge + ", Employee Id: " +
employeeId;
    }
}
```

In the `beans.xml` file, you'll find the following code:

```
...
    <bean id="employee"
    class="org.packt.Spring.chapter2.constructioninjection
.simplejavatype.Employee">
            <constructor-arg value="Ravi Kant Soni" />
            <constructor-arg value="1065" />
            <constructor-arg value="28" />
    </bean>
...
```

Spring chooses the wrong constructor to create the bean. The preceding bean definition has been written in the hope that Spring will choose the second constructor as `Ravi Kant Soni` for `employeeName`, `1065` for `employeeId`, and `28` for `employeeAge`. But the actual output will be:

```
Employee Name: Ravi Kant Soni, Employee Age: 1065, Employee Id: 28
```

The preceding result is not what we expected; the first constructor is run instead of the second constructor. In Spring, the argument type `1065` is converted to `int`, so Spring converts it and takes the first constructor even though you assume it should be a string.

In addition, if Spring can't resolve which constructor to use, it will prompt the following error message:

```
constructor arguments specified but no matching constructor
found in bean 'CustomerBean' (hint: specify index and/or
type arguments for simple parameters to avoid type ambiguities)
```

Solution – use type attribute

The solution to this problem is to use the `type` attribute to specify the exact data type for the constructor:

```
...
    <bean id="employee"
    class="org.packt.Spring.chapter2.constructioninjection.
simplejavatype.Employee">

            <constructor-arg value="Ravi Kant Soni"
type="java.lang.String"/>
            <constructor-arg value="1065" type="java.lang.String"/>
```

```
        <constructor-arg value="28" type="int"/>
    </bean>
  ...
```

Now the output will be as expected:

```
Employee Name: Ravi Kant Soni, Employee Age: 28, Employee Id: 1065
```

The setter-based Dependency Injection

The setter-based DI is the method of injecting the dependencies of an object using the setter method. In the setter injection, the Spring container uses setXXX() of the Spring bean class to assign a dependent variable to the bean property from the bean configuration file. The setter method is more convenient to inject more dependencies since a large number of constructor arguments makes it awkward.

In the EmployeeServiceImpl.java class, you'll find the following code:

```java
public class EmployeeServiceImpl implements EmployeeService {

    private EmployeeDao employeeDao;

    public void setEmployeeDao(EmployeeDao employeeDao) {
        this.employeeDao = employeeDao;
    }
}
```

In the EmployeeDaoImpl.java class, you'll find the following code:

```java
public class EmployeeDaoImpl implements EmployeeDao {
    // ...
}
```

In the preceding code snippet, the EmployeeServiceImpl class defined the setEmployeeDao() method as the setter method where EmployeeDao is the property of this class. This method injects values of the employeeDao bean from the bean configuration file before making the employeeService bean available to the application.

The Spring bean XML configuration tag <property> is used to configure properties. The ref attribute of property elements is used to define the reference of another bean.

In the `beans.xml` file, you'll find the following code:

```
. . .
    <bean id="employeeService"
    class="org.packt.Spring.chapter2.dependencyinjection.
EmployeeServiceImpl">
            <property name="employeeDao" ref="employeeDao" />
    </bean>

    <bean id="employeeDao"
    class="org.packt.Spring.chapter2.dependencyinjection.
EmployeeDaoImpl">
    </bean>
. . .
```

The <property> element

The `<property>` element invokes the setter method. The bean definition can be describing the zero or more properties to inject before making the bean object available to the application. The `<property>` element corresponds to JavaBeans' setter methods, which are exposed by bean classes. The `<property>` element supports the following three attributes:

Attributes	Description	Occurrence
name	It takes the name of Java bean-based property	Optional
value	It describes the content in a simple string representation, which is converted into the argument type using JavaBeans' PropertyEditors	Optional
ref	It refers to a bean	Optional

Setter Injection – injecting a simple Java type

Here, we inject string-based values using the setter method. The `Employee` class contains the `employeeName` field with its setter method.

In the `Employee.java` class, you'll find the following code:

```
package org.packt.Spring.chapter2.setterinjection;

public class Employee {
```

```
String employeeName;

public void setEmployeeName(String employeeName) {
      this.employeeName = employeeName;
}

@Override
public String toString() {
      return "Employee Name: " + employeeName;
}
}
```

In the beans.xml file, you'll find the following code:

```
. . .
   <bean id="employee" class="org.packt.Spring.chapter2.
setterinjection.Employee">
         <property name="employeeName" value="Ravi Kant Soni" />
   </bean>
. . .
```

In the preceding code snippet, the bean configuration file set the property value.

In the PayrollSystem.java class, you'll find the following code:

```
package org.packt.Spring.chapter2.setterinjection;

import org.springframework.context.ApplicationContext;
import org.springframework.context.support.ClassPathXml
ApplicationContext;

public class PayrollSystem {

   public static void main(String[] args) {
         ApplicationContext context = new
ClassPathXmlApplicationContext(
                      "beans.xml");
         Employee employee = (Employee)
context.getBean("employee");
         System.out.println(employee);
   }
}
```

The output after running the `PayrollSystem` class will be as follows:

```
INFO: Refreshing org.springframework.context.support.
ClassPathXmlApplicationContext
@1ba94d: startup date [Sun Jan 25 10:11:36 IST 2015]; root of
context hierarchy
Jan 25, 2015 10:11:36 AM org.springframework.beans.factory.xml.
XmlBeanDefinitionReader
loadBeanDefinitions
INFO: Loading XML bean definitions from class path resource
[beans.xml]
Employee Name: Ravi Kant Soni
```

Setter Injection – injecting collections

In the Spring IoC container, beans can also access collections of objects. Spring allows you to inject a collection of objects in a bean using Java's collection framework. Setter Injection can be used to inject collection values in the Spring Framework. If we have a dependent object in the collection, we can inject this information using the `ref` element inside the list, set, or map. Let's discuss them in more detail:

- `<list>`: This element describes a `java.util.List` type. A list can contain multiple `bean`, `ref`, `value`, `null`, another `list`, `set`, and `map` elements. The necessary conversion is automatically performed by `BeanFactory`.

- `<set>`: This element describes a `java.util.Set` type. A set can contain multiple `bean`, `ref`, `value`, `null`, another `set`, `list`, and `map` elements.

- `<map>`: This element describes a `java.util.Map` type. A map can contain zero or more `<entry>` elements, which describes a key and value.

The `Employee` class is a class with an injecting collection.

In the `Employee.java` class, you'll find the following code:

```java
package org.packt.Spring.chapter2.setterinjection;

import java.util.List;
import java.util.Map;
import java.util.Set;

public class Employee {

    private List<Object> lists;
    private Set<Object> sets;
    private Map<Object, Object> maps;
```

```
    public void setLists(List<Object> lists) {
          this.lists = lists;
    }

    public void setSets(Set<Object> sets) {
          this.sets = sets;
    }

    public void setMaps(Map<Object, Object> maps) {
          this.maps = maps;
    }
}
```

The bean configuration file is the one that injects each and every property of the Employee class.

In the beans.xml file, you'll find the following code:

```
...
<bean id="employee" class="org.packt.Spring.chapter2.setterinjection.
Employee">
  <property name="lists">
    <list>
      <value>Ravi Kant Soni</value>
      <value>Shashi Kant Soni</value>
      <value>Shree Kant Soni</value>
    </list>
  </property>
  <property name="sets">
    <set>
      <value>Namrata Soni</value>
      <value>Rishi Raj Soni</value>
    </set>
  </property>
  <property name="maps">
    <map>
      <entry key="Key 1" value="Sasaram"/>
      <entry key="Key 2" value="Bihar"/>
    </map>
  </property>
</bean>
...
```

In the preceding code snippet, we injected values of all three setter methods of the `Employee` class. The `List` and `Set` instances are injected with the `<list>` and `<set>` tags. For the `map` property of the `Employee` class, we injected a `Map` instance using the `<map>` tag. Each entry of the `<map>` tag is specified with the `<entry>` tag that contains a key-value pair of the `Map` instance.

Injecting inner beans

Similar to the concept of inner classes in Java, it is also possible to define a bean inside another bean; for example, in an **Automated Teller Machine (ATM)** system, we can have a printer bean as an inner bean of the `ATM` class.

The following are the characteristics of inner beans in Spring:

* A bean can optionally be declared as an inner bean when it doesn't need to be shared with other beans.

* An inner bean is defined within the context of its enclosing bean.

* Typically, the inner bean does not have an ID associated with it because the inner bean will not be shared outside of its enclosing bean. We can associate an ID; however, the value of this ID attribute is ignored by Spring.

* The inner class is independent of the inner bean. Any class can be defined as an inner bean; for instance, a `Printer` class is not an inner class, but a printer bean is defined as an inner bean.

* The scope of an inner bean is always a prototype.

The limitations of using inner beans are as follows:

* It cannot be reused or shared with other beans

* In practice, it affects the readability of the configuration file

An `ATM` class has a `Printer` class. We'll declare the printer bean as an inner bean (inside the enclosing ATM bean) since the `Printer` class is not referenced anywhere outside the `ATM` class. The `printBalance()` method of ATM delegates the call to the `printBalance()` method of the printer. The printer bean will be declared as an inner bean and will then be injected into the ATM bean using Setter Injection.

The `ATM` class delegates the call to print the balance to the `Printer` class.

The following code snippet can also be found in `ATM.java`:

```
package org.packt.Spring.chapter2.setterinjection;

public class ATM {
```

```
    private Printer printer;

    public Printer getPrinter() {
          return printer;
    }

    public void setPrinter(Printer printer) {
          this.printer = printer;
    }

    public void printBalance(String accountNumber) {
          getPrinter().printBalance(accountNumber);
    }
}
```

In the preceding code snippet, the ATM class has a Printer class as property and the setter, getPrinter(), and printBalance() methods.

In the Printer.java class, you'll find the following code:

```
package org.packt.Spring.chapter2.setterinjection;

public class Printer {

    private String message;

    public void setMessage(String message) {
          this.message = message;
    }

    public void printBalance(String accountNumber) {

          System.out.println(message + accountNumber);
    }
}
```

In the preceding code snippet, the Printer class has the printBalance() method. It has a message property, and a setter method sets the message value from the bean configuration file.

In the beans.xml file, you'll find the following code:

```
    ...
    <bean id="atmBean" class="org.packt.Spring.chapter2.
    setterinjection.ATM">
```

```
        <property name="printer">
            <bean
class="org.packt.Spring.chapter2.setterinjection.Printer">
                    <property name="message"
                        value="The balance information is
printed by Printer for the account number"></property>
            </bean>
        </property>

    </bean>
    ...
```

Here, we declare `atmBean`. We declare the printer bean as an inner bean by declaring inside the enclosing `atmBean`. The `id` attribute cannot be used outside the context of `atmBean` and hence hasn't been provided to the printer bean.

Injecting null and empty string values in Spring

We come across two cases while injecting null and empty string values.

Case 1 – injecting an empty string

We can pass an empty string as a value, as shown in the following code, which is like `setEmployeeName("")` in the Java code:

```
...
<bean id="employee"
class="org.packt.Spring.chapter2.setterinjection.Employee">
        <property name="employeeName" value=""></property>
</bean>
...
```

Case 2 – injecting a null value

We can pass a `null` value, as shown in the following code, which is like `setEmployeeName(null)` in the Java code:

```
...
    <bean id="employee"
class="org.packt.Spring.chapter2.setterinjection.Employee">
```

```
    <property name="employeeName">
            <null />
    </property>
</bean>
...
```

Bean definition inheritance

Bean definition inheritance means that you have lot of bean definition in the bean configuration file and you have something that is common across lots of bean. There is a common setter value that has to be initialized across multiple beans and only then bean definition inheritance can be used.

You can have one parent bean that contains all of these common definitions inside it, and then you can inherit all the common bean definitions across the other bean. This parent bean, which has all the common definitions, can be a bean in itself. This parent bean can be made into abstract bean definitions, so there are no beans created for it, and all it does is for the purpose of templating a bean definition.

From a parent bean definition, a child bean definition inherits configuration data and can override or add values, as required. In an XML-based configuration file, a child bean definition is indicated using a parent attribute that specifies the parent bean as the value of this attribute. Refer to the following table for clarity:

Beans	Description
ParentBean	`<bean id="pBean" class="ParentBean">`
ChildBean	`<bean id="cBean" class="ChildBean" parent="pBean">`

ParentBean and ChildBean are explained as follows:

- ParentBean: This is a parent bean that is used as a template to create other beans. It would be referred to in the XML file with id="pBean".

- ChildBean: This is a child bean that inherits from the parent bean defined earlier. The parent="pBean" specifies that this bean is inheriting the properties of the ParentBean bean.

The child bean must accept the parent bean's property values. The child bean definition inherits constructor argument values and property values from the parent bean definition. The child bean definition overrides the initialization method setting and destroys method setting from the parent bean definition.

Spring bean definition inheritance is not related with the Java class inheritance. A parent bean is defined as a template and child beans can inherit the required configuration from this parent bean.

Now, the following example illustrates bean definition inheritance.

In the `Employee.java` class, you'll find the following code:

```
package org.packt.Spring.chapter2.beaninheritance;

public class Employee {

    private int employeeId;
    private String employeeName;
    private String country;

    public void setEmployeeId(int employeeId) {
        this.employeeId = employeeId;
    }

    public void setEmployeeName(String employeeName) {
        this.employeeName = employeeName;
    }

    public void setCountry(String country) {
        this.country = country;
    }

    @Override
    public String toString() {
        return "Employee ID: " + employeeId + " Name: " + employeeName
                    + " Country: " + country;
    }

}
```

In the preceding code snippet, the `Employee` class contains properties named `employeeName`, `employeeId`, `country`, and their corresponding setter method. This class has also overridden the `toString()` method.

The Spring bean configuration file, `beans.xml`, where we defined the `indianEmployee` bean as a parent bean with the `country` property and its value. Next, an `employeeBean` bean has been defined as the child bean of `indianEmployee` using the `parent="indianEmployee"` parent attribute. The child bean inherits `country` properties from the parent bean and introduces two more properties, `employeeId` and `employeeName`.

In the `beans.xml` file, you'll find the following code:

```
    ...
        <bean id="indianEmployee"
    class="org.packt.Spring.chapter2.beaninheritance.Employee">
                    <property name="country"
    value="India"></property>
       </bean>

       <bean id="employeeBean" parent="indianEmployee">
               <property name="employeeId" value="1065"></property>
               <property name="employeeName" value="Ravi Kant
    Soni"></property>
       </bean>
    ...
```

In the `PayrollSystem.java` class, you'll find the following code:

```
    package org.packt.Spring.chapter2.beaninheritance;

    import org.springframework.context.ApplicationContext;
    import org.springframework.context.support.ClassPathXml
    ApplicationContext;

    public class PayrollSystem {

       public static void main(String[] args) {

           ApplicationContext context = new
    ClassPathXmlApplicationContext(
                       "beans.xml");

           // using 'employeeBean'
           Employee employeeA = (Employee)
    context.getBean("employeeBean");
           System.out.println(employeeA);

           // using 'indianEmployee'
```

```
        Employee employeeB = (Employee)
context.getBean("indianEmployee");
        System.out.println(employeeB);
    }
}
```

When we run the `PayrollSystem` class, the result will be as follows:

```
INFO: Refreshing
org.springframework.context.support.ClassPathXmlApplicationContext
@1c4f0f8: startup date [Sun Jan 25 14:31:50 IST 2015]; root of
context hierarchy
Jan 25, 2015 2:31:51 PM
org.springframework.beans.factory.xml.XmlBeanDefinitionReader
loadBeanDefinitions
INFO: Loading XML bean definitions from class path resource
[beans.xml]
Employee ID: 1065 Name: Ravi Kant Soni Country: India
Employee ID: 0 Name: null Country: India
```

Here, the `indianEmployee` bean is able to instantiate. In the `indianEmployee` bean, we have only set the value for the `country` property, so other fields get the `null` value. In the `employeeBean`, we have set only two properties, which are `employeeId` and `employeeName`, and the `country` property is inherited from the `indianEmployee` bean, so all the fields get their value for `employeeBean`.

Inheritance with abstract

Inheritance with abstract helps in creating a bean definition as a template, which cannot be instantiated and serves as a parent definition for child definitions. While defining a bean definition as a template, you should specify only the `abstract` attribute with the value `true`, for example, `abstract="true"`.

In the `beans.xml` file, you'll find the following code:

```
...
<bean id="indianEmployee"
class="org.packt.Spring.chapter2.beaninheritance.Employee"
        abstract="true">
        <property name="country" value="India"></property>
    </bean>

    <bean id="employeeBean" parent="indianEmployee">
        <property name="employeeId" value="1065"></property>
```

```
            <property name="employeeName" value="Ravi Kant
Soni"></property>
    </bean>
...
```

The parent bean `indianEmployee` cannot be instantiated on its own because it is explicitly marked as `abstract`. When a bean definition is `abstract`, that bean definition is served as a pure template bean definition and used as a parent definition for child definitions. So, while running the `PayrollSystem` class, the following code snippet will result in an error message on the console:

```
...
        // using 'indianEmployee'
        Employee employeeB = (Employee)
context.getBean("indianEmployee");
        System.out.println(employeeB);
...
```

Since the `indianEmployee` bean is a pure template, if you try to instantiate it, you will encounter the following error message:

```
org.springframework.beans.factory.BeanIsAbstractException: Error
creating bean with name 'indianEmployee': Bean definition is
abstract
```

Autowiring in Spring

Setting bean dependencies in the configuration file is a good practice to follow in the Spring Framework; however, the Spring container can automatically autowire relationships between collaborating beans by inspecting the contents of `BeanFactory`.

As we have seen, every member variable in the Spring bean has to be configured; for example, if a bean references another bean, we have to specify the reference explicitly. Autowiring is a feature provided by the Spring Framework that helps us reduce some of these configurations by intelligently guessing what the reference is.

The Spring Framework provides autowiring features where we don't need to provide bean injection details explicitly. The Spring container can autowire relationships between collaborating beans without using the `<constructor-arg>` and `<property>` elements. This immensely helps in cutting down the XML configuration. Spring is capable of automatically resolving dependencies at runtime. This automatic resolution of bean dependencies is also called `autowiring`.

Spring wires a bean's properties automatically by setting the autowire property on each <bean> tag that you want to autowire. By default, autowiring is disabled. To enable it, specify the method of autowiring you want to apply using the autowire attribute of the bean you want to autowire, as shown here:

```
<bean id="foo" class ="Foo" autowire="autowire-type" />
```

Autowiring modes

There are five modes of autowiring that Spring Container can use for autowiring. They are explained in the following table:

Mode	Description
No	By default, Spring bean autowiring is turned off, that is, no autowiring is to be performed, and you should use explicit bean reference ref for wiring.
byname	This is autowiring by property name, that is, if the bean property is the same as the other bean name, autowire it. The setter method is used for this type of autowiring to inject a dependency.
byType	The data type is used for this type of autowiring. If the data type bean property is compatible with the data type of the other bean, autowire it. Only one bean should be configured for this type in the configuration file; otherwise, a fatal exception is thrown.
constructor	This is similar to autowire byType, but here the constructor is used to inject a dependency.
autodetect	Spring first tries to autowire by the constructor; if it does not work, then Spring tries to autowire with byType. This option is deprecated.

Let's demonstrate autowiring with examples.

In the EmployeeServiceImpl.java class, you'll find the following code:

```java
package org.packt.Spring.chapter2.autowiring;

public class EmployeeServiceImpl implements EmployeeService {

    private EmployeeDao employeeDao = null;

    public void setEmployeeDao(EmployeeDao employeeDao) {
            this.employeeDao = employeeDao;
    }
}
```

In the `EmployeeDaoImpl.java` class, you'll find the following code:

```
package org.packt.Spring.chapter2.autowiring;

public class EmployeeDaoImpl implements EmployeeDao {

    // ...

}
```

In the preceding code snippet, the `EmployeeServiceImpl` class has `employeeDaofield` and a setter method.

Autowiring using the no option

This is a default mode, and you should use the explicit bean reference `ref` for wiring.

In the `beans.xml` file, you'll find the following code:

```
...
    <bean id="employeeService"
    class="org.packt.Spring.chapter2.autowiring.
EmployeeServiceImpl">
            <property name="employeeDao"
ref="employeeDaoBean"></property>
    </bean>

    <bean id="employeeDaoBean"
class="org.packt.Spring.chapter2.autowiring.EmployeeDaoImpl">
    </bean>
...
```

Autowiring using the byname option

Autowiring using the `byName` option autowires a bean by its property name.

A Spring container looks at the properties of the beans on which the `autowire` attribute is set using `byName` in the configuration file. It then tries to match and wire its properties with the beans defined by the same names in the configuration file. If such a bean is found, it is injected into the property. If no such bean is found, an error is raised.

Case 1 – if id=" employeeDao"

In the `beans.xml` file, you'll find the following code:

```
...
    <bean id="employeeService"
    class="org.packt.Spring.chapter2.autowiring.
EmployeeServiceImpl"
            autowire="byName">
    </bean>

    <bean id="employeeDao"
class="org.packt.Spring.chapter2.autowiring.EmployeeDaoImpl">
    </bean>

...
```

In this case, since the name of the `employeeDao` bean is the same as the `employeeService` bean's property (`EmployeeDao employeeDao`), Spring will autowire it via the setter method `setEmployeeDao (EmployeeDao employeeDao)`.

Case 2 – if id=" employeeDaoBean"

In the `beans.xml` file, you'll find the following code:

```
...
    <bean id="employeeService"
    class="org.packt.Spring.chapter2.autowiring.
EmployeeServiceImpl"
            autowire="byName">
    </bean>

    <bean id="employeeDaoBean" class="org.packt.Spring.chapter2.
autowiring.EmployeeDaoImpl">
    </bean>

...
```

In this case, since the name of the `employeeDaoBean` bean is not the same as the `employeeService` bean's property (`EmployeeDao employeeDao`), Spring will not autowire it via the setter method, `setEmployeeDao(EmployeeDao employeeDao)`. So, the `employeeDao` property will get a `null` value.

Autowiring using the byType option

Autowiring using byType enables Dependency Injection based on property data types.

The Spring container looks at each property's class type searching for a matching bean definition in the configuration file when autowiring a property in a bean. If no such bean is found, a fatal exception is thrown. If there is more than one bean definition found in the configuration, a fatal exception is thrown, and it will not allow byType autowiring for that bean.

If there are no matching beans, nothing happens; the property is not set. So, to throw an error, use the dependency-check="objects" attribute value.

In the beans.xml file, you'll find the following code:

```
. . .
    <bean id="employeeService"
    class="org.packt.Spring.chapter2.autowiring.
EmployeeServiceImpl"
        autowire="byType">
    </bean>

    <bean id="employeeDaoBean"
class="org.packt.Spring.chapter2.autowiring.EmployeeDaoImpl">
    </bean>
. . .
```

In this case, since the data type of the employeeDaoBean bean is the same as the data type of the employeeService bean's property (EmployeeDao employeeDao), Spring will autowire it via the setter method setEmployeeDao(EmployeeDao employeeDao).

Autowiring using the constructor

Autowiring using the constructor applies to constructor arguments.

It will look for the class type of constructor arguments and perform autowiring using byType on all constructor arguments. A fatal error is raised if there isn't exactly one bean of the constructor argument type in the container.

In the EmployeeServiceImpl.java class, you'll find the following code:

```
package org.packt.Spring.chapter2.autowiring;

public class EmployeeServiceImpl implements EmployeeService {

    private EmployeeDao employeeDao;
```

```
    public EmployeeServiceImpl(EmployeeDao employeeDao) {
        this.employeeDao = employeeDao;
    }

    public EmployeeDao getEmployeeDao() {
        return employeeDao;
    }
}
```

In the `beans.xml` file, you'll find the following code:

```
    . . .
    <bean id="employeeService"
    class="org.packt.Spring.chapter2.autowiring
.EmployeeServiceImpl"
        autowire="constructor">
    </bean>

    <bean id="employeeDaoBean" class="org.packt.Spring.chapter2.
autowiring.EmployeeDaoImpl">
    </bean>
    . . .
```

In this case, since the data type of the `employeeDaoBean` bean is the same as the constructor argument data type in the `employeeService` bean's property (`EmployeeDao employeeDao`), Spring autowires it via the `constructor: public EmployeeServiceImpl(EmployeeDao employeeDao)`.

The bean's scope

Spring provides us with beans after instantiating and configuring them. Spring Container manages objects. This means that any object can refer to any other object from Spring Container using the bean's ID, and Spring Container provides an instance of the requesting object.

When we start Spring Container, `ApplicationContext` reads the Spring configuration, file looks for all bean definitions available there, and then initializes beans before any call to the `getBean()` method.

During initialization, `ApplicationContext` itself has initialized all the Spring beans configured in Spring XML. When another object makes a call to the `getBean()` method, `ApplicationContext` returns the same reference of bean that has already been initialized. This is the default behavior of beans.

This leads to the concept of a bean's scope. We can choose the number of instances of beans depending on the scope. There are different scopes in which a bean can be configured. The `<bean>` tag has a `scope` attribute that is used to configure the scope of the bean. There are different bean scopes in Spring, such as singleton, prototype, request, session, and global session. We will understand each session one by one.

Let's understand this by considering the following example, where we have the `EmployeeService` interface, `EmployeeServiceImpl` class, and `PayrollSystem` class with the `main()` method.

In the `EmployeeService.java` interface, you'll find the following code:

```
package org.packt.Spring.chapter2.beanscope;

public interface EmployeeService {
    void setMessage(String message);
    String getMessage();
}
```

In the preceding code snippet, the `EmployeeService` interface declares two methods.

The following are the contents of the `EmployeeServiceImpl.java` class:

```
package org.packt.Spring.chapter2.beanscope;

import org.springframework.beans.factory.InitializingBean;

public class EmployeeServiceImp implements EmployeeService {

    private String message;

    @Override
    public void setMessage(String message) {
        this.message = message;
    }

    @Override
    public String getMessage() {
        return this.message;
    }
}
```

In the preceding code snippet, the `EmployeeServiceImpl` class implemented the `EmployeeService` interface.

In the `beans.xml` file, you'll find the following code:

```xml
<?xml version="1.0" encoding="UTF-8"?>
<beans xmlns="http://www.springframework.org/schema/beans"
    xmlns:xsi="http://www.w3.org/2001/XMLSchema-instance"
    xsi:schemaLocation="http://www.springframework.org/schema/beans
    http://www.springframework.org/schema/beans/spring-beans.xsd">

    <bean id="employeeServiceBean" class="org.packt.Spring.chapter2.
beanscope.EmployeeServiceImpl">
    </bean>

</beans>
```

In the preceding configuration file, we defined `employeeServiceBean` without any scope, to see the default nature of the bean.

In the `PayrollSystem.java` class, you'll find the following code:

```java
package org.packt.Spring.chapter2.beanscope;

import org.springframework.context.ApplicationContext;
import org.springframework.context.support.ClassPathXml
ApplicationContext;

public class PayrollSystem {

    public static void main(String[] args) {

            ApplicationContext context = new
    ClassPathXmlApplicationContext(
                        "beans.xml");

            // Retrieve for first time
            EmployeeService employeeServiceA = (EmployeeService)
    context
                        .getBean("employeeServiceBean");
            employeeServiceA.setMessage("Message by service A");

                System.out
                        .println("employeeServiceA: " +
    employeeServiceA.getMessage());
```

```
            // Retrieve it again
            EmployeeService employeeServiceB = (EmployeeService)
context
                        .getBean("employeeServiceBean");
            System.out
                        .println("employeeServiceB: " +
employeeServiceB.getMessage());
    }
}
```

In the preceding code snippet, the PayrollSystem class has the main() method. For the first time, we call getBean("employeeServiceBean"), assign the bean to the employeeServiceA variable of the EmployeeService type, and then set the message by calling the setMessage() method. Again, we call getBean("employeeServiceBean") and assign the bean to the employeeServiceB variable of the EmployeeService type. The output after calling the getMessage() method from both reference variable results is the same, as shown here:

```
org.springframework.context.support.ClassPathXmlApplicationContext
prepareRefresh
INFO: Refreshing org.springframework.context.support.
ClassPathXmlApplicationContext
@1202d69: startup date [Sat Jan 24 20:04:30 IST 2015]; root of
context hierarchy
Jan 24, 2015 8:04:30 PM org.springframework.beans.factory.xml.
XmlBeanDefinitionReader
loadBeanDefinitions
INFO: Loading XML bean definitions from class path resource
[beans.xml]
employeeServiceA: Message by service A
employeeServiceB: Message by service A
```

Singleton

By default, all Spring beans are singleton. Once ApplicationContext is initialized, it looks at all the beans in XML and initializes only one bean per bean definition in Spring Container. On each call to the getBean() method, Spring Container returns the same instance of the bean.

The first bean scope in Spring that is called is singleton, which initializes only one bean per bean definition in the container and returns the same instance reference on each call to the getBean() method. This scope makes Spring initialize all beans during the load time itself without waiting for the getBean() call.

In the `beans.xml` file, you'll find the following code:

```
...
<bean id="employeeServiceBean" class="org.packt.Spring.chapter2.
beanscope.EmployeeServiceImpl"
        scope="singleton">
</bean>
...
```

In the preceding configuration file, we have a bean with a singleton scope. When we run `PayrollSystem.java`, the output will be as follows:

```
org.springframework.context.support.ClassPathXmlApplicationContext
prepareRefresh
INFO: Refreshing org.springframework.context.support.
ClassPathXmlApplicationContext
@1855562: startup date [Sat Jan 24 20:36:27 IST 2015]; root of
context hierarchy
Jan 24, 2015 8:36:28 PM
org.springframework.beans.factory.xml.XmlBeanDefinitionReader
loadBeanDefinitions
INFO: Loading XML bean definitions from class path resource
[beans.xml]
employeeServiceA: Message by service A
employeeServiceB: Message by service A
```

Since the `EmployeeServiceImpl` bean is in the singleton scope, the second retrieval by `employeeServiceB` will display the message set by `employeeServiceA` even though it's retrieved by calling a new `getBean()` method.

The singleton pattern in general says that overall there will be only one instance of the object. But when we talk about singleton in the Spring Framework, we are talking about Spring Container alone.

We can have multiple containers running in the same JVM, so we can have multiple instances of the same bean in same JVM.

So, singleton in Spring represents in a particular Spring container, and there is only one instance of a bean created in that container that is used across different references.

Prototype

The prototype is second bean scope in Spring, which returns a brand-new instance of a bean on each call to the getBean() method. When a bean is defined as a prototype, Spring waits for getBean() to happen and only then does it initialize the prototype. For every getBean() call, Spring has to perform initialization, so instead of doing default initialization while a context is being created, it waits for a getBean() call. So, every time getBean() gets called, it creates a new instance.

In the beans.xml file, you'll find the following code:

```
. . .
    <bean id="employeeServiceBean" class="org.packt.Spring.chapter2.
beanscope.EmployeeServiceImpl"
        scope="prototype">
    </bean>
. . .
```

In the preceding configuration file, we have a bean with scope as a prototype. When we run the PayrollSystem.java file, the output will be as follows:

```
org.springframework.context.support.ClassPathXmlApplicationContext
prepareRefresh
INFO: Refreshing
org.springframework.context.support.ClassPathXmlApplicationContext
@1855562: startup date [Sat Jan 24 21:05:14 IST 2015]; root of
context hierarchy
Jan 24, 2015 9:05:15 PM
org.springframework.beans.factory.xml.XmlBeanDefinitionReader
loadBeanDefinitions
INFO: Loading XML bean definitions from class path resource
[beans.xml]
employeeServiceA: Message by service A
employeeServiceB: null
```

The configured destruction life cycle callbacks are not called in the case of a prototype. Spring doesn't maintain the complete life cycle of the prototype. Here, the container instantiates and configures prototype beans and returns this bean to the client with no further record of this prototype instance.

Since every getBean() call creates a new instance of the prototype bean, this could lead to performance issues when beans use limited resources such as network connections, whereas it may be useful if you would like to get a new instance of a domain object, such as an employee object.

Request

The third bean scope in Spring is request, which is available only in web applications that use Spring and create an instance of bean for every HTTP request. Here, a new bean is created per Servlet request. Spring will be aware of when a new request is happening because it ties well with the Servlet APIs, and depending on the request, Spring creates a new bean. So, if the request scope has getBean() inside it, for every new request, there will be a new bean. However, as long as it's in the same request scope, the same bean is going to be used.

Session

The session is the fourth bean scope in Spring, which is available only in web applications that use Spring and create an instance of bean for every HTTP session. Here, a new bean is created per session. As long as there is one user accessing in a single session, each call to getBean() will return same instance of the bean. But if it's a new user in a different session, then a new bean instance is created.

Global session

The global session is the fifth bean scope in Spring, which works only in portlet environments that use Spring and create a bean for every new portlet session.

The Spring bean life cycle

As long as Spring beans are required by the application, they exist within the container. For a bean to get into a usable state after instantiation, it needs to perform some initialization. Likewise, some clean up may be necessary when the bean is no longer required and is removed from the container.

Spring provides us with callback methods for the life cycle of the bean. You can have a method in your bean that runs when the bean has been created, and you can also have a method in your bean that is run when the bean is about to be destroyed.

Spring's BeanFactory manages the life cycle of beans created through the Spring IoC container. The life cycle of beans consist of callback methods, which can be categorized broadly into the following two groups:

- Post-initialization callback methods
- Pre-destruction callback methods

The following figure illustrates the two groups:

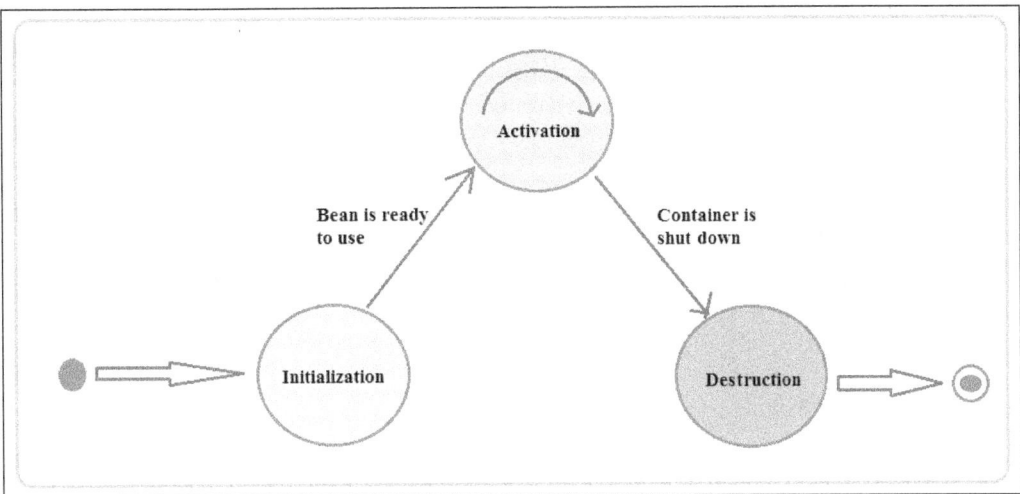

Initialization

It represents a sequence of activities that take place between the bean instantiation and the handover of its reference to the client application:

- The bean container finds the definition of the Spring bean in the configuration file and creates an instance of the bean

- If any properties are mentioned, populate the properties using setters

- If the Bean class implements the BeanNameAware interface, then call the setBeanName() method

- If the Bean class implements the BeanFactoryAware interface, then call the setBeanFactory() method

- If the Bean class implements the ApplicationContextAware interface, then call the setApplicationContext() method

- If there are any BeanPostProcessors objects associated with the BeanFactory interface that loaded the bean, then Spring will call the postProcessBeforeInitialization() method before the properties for the bean are injected

- If the Bean class implements the InitializingBean interface, then call the afterPropertiesSet() method once all the bean properties defined in the configuration file are injected

- If the bean definition in the configuration file contains the `init-method` attribute, then call this method after resolving the value for the attribute to a method name in the `Bean` class

- The `postProcessAfterInitialization()` method will be called if there are any bean post processors attached to the `BeanFactory` interface that loads the bean

Activation

The bean has been initialized and the dependency has been injected. Now the bean is ready to be used by the application.

Destruction

This represents the following sequence of activities:

- If the `Bean` class implements the `DisposableBean` interface, then call the `destroy()` method when the application no longer needs the bean reference

- If the bean definition in the configuration file contains the `destroy-method` attribute, then call this method after resolving the value for the attribute to a method name in the `Bean` class.

There are two important bean life cycle callback methods that are required at the time of bean initialization and its destruction.

- Initialization callbacks
- Destruction callbacks

Initialization callbacks

There are two ways in which you can achieve the initialization work after all necessary properties on the bean are set by the container:

- Implementing the `org.springframework.beans.factory.InitializingBean` interface

- Using `init-method` in the XML configuration

In the `EmployeeService.java` class, you'll find the following code:

```
package org.packt.Spring.chapter2.callbacks;

public interface EmployeeService {
```

```
public Long generateEmployeeID();

}
```

Implementing the org.springframework.beans.factory.InitializingBean interface

The `org.springframework.beans.factory.InitializingBean` interface is used to specify a single method in a bean, as follows:

```
void afterPropertiesSet()throws Exception;
```

This method gets initialized whenever the bean containing this method is called.

In the `EmployeeServiceImpl.java` class, you'll find the following code:

```java
package org.packt.Spring.chapter2.callbacks;

import org.springframework.beans.factory.InitializingBean;

public class EmployeeServiceImpl implements EmployeeService,
InitializingBean {

    @Override
    public Long generateEmployeeID() {

            return System.currentTimeMillis();
    }

    @Override
    public void afterPropertiesSet() throws Exception {
        System.out.println("Employee afterPropertiesSet... ");
    }
}
```

In the `beans.xml` file, you'll find the following code:

```xml
...
<bean id="employeeServiceBean"
class="org.packt.Spring.chapter2.callbacks.EmployeeServiceImpl">
</bean>
...
```

Here, the `InitializingBean` interface tells Spring that the `EmployeeServiceImpl` bean needs to know when it's being initialized. A method of this bean needs to be called when the bean is initialized. The `InitializingBean` interface has `afterPropertiesSet()`, which needs to be implemented, and it will be called by Spring when this bean is initialized and all properties are set. This `InitializingBean` interface is a marker for the bean to know that the `afterPropertiesSet()` method of this bean needs to be called after initialization.

Using init-method in the XML configuration

In the case of XML-based configuration metadata, you can use the `init-method` attribute to specify the name of the method that has a void no-argument signature, which is to be called on the bean immediately upon instantiation.

In the `beans.xml` file, you'll find the following code:

```
. . .
<bean id="employeeServiceBean" class="org.packt.Spring.chapter2.
callbacks.xml.EmployeeServiceImpl"
init-method="myInit">
</bean>
. . .
```

In the `EmployeeServiceImpl.java` class, you'll find the following code:

```
package org.packt.Spring.chapter2.callbacks.xml;

public class EmployeeServiceImpl implements EmployeeService {

    @Override
    public Long generateEmployeeID() {
            return System.currentTimeMillis();
    }

    public void myInit() {
            System.out.println("Employee myInit... ");
    }
}
```

Now we have `init-method` in the configuration `beans.xml` file, which will take the method name as the value from the bean. So, instead of implementing an interface to this bean, we have a simple method that is called by Spring.

Destruction callbacks

There are two ways you can do a destruction callback:

- Implementing the `org.springframework.beans.factory.DisposableBean` interface
- Using `destroy-method` in the XML configuration

Implementing the org.springframework.beans. factory.DisposableBean interface

The `org.springframework.beans.factory.DisposableBean` interface is used to specify a single method in a bean, as follows:

```
void destroy() throws Exception;
```

This method allows a bean to get a callback whenever the Spring container containing this bean is destroyed.

In the `EmployeeServiceImp.java` class, you'll find the following code:

```
package org.packt.Spring.chapter2.callbacks;

import org.springframework.beans.factory.DisposableBean;

public class EmployeeServiceImp implements EmployeeService,
DisposableBean {

    @Override    public Long generateEmployeeID() {
            return System.currentTimeMillis();
    }

    @Override
    public void destroy() throws Exception {
            System.out.println("Employee destroy... ");
    }
}
```

In the `beans.xml` file, you'll find the following code:

```
. . .
<bean id="employeeServiceBean" class="org.packt.Spring.chapter2.
callbacks.EmployeeServiceImpl">
</bean>
. . .
```

The `DisposableBean` interface has a `destroy()` method. If a bean implements a `DisposableBean` interface, then Spring will automatically call the `destroy()` method of that bean before actually destroying the bean.

Using destroy-method in the XML configuration

In the case of XML-based configuration metadata, you can use the `destroy-method` attribute to specify the name of the method that has a void no-argument signature, which is called just before a bean is removed from the container.

In the `beans.xml` file, you'll find the following code:

```
<bean id="employeeServiceBean" class="org.packt.Spring.chapter2.
callbacks.xml.EmployeeServiceImpl"
destroy-method="cleanUp">
</bean>
```

In the `EmployeeServiceImpl.java` class, you'll find the following code:

```java
package org.packt.Spring.chapter2.callbacks.xml;

public class EmployeeServiceImpl implements EmployeeService {

    @Override
    public Long generateEmployeeID() {
            return System.currentTimeMillis();
    }

    public void cleanUp() {
            System.out.println("Employee Cleanup... ");
    }
}
```

Now we have `destroy-method` in the configuration `beans.xml` file, which will take the method name as a value from the bean. So, instead of implementing the interface to this bean, we have a simple method that is called by Spring.

In the `PayrollSystem.java` class, you'll find the following code:

```
package org.packt.Spring.chapter2.callbacks.xml;

import org.springframework.context.ConfigurableApplicationContext;
import org.springframework.context.support.ClassPathXmlApplication
Context;

public class PayrollSystem {

    public static void main(String[] args) {
        ConfigurableApplicationContext context = new
ClassPathXmlApplicationContext("beans.xml");
        EmployeeService employeeService = (EmployeeService)
context.getBean("employeeServiceBean");
        System.out.println(employeeService.generateEmployeeID());
        context.close();
    }
}
```

Exercise

Q1. What are Inversion of Control (IoC) and Dependency Injection (DI)?

Q2. What are the different types of Dependency Injection in Spring?

Q3. Explain autowiring in Spring. What are the different modes of autowiring.

Q4. Explain the different Spring bean scopes.

 The answers to these are provided in *Appendix A, Solution to Exercises*.

Summary

In this chapter, you learned about the Spring IoC container and the `BeanFactory` and `ApplicationContext` interfaces. You also learned about DI in Spring and their types. We saw the bean's scope in Spring. Finally, we went through the life cycle of the Spring bean.

In the next chapter, we will cover the DAO design pattern. We will take a look at a simplified spring JDBC abstraction framework. We will implement the JDBC code using the Spring JDBC support and discuss how Spring manages `DataSource` and the data sources you can use in your applications. We will also discuss data support in Spring applications.

3
DAO and JDBC in Spring

In the previous chapter, you explored the concept of **Inversion of Control** (**IoC**). We then explored concepts such as, Spring Core Container, `BeanFactory`, and `ApplicationContext`, and then you learned how to implement them. We looked at **Dependency Injection** (**DI**) in Spring and their types: setter and constructor. We also wired beans using setter- and constructor-based Dependency Injection for the different data types.

In this chapter, we will cover the **Data Access Object** (**DAO**) design pattern. We will look at the simplified spring JDBC abstraction framework. We will implement the JDBC code using the Spring JDBC support and discuss how Spring manages `DataSource` that you can use in your applications. We will discuss data support in the Spring application.

When we talk about the Spring data support, it's specifically for the purpose of your application interacting with the data or the database, and you can typically write the Java code that interacts with the database. There are a few things that you have to do irrespective of what code you are going to write. You need to open the connection, manage the transaction, and then close the connection to write some boilerplate code. The whole point of using the Spring data support is that you can do away with all the extra boilerplate code and the code that you write specifically for the business case and the business problem that you want to resolve.

When we talk about writing a code that interacts with the database in Java, there are numerous ways we can do that. It could be as simple as JDBC or it could be some kind of framework, such as **Hibernate** or **iBATIS**. Spring supports lots of these technologies. The Spring JDBC module provides a kind of an abstraction layer and all the tedious JDBC code that we would otherwise have to write is provided by the JDBC module, which is in the Spring Framework.

The topics covered in this chapter are listed as follows:

- Overview of database
- The DAO design pattern
- JDBC without Spring
- The Spring JDBC packages
- JDBC with Spring
- What is `JdbcTemplate`
- The JDBC batch operation in Spring
- Calling the stored procedure

Overview of database

Databases are everywhere, but you never see them. They are concealed behind the tools and services that you use every day. Ever wondered where Facebook, Twitter, and Tumbler store their data? The answer is a database. Where does Google keep the details of the pages that it indexes from the Internet and where are the contacts stored in your mobile phone? Again, the answer is a database. In the information system, databases do most of the work that we do in our day-to-day lives. So, what is a database?

A database is a place where we store data. Databases are organized and structured. All the data that we store in the database fits into the database structure. Flat-file databases are simple databases. They store data in columns and rows.

Let's look at an Employee table:

Employee ID	First name	Last name	Age	Contact number
1	Ravi	Soni	28	+91-9986XXXXXX
2	Shree	Kant	22	+91-9986XXXXXX

Let's think about a simple database that the **Human Resource (HR)** has used to store his/her employee details. This database contains the name, address, birth date, and contact number of each employee. If the HR hires a new employee and would like to add the employee details to the database, then the HR will store the employee's first name, last name, address, date of birth, and mobile number in the database. The employee details that the HR writes down are stored in the fields of his employee address database. Each row is called a record, and each of the rows holds the information about the different employees in his/her employee address database. So, unlike a paper employee address book, the HR can carry out employee-related operations on his/her stored database. They can use the search option to find a particular employee's details.

In almost any business these days, there is a database or a collection of databases, and these are the main pieces of the backend infrastructure. Database is nothing but collection of data. There are different kinds of databases, such as Oracle, PostgreSQL, MySQL, and so on. The database software is called a **relational database management system (RDBMS)** and its instance is called a database engine. The database server is a machine that runs the database engine. We refer to the RDBMS, when we mention the term database throughout this book.

[ Refer to *Appendix B, Apache Derby Database*, to set up the Apache Derby database.]

The DAO design pattern

The DAO design pattern can be used to provide a separation between the low-level data accessing operations and the high-level business services, as shown here:

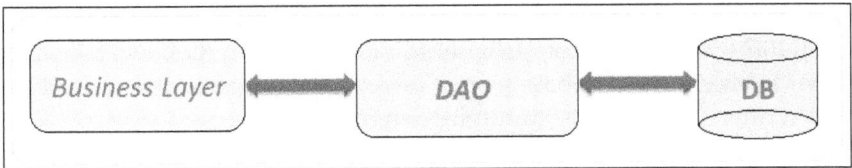

The DAO layer

In between the database and the business layer, there is a layer called the DAO layer. The DAO layer is mainly used to perform the **Create-Retrieve-Update-Delete (CRUD)** operation. The DAO layer is responsible for creating, obtaining, updating, or deleting records in the database table. To perform this CRUD operation, DAO uses a low-level API, such as the JDBC API or the Hibernate API. This DAO layer will have a method for performing the CRUD operation. It is the intermediate layer between the **Business Layer** and the **DB**. It is used to separate the low-level accessing API from the high-level business service. The DAO layer decouples the implementation of persistent storage from the rest of your application.

The advantages of using DAO are as follows:

* Its application is independent of the data access techniques and database dependency

* It offers loose coupling with the other layers of the application

* It helps the unit test the service layer using a mock object without connecting to the database

JDBC without Spring

As Java developers, we work with data all the time and develop almost all the applications that interact with some sort of database and most of the times it's relational. Generally, the application needs to interact with a database in order to get data from it. And the typical way for connecting a Java application to a database would be through JDBC.

Java Database Connectivity (JDBC) is a standard Java API. It is used for database connectivity between the Java programming language and a great variety of databases. JDBC is an application programming interface that allows a Java programmer to access the database from a Java code using sets of standard interfaces and classes written in a Java programming language.

JDBC provides several methods for querying, updating, and deleting data in RDBMS, such as SQL, Oracle, and so on. The JDBC library provides APIs for tasks such as:

* Making a connection to a database

* Creating the SQL statements

* Executing the SQL queries in the database

- Viewing and modifying the resulting records
- Closing a database connection

It is generally considered a pain to write a code to get JDBC to work. We need to write a boilerplate code to open a connection and to handle the data. Another problem with JDBC is that of poor exception hierarchy, such as SQLException, DataTruncation, SQLWarning, and BatchUpdateException. These require less explanation and a major problem is that all of these exceptions are deployed as checked exceptions, which mandate the developer to go ahead to implement a try block. It's very difficult to recover from a catch block, when an exception is thrown even during the statement execution, and most of the time these catch blocks are used for generating log messages for those exceptions.

Sample code

Here, we will take the example of JdbcHrPayrollSystem, which connects to the Apache Derby database that we saw in the previous section. We will write a query to retrieve the record, we will look at the code required to run this query, and then we will print out the retrieved record.

ADD drivers specific to database into the project

Whenever we need to write a code to access the database, we have to make sure that the drivers for the database that we are trying to connect to are available for the project. For Apache Derby, we need to include a driver so that the project can connect to the database, as shown here:

```
project > properties > Libraries > Add External jars > (navigate
to the derby folder) > lib folder > select (derby.jar and
derbyclient.jar) > ok
```

Directory structure of the application

The final directory structure of the application is shown in the following screenshot:

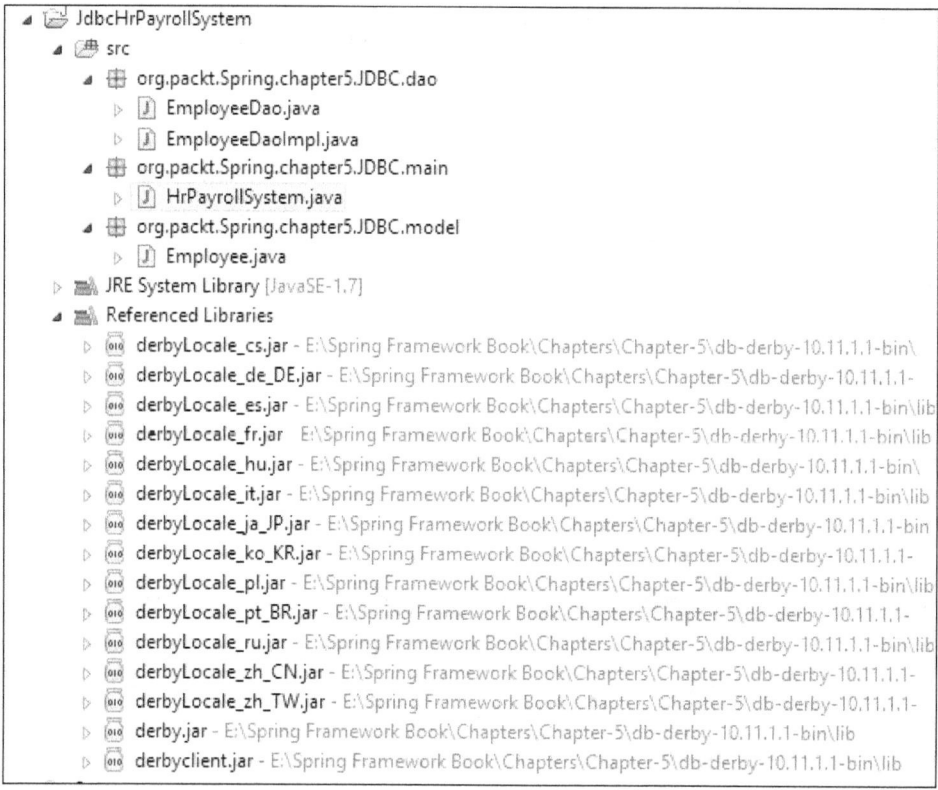

It is a good practice to design DAO using the **program to an interface** principle, which states that concrete implementations must implement the interface that is used in the program that wants to use the implementation rather than the implementation class itself. Following this principle, we will first define an interface for EmployeeDao and declare some data access methods that include the methods for creating new employee details, or getting employee details using the employee ID, and then inserting the employee details into the table.

The Employee.java file

We have package org.packt.Spring.chapter5.JDBC.model that contains the class named employee, which is a simple model class containing the employee ID, name, and its corresponding getter and setter. This employee class also has a parameterized constructor with parameters, such as id and name that set the instance variable:

```
package org.packt.Spring.chapter5.JDBC.model;

public class Employee {

    private int id;
    private String name;

    public Employee(int id, String name) {
            setId(id);
            setName(name);
    }

    // setter and getter
}
```

The EmployeeDao.java file

We have package org.packt.Spring.chapter5.JDBC.dao that has the interface EmployeeDao and the class EmployeeDaoImp. This interface contains the method for creating the Employee table, inserting the values into the table, and fetching the employee data from the table based on the employee ID, as shown here:

```
package org.packt.Spring.chapter5.JDBC.dao;

import org.packt.Spring.chapter5.JDBC.model.Employee;

public interface EmployeeDao {
    // get employee data based on employee id
    Employee getEmployeeById(int id);
    // create employee table
    void createEmployee();
    // insert values to employee table
    void insertEmployee(Employee employee);
}
```

The EmployeeDaoImpl.java file

Now, we will provide an implementation for the `EmployeeDao` interface. The `EmployeeDaoImpl` class is responsible for connecting to the database and getting or setting the values. The complexity lies in the JDBC code that goes inside the methods that connect to the database. First, we need to have a connection object, and then we need to initialize `ClientDriver`, which in our case, is specific to the Apache Derby driver. Now, we need to open a connection using the database URL. Then, based on the functionality, we need to prepare and execute a query:

```java
package org.packt.Spring.chapter5.JDBC.dao;

import java.sql.Connection;
import java.sql.DriverManager;
import java.sql.PreparedStatement;
import java.sql.ResultSet;
import java.sql.SQLException;
import java.sql.Statement;
import org.packt.Spring.chapter5.JDBC.model.Employee;

public class EmployeeDaoImpl implements EmployeeDao {
    // JDBC driver name and database URL
    static final String JDBC_DRIVER =
"org.apache.derby.jdbc.ClientDriver";
    static final String DB_URL = "jdbc:derby://localhost:1527/db";

    private void registerDriver() {
        try {
                Class.forName(JDBC_DRIVER).newInstance();
        } catch (InstantiationException e) {
        } catch (IllegalAccessException e) {
        } catch (ClassNotFoundException e) {
        }
    }
```

Here, the `getEmployeeById(int id)` method will fetch the employee information based on the employee ID:

```java
@Override
public Employee getEmployeeById(int id) {
        Connection conn = null;
        Employee employee = null;
```

```
        try {
                // register apache derby driver
                registerDriver();
                // open a connection using DB url
                conn = DriverManager.getConnection(DB_URL);
                // Creates a PreparedStatement object for sending
parameterized SQL
                // statements to the database
                PreparedStatement ps = conn
                            .prepareStatement("select * from
employee where id = ?");
                // Sets the designated parameter to the given Java
int value
                ps.setInt(1, id);
                // Executes the SQL query in this PreparedStatement
object and
                // returns the ResultSet object
                ResultSet rs = ps.executeQuery();
                if (rs.next()) {
                        employee = new Employee(id,
rs.getString("name"));
                }
                rs.close();
                ps.close();
        } catch (SQLException e) {
                throw new RuntimeException(e);
        } finally {
                if (conn != null) {
                        try {
                                conn.close();
                        } catch (SQLException e) {
                        }
                }
        }
        return employee;
    }
```

The createEmployee() method creates an Employee table with the column ID and name, as shown in the following code snippet:

```
@Override
public void createEmployee() {
        Connection conn = null;
        try {
                // register apache derby driver
                registerDriver();
                // open a connection using DB url
                conn = DriverManager.getConnection(DB_URL);
                Statement stmt = conn.createStatement();
                stmt.executeUpdate("create table employee (id
integer, name char(30))");
                stmt.close();
        } catch (SQLException e) {
            throw new RuntimeException(e);
        } finally {
            if (conn != null) {
                    try {
                            conn.close();
                    } catch (SQLException e) {
                    }
            }
        }
    }
```

In the following code snippet, the insertEmployee(Employee employee) method will insert the employee information into the Employee table:

```
@Override
public void insertEmployee(Employee employee) {
        Connection conn = null;
        try {
                // register apache derby driver
                registerDriver();
                // open a connection using DB url
                conn = DriverManager.getConnection(DB_URL);
                Statement stmt = conn.createStatement();
                stmt.executeUpdate("insert into employee values ("
                            + employee.getId() + ",'" +
employee.getName() + "')");
                    stmt.close();
            } catch (SQLException e) {
```

```
                throw new RuntimeException(e);
        } finally {
            if (conn != null) {
                try {
                    conn.close();
                } catch (SQLException e) {
                }
            }
        }
    }
}
```

The HrPayrollSystem.java file

We have `package org.packt.Spring.chapter5.JDBC.main` that contains the class `HrPayrollSystem` with the `main()` method. In the `main()` method, we will initialize DAO and call the methods of DAO to create a table, insert the data, and then fetch the data from the table, as shown here:

```
package org.packt.Spring.chapter5.JDBC.main;

import org.packt.Spring.chapter5.JDBC.dao.EmployeeDao;
import org.packt.Spring.chapter5.JDBC.dao.EmployeeDaoImpl;
import org.packt.Spring.chapter5.JDBC.model.Employee;

public class HrPayrollSystem {

    public static void main(String[] args) {
        EmployeeDao employeeDao = new EmployeeDaoImpl();
        // create employee table
        employeeDao.createEmployee();
        // insert into employee table
        employeeDao.insertEmployee(new Employee(1, "Ravi"));
        // get employee based on id
        Employee employee = employeeDao.getEmployeeById(1);
        System.out.println("Employee name: " +
employee.getName());
    }
}
```

Having shown the trouble in using JDBC, in the next section, we will be discussing the DAO support in the Spring Framework to remove the troubling points one after the other.

Spring JDBC packages

In the previous section, we have seen the shortcomings of using the JDBC API as a low-level data access API for implementing the DAOs. These shortcomings are as follows:

- **Code duplication**: As we know, writing the boilerplate code over and over again in code duplication violates the **Don't repeat yourself (DRY)** principle. This has some side effects in terms of the project costs, efforts, and timelines.

- **Resource leakage**: The DAO methods must hand over the control of the obtained database resources, such as connection, statements, or result sets after calling the `close()` method. This is a risky plan because a novice programmer might very easily skip some of the code fragments. As a result, the resources would run out and bring the system to a stop.

- **Error handling**: When using JDBC directly we need to handle `SQLException`, since the JDBC drivers report all the errors suitable by raising `SQLException`. It is not possible to recover these exceptions. Moreover, the message and the error code obtained from the `SQLException` object are database vendor-specific, so it is difficult to write a portable DAO error messaging code.

To solve the aforementioned problems, we need to identify the parts of the code that are fixed and then encapsulate them into some reusable objects. The Spring Framework provides a solution for these problems by giving a thin, robust, and highly extensible JDBC abstraction framework.

The JDBC abstraction framework provided under the Spring Framework is considered to be a value-added service that takes care of all the low-level details, such as retrieving connection, preparing the statement object, executing the query, and releasing the database resources. While using it for data access, the application developer needs to specify the SQL statement for executing and retrieving the result.

To handle the different aspects of JDBC, Spring JDBC is divided into packages, as shown in the following table:

Spring JDBC package	Description
org.springframework.jdbc.core	In the Spring Framework, this package contains the foundation of the JDBC classes, which includes the core JDBC class and JdbcTemplate. It simplifies the database operation using JDBC.
org.springframework.jdbc.datasource	This package contains DataSource implementations and helper classes, which can be used to run the JDBC code outside the JEE container.
org.springframework.jdbc.object	In the Spring Framework, this package contains the classes that help in converting the data returned from the database into plain Java objects.
org.springframework.jdbc.support	SQLExceptionTranslator is the most important class in this package of the Spring Framework. The Spring Framework recognizes the error code used by the database. This is done by using this class and mapping the error code to a higher level of exception.
org.springframework.jdbc.config	This package contains the classes that support JDBC configuration within ApplicationContext of the Spring Framework.

JDBC with Spring

In the earlier section, we did not include any Spring-related functionality, and we implemented a Java class that had DAO implementation, which connected to a database to fetch a particular record using JDBC. Now in this section, we will look at some of the features of the Spring Framework that make our job easier by eliminating the boilerplate code. Here, we will look into the connection support provided by Spring that makes it easy to handle the connections.

DataSource

The `DriverManagerDataSource` class is used for configuring the `DataSource` for application, which is defined in the configuration file, that is, `Spring.xml`. So, first of all, we need to add the Spring JAR that will have the `DriverManagerDataSource` class to our project. The Spring Framework provides the JAR for JDBC `spring-jdbc-4.1.4.RELEASE.jar` containing the package named `DataSource`, which will have the class `DriverManagerDataSource.class`, as shown in the following screenshot:

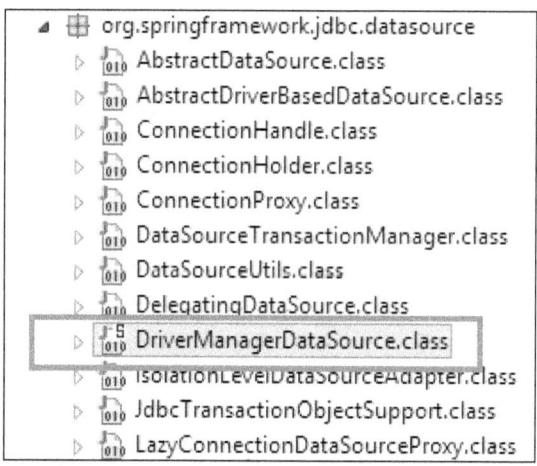

The configuration of `DriverManagerDataSource` is shown here. We need to provide the driver class name and the connection URL. We can also add the username and the password in the property if the database requires it.

Check out the file `Spring.xml` using the following code snippet:

```
...
    <context:annotation-config />

    <context:component-scan base-
package="org.packt.Spring.chapter5.JDBC.dao" />

    <bean id="dataSource"
    class="org.springframework.jdbc.datasource.
DriverManagerDataSource">
            <property name="driverClassName"
value="${jdbc.driverClassName}" />
```

```
            <property name="url" value="${jdbc.url}" />
    </bean>

    <context:property-placeholder location="jdbc.properties" />
    ...
```

The bold properties in the aforementioned configuration code represent the values that you normally pass to JDBC to connect it with the interface. For easy substitution in the different deployment environments and for easy maintenance, the database connection information is stored in the properties file, and the Spring's property placeholder will load the connection information from the jdbc.properties file:

```
jdbc.driverClassName=org.apache.derby.jdbc.ClientDriver
jdbc.url=jdbc:derby://localhost:1527/db
```

DataSource in the DAO class

In the previous section, we added the properties for the DataSource in the configuration file Spring.xml. So, we will look into the DAOs class to see the benefit of using DataSource. We will implement the EmployeeDao interface that we defined in the earlier section.

Directory structure of the application

The final directory structure of the application is shown in the following screenshot:

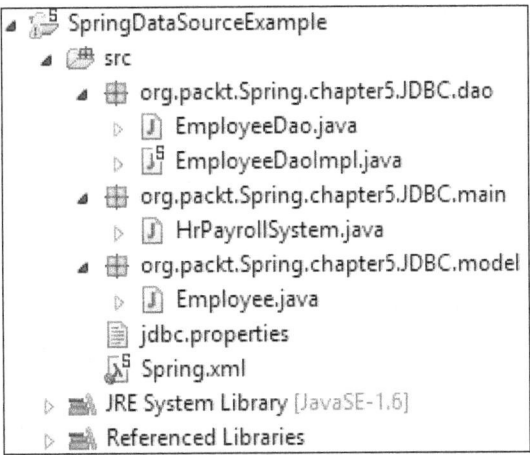

The EmployeeDaoImpl.java file

In the earlier section, we were trying to perform a few basic steps, which are common for methods such as:

- Set up connection to a database
- Create a prepared statement

The first step is to connect to the database that is common for all the methods of the application. We will take out the boilerplate code for this step from the methods defined in the EmployeeDaoImpl class.

We have defined DataSource as a member variable and annotated it by the @Autowired annotation. We have called the getConnection() method of this DataSource to get the connection based on the definition provided in the configuration file.

Checkout the file EmployeeDaoImpl.java for the following code snippet:

```
package org.packt.Spring.chapter5.JDBC.dao;

import java.sql.Connection;
import java.sql.PreparedStatement;
import java.sql.ResultSet;
import java.sql.SQLException;
import java.sql.Statement;
import javax.sql.DataSource;
import org.packt.Spring.chapter5.JDBC.model.Employee;
import org.springframework.beans.factory.annotation.Autowired;
import org.springframework.stereotype.Repository;

@Repository
public class EmployeeDaoImpl implements EmployeeDao {
    @Autowired
    private DataSource dataSource;
```

Here, the EmployeeDaoImpl class is annotated by the stereotypical annotation, @Repository, so that Spring automatically scans this class and registers it as the Spring bean employeeDaoImpl.

The getEmployeeById(int id) method is used to get the employee details based on the employee ID, as shown here:

```
@Override
public Employee getEmployeeById(int id) {
    Employee employee = null;
```

```
        Connection conn = null;
        try {
                conn = dataSource.getConnection();
                PreparedStatement ps = conn
                            .prepareStatement("select * from
employee where id = ?");
                ps.setInt(1, id);
                ResultSet rs = ps.executeQuery();
                if (rs.next()) {
                        employee = new Employee(id,
rs.getString("name"));
                }
                rs.close();
                ps.close();
        } catch (SQLException e) {
                throw new RuntimeException(e);
        } finally {
                if (conn != null) {
                        try {
                                conn.close();
                        } catch (SQLException e) {
                        }
                }
        }
        return employee;
    }
```

The createEmployee() method is used for creating the Employee table, as shown in the following code snippet:

```
    @Override
    public void createEmployee() {
            Connection conn = null;
            try {
                    conn = dataSource.getConnection();
                    Statement stmt = conn.createStatement();
                    stmt.executeUpdate("create table employee (id
integer, name char(30))");
                    stmt.close();
            } catch (SQLException e) {
                    throw new RuntimeException(e);
            } finally {
                    if (conn != null) {
                            try {
```

```
                conn.close();
            } catch (SQLException e) {
            }
        }
    }
}
```

The `insertEmployee(Employee employee)` method is used for inserting the data into the Employee table, as shown here:

```
@Override
public void insertEmployee(Employee employee) {
    Connection conn = null;
    try {
        conn = dataSource.getConnection();
        Statement stmt = conn.createStatement();
        stmt.executeUpdate("insert into employee values ("
                + employee.getId() + ",'" +
employee.getName() + "')");
        stmt.close();
    } catch (SQLException e) {
        throw new RuntimeException(e);
    } finally {
        if (conn != null) {
            try {
                conn.close();
            } catch (SQLException e) {
            }
        }
    }
}
```

The HrPayrollSystem.java file

We have `package org.packt.Spring.chapter5.JDBC.main` that contains the class `HrPayrollSystem` with the `main()` method:

```
package org.packt.Spring.chapter5.JDBC.main;

import org.packt.Spring.chapter5.JDBC.dao.EmployeeDao;
import org.packt.Spring.chapter5.JDBC.model.Employee;
import org.springframework.context.ApplicationContext;
import org.springframework.context.support.
ClassPathXmlApplicationContext;
```

```
public class HrPayrollSystem {

    public static void main(String[] args) {
            @SuppressWarnings("resource")
            ApplicationContext context = new
ClassPathXmlApplicationContext(
                            "Spring.xml");
            EmployeeDao employeeDao =
context.getBean("employeeDaoImpl",
                            EmployeeDao.class);
            // create employee table
            employeeDao.createEmployee();
            // insert into employee table
            employeeDao.insertEmployee(new Employee(1, "Ravi"));
            // get employee based on id
            Employee employee = employeeDao.getEmployeeById(1);
            System.out.println("Employee name: " +
employee.getName());
    }
}
```

The types of code that we have discussed so far use the Spring Framework to manage `DataSource` and this makes things simple. We have taken all the connection parameters from the class and set them to bean defined by an XML file. In DAO, we have used the method of the new bean to get the connection of the database.

What is JdbcTemplate

The central class of the Spring JDBC abstraction framework is the `JdbcTemplate` class that includes the most common logic in using the JDBC API to access data, such as handling the creation of connection, statement creation, statement execution, and release of resource. The `JdbcTemplate` class can be found in the `org.springframework.jdbc.core` package.

The `JdbcTemplate` class instances are thread-safe once configured. A single `JdbcTemplate` can be configured and injected into multiple DAOs.

We can use the `JdbcTemplate` to execute the different types of SQL statements. **Data Manipulation Language (DML)** is used for inserting, retrieving, updating, and deleting the data in the database. `SELECT`, `INSERT`, or `UPDATE` statements are examples of DML. **Data Definition Language (DDL)** is used for either creating or modifying the structure of the database objects in the database. `CREATE`, `ALTER`, and `DROP` statements are examples of DDL.

The JdbcTemplate class is in the org.springframework.jdbc.core package. It is a non-abstract class. It can be initiated using any of the following constructors:

- JdbcTemplate: Construct a new JdbcTemplate object. When constructing an object using this constructor, we need to use the setDataSource() method to set the DataSource before using this object for executing the statement.

- JdbcTemplate(DataSource): Construct a new JdbcTemplate object, and initialize it with a given DataSource to obtain the connections for executing the requested statements.

- JdbcTemplate(DataSource, Boolean): Construct a new JdbcTemplate object, and initialize it by a given DataSource to obtain the connections for executing the requested statements, and the Boolean value describing the lazy initialization of the SQL exception translator.

  If the Boolean argument value is true, then the exception translator will not be initialized immediately. Instead, it will wait until the JdbcTemplate object is used for executing the statement. If the Boolean argument value is false, then the exception translator will be initialized while constructing the JdbcTemplate object.

It also catches the JDBC exception and translates it into the generic and more informatics exception hierarchy, which is defined in the org.springframework.dao package. This class avoids common error and executes the SQL queries, updates the statements, stores the procedure calls, or extracts the results.

While using the JdbcTemplate, the application developer has to provide the code for preparing the SQL statement and the extract result. In this section, we will look into operations such as, query, update, and so on using the JdbcTemplate in Spring.

Configuring the JdbcTemplate object as Spring bean

The Spring JdbcTemplate makes the application developer's life a lot easier by taking care of all the boilerplate code required for creating and releasing database connection, which saves development time. In the earlier section, we saw how to define the DataSource bean in the configuration file. To initialize the JdbcTemplate object, we will use the DataSource bean as ref. This is discussed while explaining the configuration file, Spring.xml.

The Spring.xml file

The following code snippet shows the `Spring.xml` file:

```
<?xml version="1.0" encoding="UTF-8"?>
<beans xmlns="http://www.springframework.org/schema/beans"
    xmlns:xsi="http://www.w3.org/2001/XMLSchema-instance"
xmlns:context="http://www.springframework.org/schema/context"
    xmlns:jdbc="http://www.springframework.org/schema/jdbc"
    xsi:schemaLocation="http://www.springframework.org/schema/beans
http://www.springframework.org/schema/beans/spring-beans.xsd
        http://www.springframework.org/schema/context
http://www.springframework.org/schema/context/spring-context-
3.2.xsd
        http://www.springframework.org/schema/jdbc
http://www.springframework.org/schema/jdbc/spring-jdbc-3.2.xsd">

    <context:annotation-config />

    <context:component-scan base-
package="org.packt.Spring.chapter5.JDBC.dao" />

    <bean id="dataSource"
    class="org.springframework.jdbc.datasource.
DriverManagerDataSource">
        <property name="driverClassName">
            <value={jdbc.driverClassName}></value>
        </property>
        <property name="url">
            <value={jdbc.url}></value>
        </property>
    </bean>

     <bean id="jdbcTemplate" class="org.springframework.jdbc.core.
JdbcTemplate">
        <property name="dataSource" ref="dataSource" />
    </bean>

    <context:property-placeholder location="jdbc.properties"/>

</beans>
```

Functionality exposed by the JdbcTemplate class

The Spring `JdbcTemplate` provides many helpful methods for the CRUD operations for the database.

Querying (select)

Here, we use the `select` command to query the database using the `JdbcTemplate` class. Depending upon the following application requirements, the database table can be queried:

- The following is a simple query to get the number of rows in a relation:

```
int rowCount = this.jdbcTemplate.queryForObject("select
count(*) from employee ", Integer.class);
```

- A simple query that uses the bind variable is shown here:

```
int countOfEmployeesNamedRavi =
this.jdbcTemplate.queryForObject(
        "select count(*) from employee where Name = ?",
Integer.class, "Ravi");
```

- The following is a simple query for String:

```
String empName = this.jdbcTemplate.queryForObject(
        "select Name from employee where EmpId = ?",
        new Object[]{12121}, String.class);
```

- The code block to populate a domain object after querying is shown here:

```
Employee employee = this.jdbcTemplate.queryForObject(
        "select Name, Age from employee where EmpId = ?",
        new Object[]{1212},
        new RowMapper<Employee>() {
            public Employee mapRow(ResultSet rs, int
rowNum) throws SQLException {
                Employee emp = new Employee(rs.getString("Name"),
rs.getString("Age"));
                return emp;
            }
        });
```

- The code block to populate a list of the domain objects after querying is given here:

```
List<Employee> employee = this.jdbcTemplate.query(
        "select Name, Age from employee",
        new RowMapper<Employee>() {
            public Employee mapRow(ResultSet rs, int
rowNum) throws SQLException {
                Employee emp = new Employee(rs.getString("Name"),
rs.getString("Age"));
                return emp;
            }
        });
```

Apart from querying the database table, the operation for updating the record can also be performed as discussed in the next section.

Updating (Insert-Update-Delete)

When we talk about updating a record, it simply implies inserting a new record, making a change in an existing record, or deleting an existing record.

The `Update()` method is used to perform operations such as insert, update, or delete. The parameter values are usually provided as an object array or var args. Consider the following cases:

- The following shows an `Insert` operation:

```
this.jdbcTemplate.update("insert into employee (EmpId,
Name, Age) values (?, ?, ?)", 12121, "Ravi", "Soni");
```

- An `Update` operation is shown here:

```
this.jdbcTemplate.update("update employee set Name = ?
where EmpId = ?", "Shree", 12121);
```

- A `Delete` operation is given here:

```
this.jdbcTemplate.update("delete from employee where EmpId
= ?",Long.valueOf(empId));
```

Other JdbcTemplate operations

The `execute()` method is used for executing any arbitrary SQL:

```
this.jdbcTemplate.execute("create table employee (EmpId integer,
Name varchar(30), Age integer)");
```

Directory structure of the application

The final directory structure of the application is shown here:

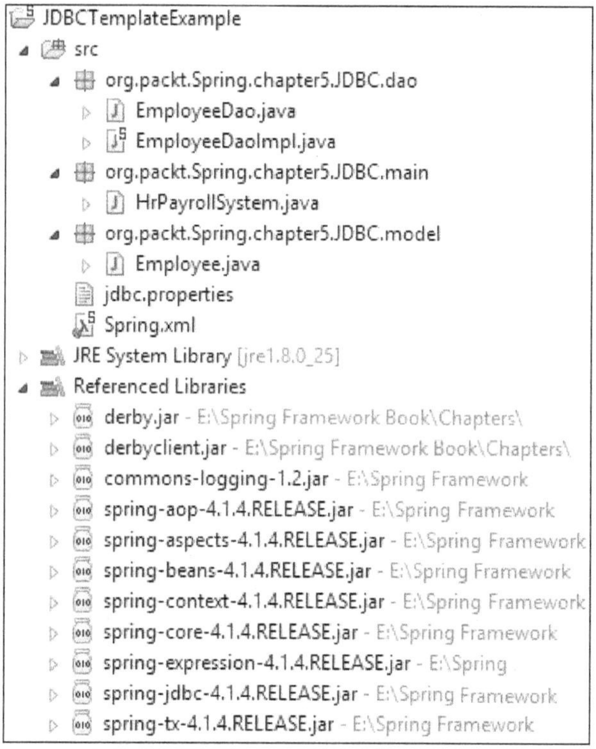

The Employee.java file

The Employee class has parameterized the constructor with three parameters, namely, empId, name, and age:

```java
package org.packt.Spring.chapter5.JDBC.model;

public class Employee {

    private int empId;
    private String name;
    private int age;

    public Employee(int empId, String name, int age) {
        setEmpId(empId);
```

```
        setName(name);
        setAge(age);
    }

// setter and getter
```

The EmployeeDao.java file

The `EmployeeDao` interface contains the declaration of a method whose implementation is provided in `EmployeeDaoImpl.java`:

```
package org.packt.Spring.chapter5.JDBC.dao;
import org.packt.Spring.chapter5.JDBC.model.Employee;
public interface EmployeeDao {
    void createEmployee();
    int getEmployeeCount();
    int insertEmployee(Employee employee);
    int deleteEmployeeById(int empId);
    Employee getEmployeeById(int empId);
}
```

The EmployeeDaoImpl.java file

Now let's look at the implementation of `EmployeeDao`, where we will use the `JdbcTemplate` class to execute the different types of queries:

```
package org.packt.Spring.chapter5.JDBC.dao;

import java.sql.ResultSet;
import java.sql.SQLException;
import java.sql.Types;

import org.packt.Spring.chapter5.JDBC.model.Employee;
import org.springframework.beans.factory.annotation.Autowired;
import org.springframework.jdbc.core.JdbcTemplate;
import org.springframework.jdbc.core.RowMapper;
import org.springframework.stereotype.Repository;

@Repository
public class EmployeeDaoImpl implements EmployeeDao {
    @Autowired
    private JdbcTemplate jdbcTemplate;

    @Override
    public int getEmployeeCount() {
```

```
                    String sql = "select count(*) from employee";
                    return jdbcTemplate.queryForInt(sql);
        }


        @Override
        public int insertEmployee(Employee employee) {
                String insertQuery = "insert into employee (EmpId, Name,
Age) values (?, ?, ?) ";
                Object[] params = new Object[] { employee.getEmpId(),
                            employee.getName(), employee.getAge() };
                int[] types = new int[] { Types.INTEGER, Types.VARCHAR,
Types.INTEGER };
                return jdbcTemplate.update(insertQuery, params, types);
        }


        @Override
        public Employee getEmployeeById(int empId) {
                String query = "select * from Employee where EmpId = ?";
                // using RowMapper anonymous class, we can create a
separate RowMapper
                // for reuse
                Employee employee = jdbcTemplate.queryForObject(query,
                            new Object[] { empId }, new
RowMapper<Employee>() {
                                    @Override
                                    public Employee mapRow(ResultSet rs,
int rowNum)
                                                throws SQLException {
                                            Employee employee = new
Employee(rs.getInt("EmpId"), rs

    .getString("Name"), rs.getInt("Age"));
                                            return employee;
                                    }
                            });
                return employee;
        }


        @Override
        public int deleteEmployeeById(int empId) {
                String delQuery = "delete from employee where EmpId =
?";
                return jdbcTemplate.update(delQuery, new Object[] {
empId });
        }
}
```

JDBC batch operation in Spring

The single executable unit for performing multiple operations is known as a batch. If you batch multiple calls to the same prepared statement, then most of the JDBC drivers show improved performance. Moreover, if you group the updates into batches, then you can limit the number of round trips to the database, as shown in the following diagram:

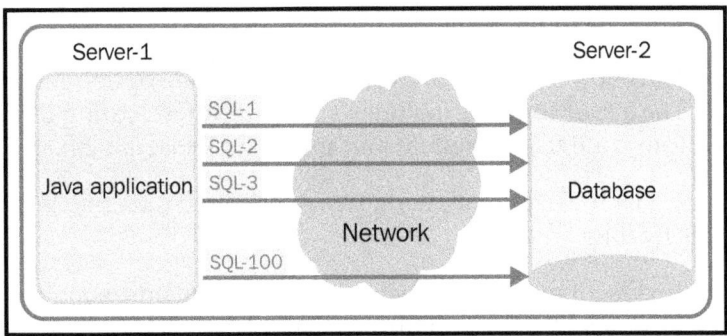

As shown in the aforementioned figure, we have **Server-1**, where our Java application is running, and in **Server-2**, the database is running. Both the servers are situated in different locations. Let's assume that we have to execute 100 queries. Generally, we send each query from the Java application to the database server and execute them one by one. Here, we have sent the **SQL-1** query from the Java application to the database server for execution, and then the **SQL-2** query, and so on till the **SQL-100** query. So here, for 100 queries, we have to send the SQL queries from the Java application to the database server through the network. This will add a communication overhead and reduce the performance. So to improve the performance and reduce the communication overhead, we use the JDBC batch processing, as shown here:

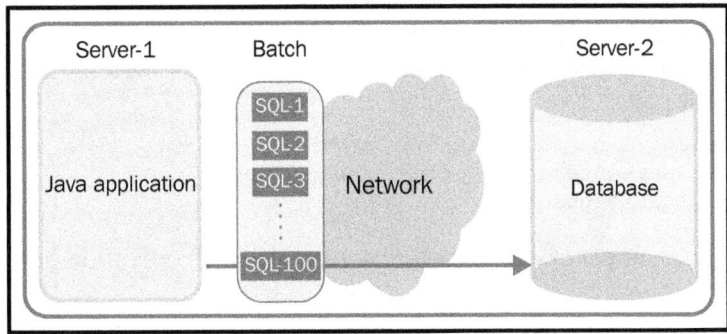

JDBC with batch processing

In the preceding figure, we have a batch with 100 SQL queries, which will be sent from the Java application server to the database server only once, and they will still be executed. So, there is no need to send each SQL query from the Java application server to the database server. In this way, it will reduce the communication overhead and improve the performance.

The batch update operation allows you to submit multiple SQL queries to the DataSource for processing at once. Submitting multiple SQL queries at once instead of submitting them individually, improves the performance.

This section explains how to use an important batch update option with the JdbcTemplate. The JdbcTemplate includes a support for executing the batch of statements through a JDBC statement and through PreparedStatement.

The JdbcTemplate includes the following two overloaded batchUpdate() methods that support this feature:

- One method is for executing a batch of SQL statements using the JDBC statement. This method's signature is that it issues multiple SQL updates, as shown here:

```
public int[] batchUpdate(String[] sql) throws
DataAccessException
```

  The following sample code shows how to use this method:

```
jdbcTemplate.batchUpdate (new String [] {
                "update emp set salary = salary * 1.5 where
empId = 10101",
                 "update emp set salary = salary * 1.2 where
empId = 10231",
                  "update dept set location = 'Bangalore'
where deptNo = 304"
});
```

- The other method is for executing the SQL statement multiple times with different parameters using PreparedStatement, as shown by the following code snippet:

```
public int[] batchUpdate(String sql,
BatchPreparedStatementSetter bPSS) throws
DataAccessException
```

Let's consider an example of a code, where an update batch operation performs actions.

Directory structure of the application

The final directory structure of the application is shown here:

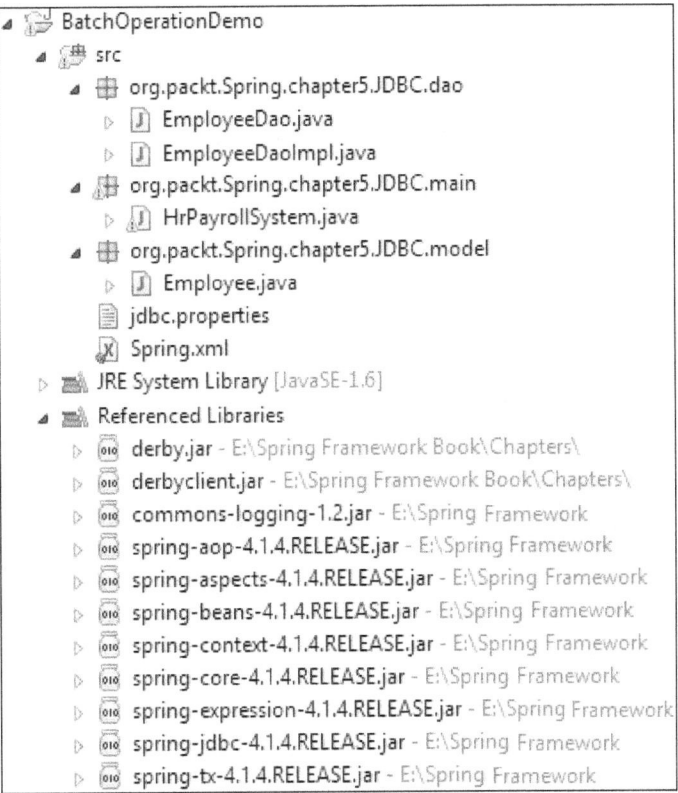

The EmployeeDaoImpl.java file

The EmployeeDaoImp class has the method insertEmployees() that performs the batch insert operation, as shown here:

```
package org.packt.Spring.chapter5.JDBC.dao;

import java.sql.PreparedStatement;
import java.sql.SQLException;
import java.util.List;

import org.packt.Spring.chapter5.JDBC.model.Employee;
import org.springframework.beans.factory.annotation.Autowired;
import org.springframework.jdbc.core.BatchPreparedStatementSetter;
```

```
import org.springframework.jdbc.core.JdbcTemplate;
import org.springframework.stereotype.Repository;

@Repository
public class EmployeeDaoImpl {
   @Autowired
   private JdbcTemplate jdbcTemplate;

   public void insertEmployees(final List<Employee> employees) {
        jdbcTemplate.batchUpdate("INSERT INTO employee "
                   + "(id, name) VALUES (?, ?)",
                   new BatchPreparedStatementSetter() {

                        public void
setValues(PreparedStatement ps, int i)
                                            throws SQLException {
                                 Employee employee =
employees.get(i);
                                 ps.setLong(1,
employee.getId());
                                 ps.setString(2,
employee.getName());
                        }

                        public int getBatchSize() {
                                return employees.size();
                        }
                   });
   }

   public int getEmployeeCount() {
        String sql = "select count(*) from employee";
        return jdbcTemplate.queryForInt(sql);
   }

}
```

The HrPayrollBatchUpdate.java file

The `HrPayrollBatchUpdate` class calls a method from `EmployeeDaoImp` to perform a batch update operation:

```
package org.packt.Spring.chapter5.JDBC.batchupdate;

public class HrPayrollBatchUpdate {
```

```
public static void main(String[] args) {

        ApplicationContext context = new
ClassPathXmlApplicationContext(
                    "Spring.xml");
        EmployeeDaoImp employeeDaoImp = (EmployeeDaoImp) context
                    .getBean("employeeDaoImp");

        List<Employee> employeeList = new ArrayList<Employee>();
        Employee employee1 = new Employee(10001, "Ravi");
        Employee employee2 = new Employee(23330, "Kant");
        Employee employee3 = new Employee(12568, "Soni");
        employeeList.add(employee1);
        employeeList.add(employee2);
        employeeList.add(employee3);
        employeeDaoImp.insertEmployees(employeeList);
        System.out.println(employeeDaoImp.getEmployeeCount());
    }
}
```

The preceding code shows how to use the `batchUpdate()` method with string and `BatchPreparedStatementSetter` for executing a SQL statement multiple times with different parameter values. In this section, we have seen how to execute batch statements using a `JdbcTemplate`.

Calling a stored procedure

A stored procedure is a group of transact SQL statements. If you have a situation where you write the same query over and over again, then you can save that specific query as a stored procedure and call it just by calling its name. Stored procedures are a block of SQL statements that are stored as basic objects within your database.

Let's take our Employee table that has columns as `EmpId`, `Name`, and `Age`. Let's say that we need the name and age of an employee, we will write the query as `Select Name, Age from employee`. So every time we need the name and age of the employee, we will need to write this query. Instead, we can add this query to the stored procedure and call that stored procedure rather than writing this query again and again.

The advantages and disadvantages of using the stored procedure are as follows:

Advantages	Disadvantages
Stored procedure helps in increasing the performance of an application. Stored procedures, once created, are compiled and stored in the database. And this compiled version of the stored procedures is used if an application uses the stored procedures multiple times in a single connection.	Stored procedures are difficult to debug and only a few DBMS allow you to debug it.
It helps in reducing the traffic between the application and the database server. Because, the application has to send the name and the parameter of the stored procedures rather than sending the multiple length SQL statements.	Developing and maintaining the stored procedures is not easy and leads to problems in the development and the maintenance phases, as it requires a specialized skill set, which the average developer has no interest in learning.

Using the SimpleJdbcCall class

An instance of the SimpleJdbcCall class is that of a multithreaded and reusable object, representing a call to a stored procedure. It provides the metadata processing to simplify the code required for accessing the basic stored procedure. While executing a call, you only have to provide the name of the stored procedure. The names of the supplied parameters are matched with the in and out parameters, specified during the declaration of a stored procedure. Here, we will discuss the calling of a stored procedure and a stored function using the SimpleJdbcCall class.

Calling a stored procedure

The SimpleJdbcCall class takes the advantage of the metadata present in the database to look up the names of the IN and OUT parameters, and thereby there is no need to explicitly declare the parameters. However, you can still declare them if you have the parameters that don't have the automatic mapping of the class, such as the array parameters.

In MYSQL, we declare a stored procedure named getEmployee, which contains an IN parameter ID and two OUT parameter IDs, named Emp_Name and Emp_Age. The query lies between BEGIN and END:

```
IN MYSQL

DROP PROCEDURE IF EXISTS getEmployee
CREATE PROCEDURE getEmployee
(
```

```
    IN id INTEGER,
    OUT Emp_Name VARCHAR(20),
    OUT Emp_Age INTEGER
)
BEGIN
    SELECT Name, Age
    INTO Emp_Name, Emp_Age
    FROM employee where EmpId = id;
END;
```

In the preceding code snippet, three parameters were specified. First was the IN parameter id, containing the ID of the employee. The remaining parameters were the OUT parameters, which were used for returning the data retrieved from table.

In Apache Derby, we declare a stored procedure named getEmployee as shown here:

```
IN Apache Derby

CREATE PROCEDURE getEmployee(IN id INTEGER,  OUT name varchar(30))
LANGUAGE JAVA EXTERNAL NAME
'org.packt.Spring.chapter5.JDBC.dao.EmployeeDaoImp.getEmployee'
PARAMETER STYLE JAVA;
```

The CREATE PROCEDURE statement, as shown in aforementioned code snippet, allows us to create the Java stored procedures that can be called by using the CALL PROCEDURE statement. The getEmployee is a procedure name that is created in the database. The LANGUAGE JAVA makes the database manager call the procedure as a public static method in a Java class. The EXTERNAL NAME 'package.class_name.method_name' makes the method_name method to be called when the procedure is executed. Here, the EXTERNAL NAME 'org.packt.Spring.chapter5.JDBC.dao.EmployeeDaoImp.getEmployee' makes the getEmployee method get called during the execution of the procedure. The Java method created org.packt.Spring.chapter5.JDBC.dao.EmployeeDaoImp.getEmployee is specified as the EXTERNAL NAME.

Now, let's discuss the implementation of SimpleJdbcCall for calling the getEmployee stored procedure. The following code snippet shows us how to read the getEmployee stored procedure.

The EmployeeDaoImpl.java file

The following code snippet gives the EmployeeDaoImpl.java class:

```
package org.packt.Spring.chapter5.JDBC.dao;

import java.util.Map;
```

```java
import javax.sql.DataSource;

import org.packt.Spring.chapter5.JDBC.model.Employee;
import org.springframework.beans.factory.annotation.Autowired;
import org.springframework.jdbc.core.JdbcTemplate;
import org.springframework.jdbc.core.namedparam.MapSqlParameterSource;
import org.springframework.jdbc.core.namedparam.SqlParameterSource;
import org.springframework.jdbc.core.simple.SimpleJdbcCall;
import org.springframework.stereotype.Repository;

@Repository
public class EmployeeDaoImpl implements EmployeeDao {
    @Autowired
    private DataSource dataSource;
    @Autowired
    private JdbcTemplate jdbcTemplate;
    private SimpleJdbcCall jdbcCall;

    public void setJdbcTemplateObject(JdbcTemplate jdbcTemplate) {
        this.jdbcTemplate = jdbcTemplate;
    }

    @Autowired
    public void setDataSource(DataSource dataSource) {
        this.dataSource = dataSource;
        this.jdbcCall = new SimpleJdbcCall(this.dataSource)
                    .withProcedureName("getEmployee");
    }

    @Override
    public Employee getEmployee(Integer id) {
        SqlParameterSource in = new
MapSqlParameterSource().addValue("id", id);
        Map<String, Object> simpleJdbcCallResult =
jdbcCall.execute(in);
        Employee employee = new Employee(id,
                    (String) simpleJdbcCallResult.get("name"));
        return employee;
    }
}
```

In the preceding code snippet, the instance of the `SqlParameterSource` interface was created, which contained the parameters that must match the name of the parameter declared in the stored procedure. The `execute()` method accepts the `IN` parameter as an argument and returns a map containing the `OUT` parameters, keyed by the name, as specified in the stored procedure. Here the `OUT` parameter is `name`. The retrieved value is set to the employee instance of employee.

Exercise

Q1. Explain the Spring JDBC packages.

Q2. What is `JdbcTemplate`?

Q3. Explain the JDBC batch operation in Spring.

 The answers to these are provided in *Appendix A, Solution to Exercises.*

Summary

In this chapter, we understood the overview of database and covered the DAO design pattern. We looked at JDBC without the Spring Framework and the simplified Spring JDBC abstraction framework. We implemented the JDBC code using the Spring JDBC support. We discussed how Spring manages the `DataSource` and which data sources can be used in our applications. We also discussed the data support in the Spring application. We looked at the JDBC batch operation in Spring and calling the stored procedure by using `SimpleJdbcCall`.

In the next chapter, you will learn about ORM and understand the concept of Hibernate. Then, we will discuss the important elements of the Hibernate architecture. We will also learn how to use HQL and HCQL to query the persistent object.

4
Hibernate with Spring

While developing a real-world application using the Spring Framework, we often store and retrieve data to and from the relational database in the form of objects. These objects are non-scalar values that can't be directly stored and retrieved to and from the database, as only scalar values can be directly stored in the relational database, which is technically defined as impedance mismatch. In the previous section, we took a look at using JDBC in Spring applications.

Data persistence is the ability to preserve the state of an object so that it can regain the same state in the future. In this chapter, we will be focused on saving in-memory objects into the database using ORM tools that have wide support in Spring **Hibernate**.

As we have understood from earlier chapters, Spring uses POJO-based development and also uses declarative configuration management to overcome EJB's clumsy and heavy setup (EJB architecture was released a lot of time ago and is just not feasible).

The developer community realized that the development of data access logic could be easy using a simple, lightweight POJO-based framework. This resulted in the introduction of ORM. The objective of ORM libraries was to close the gap between the data structure in the RDBMS and the object-oriented model in Java. It helped developers focus on programming with the object model.

Hibernate is one of the most successful ORM libraries available in the open source community. It won the heart of the Java developer community with features such as its POJO-based approach, support of relationship definitions, and ease of development.

This chapter will cover the basic ideas and main use cases of Hibernate in Spring when developing data access logic. Hibernate is an extensive ORM library, so it is not possible to cover every aspect of Hibernate in just one chapter.

The list of topics that will be covered in this chapter are:

- Why Object/Relational Mapping (ORM)?
- Introducing ORM, O/RM, and O/R mapping
- Introducing Hibernate
- Integrating Hibernate with the Spring Framework
- Hibernate Criteria Query Language (HCQL)

Why Object/Relational Mapping?

Object-oriented languages such as Java represent data as an interconnected **Graph of Objects**, whereas relational database systems represent data in a table-like format. Relational databases normally work with tables; data is stored in different types of tables. Java implements the object model whereas **relational database management systems (RDBMS)** implement the relational model. Because both the models are quite different in the way they represent data, when we load or store graphs of objects using relational databases, it causes mismatch problems. Refer to the following figure for clarity:

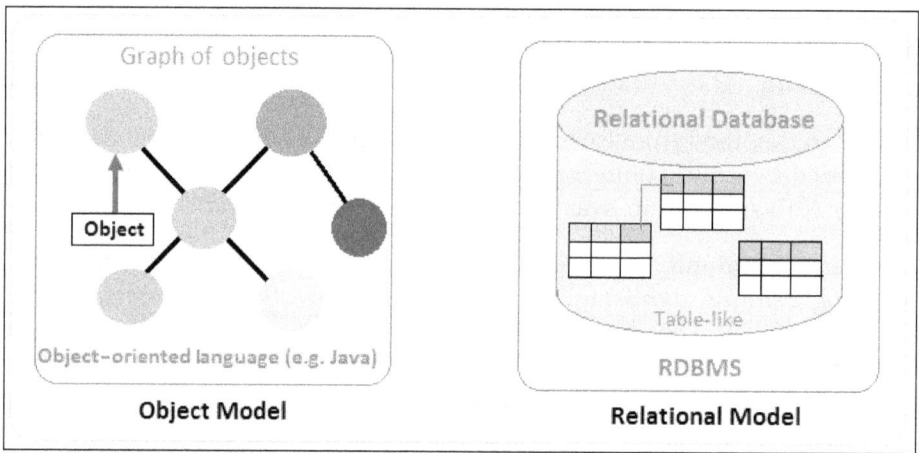

Enterprise-level applications implemented using object-oriented languages such as Java manage the data in the form of objects. Most of these applications use relational databases such as RDBMS to maintain persistence of data in the form of tables with rows and columns. Implementing the data access layer using low-level APIs such as JDBC includes huge boilerplate code, which affects the productivity of the system, increasing the cost of application development.

Let's say we have an `Employee` class in our application, having fields named `empId`, `firstName`, `dateOfBirth`, and `phone`. In the running application, there will be many instances of this class in memory. Say we have four employee objects in memory and we want to save these employee objects into the relational database as a common database.

We will be having an Employee table with column names the same as the fields in the `Employee` class. Each of these employee objects contains data for a particular employee, which will be persisted as rows in that table. A class corresponds to a table and an object of this class corresponds to a row in that table, as shown here:

Employee Class	EmpId	FirstName	DOB	Phone
EmpId	100101	Ravi	03-Nov-86	4568799
FirstName	100102	Shashi	10-Oct-88	4566887
DateOfBirth	100103	Shree	10-Aug-91	9856756
Phone	100106	Namrata	06-Sep-98	6895456
Object Mapping			**Relational**	

This is what we have followed as our traditional approach in Java applications over the years. We connect to a database using a JDBC connection and create a SQL query to perform an `INSERT` operation. So, that data will execute in the form of SQL queries to perform `INSERT`. Similarly, we create an object using setter methods after performing the `SELECT` query. By using boilerplate code, the object will get converted into a data model and vice versa, which results in a painful mapping process. This is a common problem in every Java application that has a persistence layer and that connects to the database in order to save and retrieve values.

Mapping relationships is another issue that needs to be addressed. Let's say we have another table called Address table and an object called `address` object. Let's also say the `employee` object has a reference to this `address` object. In this case, the primary key of the Address table will be mapped to a foreign key of the Employee table.

Another issue that needs to be addressed is data types. Let's say we have an object with a Boolean data type whereas most of the database doesn't have Boolean data type and probably used as char for `Y`/`N` or integer for `0`/`1`, which need to be handled during data type conversion while writing code.

Managing changes to object state is another issue that needs to be addressed. If there are some changes to object state, then we need to manually execute the procedure to make these changes and we also need to reframe the SQL queries and update the database by ourselves.

To solve these problems, we need a customizable generic system that can take the responsibility of filling the gap between the object and relational models for our application. This requirement has resulted in the introduction of ORM, which provides an elegant way to handle the mentioned issues.

Introducing ORM, O/RM, and O/R mapping

ORM is the process of persisting objects in a relational database such as RDBMS. ORM bridges the gap between object and relational schemas, allowing object-oriented applications to persist objects directly without having the need to convert objects to and from a relational format.

ORM creates a virtual object database that can be accessed via a programming language and simplifies the data access layer of complex enterprise applications using a relational database as its persistence store. ORM simplifies the job of implementing the data access layer for enterprise applications implemented using object-oriented programming languages and the relational database as its persistence store, as illustrated by the following figure:

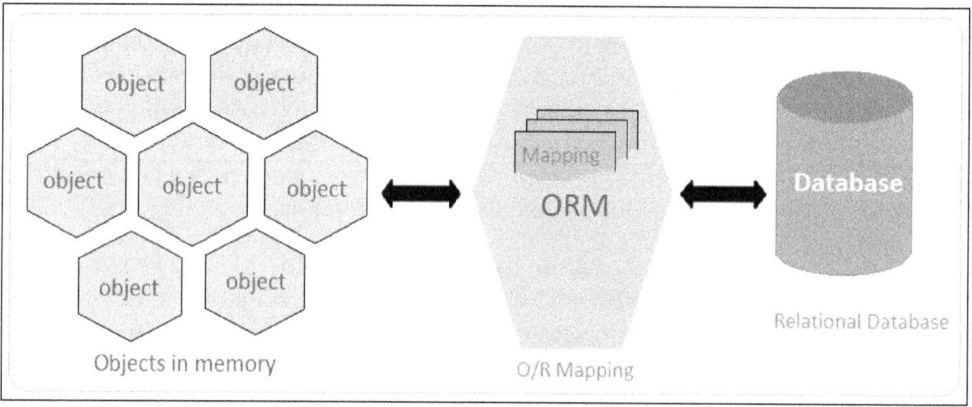

ORM is about mapping object representations to JDBC statement parameters and in turn mapping JDBC query results back to object representations. Database columns are mapped to the instance fields of domain objects or JavaBeans' properties.

Usually, ORM doesn't work at the SQL level but rather refers its own Object Query Language, which gets translated into SQL at runtime. The mapping information is kept as metadata (in XML files or as annotations on mapped objects), which defines how to map a persistent class and its fields into database tables and theirs columns. The database dialect is configured to address database specifics. For example, ID generation is configured in the metadata and is automatically translated into sequences or autoincrement columns.

Until now, we have understood how ORM implementations in Java help us to quickly implement a reliable data access layer to concentrate on other tiers of the application. In the next section, we will understand the features of Hibernate and their uses in a Spring application.

Introducing Hibernate

Hibernate, by definition, is an ORM solution for Java. Hibernate is an open source, full-fledged persistence framework. It is used to map **plain old Java objects (POJOs)** to the tables of a relational database and vice versa. Hibernate is used to persist application data into a data layer. Hibernate implements **Java Persistence API (JPA)**, which is a set of standards that has been prescribed for any persistence implementation and that needs to be met in order to get certified as a Java persistent API implementation.

Hibernate sits between Java objects in memory and the relational database server to handle the persistence of objects based on O/R mapping. Hibernate supports almost all relational database engines such as the HSQL database engine, MySQL, PostgreSQL, Oracle, and so on.

The object query language used by Hibernate is called **Hibernate Query Language (HQL)**. HQL is a SQL-like textual query language that works at the class- or field-level. Let's start learning about the architecture of Hibernate.

Hibernate architecture

In this section, we will discuss all the important elements of the Hibernate system and see how they fit into its architecture. The following figure shows the Hibernate architecture:

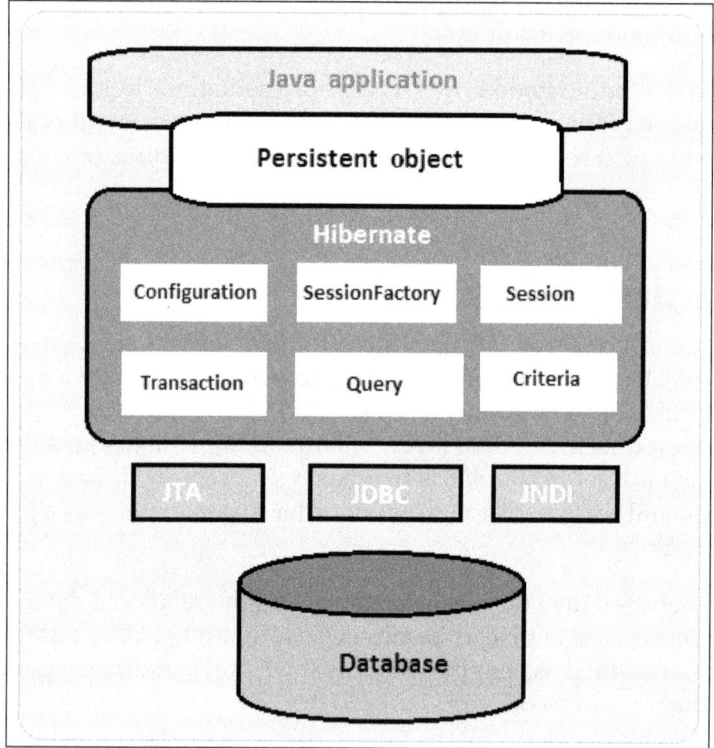

Hibernate makes use of various existing Java APIs such as **Java Database Connectivity (JDBC)**, **Java Naming and Directory Interface (JNDI)**, and **Java Transaction API (JTA)**. JDBC supports functionality common to relational databases, which allows almost any database with a JDBC driver to be supported by Hibernate, whereas JTA and JNDI allow Hibernate to be integrated with Java EE application servers. The basics elements of the Hibernate architecture are described in the following sections.

Configuration

The `org.hibernate.cfg.Configuration` class is the basic element of the Hibernate API, which allows us to build `SessionFactory`. Configuration can be thought of as the factory class that can produce `SessionFactory`. The first object of Hibernate is the `configuration` object, created only once during the initialization of the application. The `configuration` object encapsulates the Hibernate configuration details such as connection properties and dialect, which are used to build `SessionFactory` as shown in the following figure:

The `hibernate.properties` and `hibernate.cfg.xml` files are configurations files that are supported by Hibernate. We can use the `hibernate.properties` file to specify the default values for the new configuration object.

SessionFactory

The `org.hibernate.SessionFactory` interface provides an abstraction for the application to obtain the Hibernate session object. The `SessionFactory` initialization process includes various operations that consume huge resources and extra time, so it is generally recommended to use a single `SessionFactory` per JVM instance. For each database, we need to have one `SessionFactory` using a separate configuration file. So we have to create multiple `SessionFactory` if we are using multiple databases.

The `SessionFactory` is a heavyweight and immutable towards the application; that is, it is a thread safe object. It is mostly configured as a singleton in an application so that there will be only one object per application. It is usually created during the startup of an application and is kept for later reference. The `SessionFactory` is used by all threads of the application. We can open multiple sessions using a single `SessionFactory`.

Session

The `org.hibernate.Session` interface is an interface between the Hibernate system and the application. It is used to get the connection with a database. It is light weight and is initiated each time an interaction is needed with the database.

Session objects are not usually thread safe and it is recommended to obtain a separate session for each thread or transaction. After we are done using session, it has to be closed to release all the resources such as cached entity objects and the JDBC connection.

The `Session` interface provides an abstraction for Java application to perform CRUD operations on the instance of mapped persistent classes. We will look into the methods provided by the `Session` interface in a later section of his chapter.

Transaction

The `Transaction` interface is an optional interface that represents a unit of work with the database. It is supported by most RDBMS systems. In Hibernate, `Transaction` is handled by the underlying transaction manager.

Query

The `org.hibernate.Query` interface provides an abstraction to execute the Hibernate query and to retrieve the results. The `Query` object represents the Hibernate query built using the HQL. We will learn about the `Query` interface in more detail in a later section of this chapter.

Criteria

The `org.hibernate.Criteria` interface is an interface to use the criterion API and is used to create and execute object-oriented criteria queries, which is an alternative to HQL or SQL.

The Persistent object

Persistent classes are the entity classes in an application. Persistent objects are objects that are managed to be in the persistent state. Persistent objects are associated with exactly one `org.hibernate.Session`. And once the `org.hibernate.Session` is closed, these objects will be detached and will be free to be used in any layer of the application.

Integrating Hibernate with the Spring Framework

While using the Hibernate framework, you do not write the code to manage the connection or to deal with statements and result sets. Instead, all the details for accessing a particular data source are configured in the XML files and/or in the Java annotations.

While integrating the Hibernate framework with the Spring Framework, the business objects are configured with the help of the IoC container and can be externalized from the application code. Hibernate objects can be used as Spring beans in your application and you can avail all the benefits of the Spring Framework.

In this section, we will set up the Hibernate environment and create a Spring Hibernate project in STS. The simplest way to integrate Hibernate with Spring is to have a bean for `SessionFactory` and make it a singleton and the DAOs classes just get that bean and inject its dependency and get the session from the SessionFactory. The first step in creating a Spring Hibernate project is to integrate Hibernate and connect with the database.

Sample data model for example code

In this chapter, we will use a PostgreSQL database. Please refer to `http://www. postgresqltutorial.com/install-postgresql/` to set up a PostgreSQL database server on your machine and download the JDBC driver for the PostgreSQL database; we have used the `postgresql-9.3-1102.jdbc3.jar` JDBC connector for PostgreSQL.

We will create a database named `ehrpayroll_db` that will contain a table named employee and will populate dummy data to the table. The following is a sample data creation script for a PostgreSQL database.

Let's first create a database for our project in the PostgreSQL database:

1. Type in the following script to create a database named `ehrpayroll_db`:

    ```
    CREATE DATABASE ehrpayroll_db
    ```

2. Now enter the given script to create a table named `EMPLOYEE_INFO`:

    ```
    CREATE TABLE EMPLOYEE_INFO(
        ID serial NOT NULL Primary key,
        FIRST_NAME varchar(30) not null,
        LAST_NAME varchar(30) not null,
    ```

```
     JOB_TITLE varchar(100) not null,
     DEPARTMENT varchar(100) not null,
     SALARY INTEGER
);
```

3.   The next script helps you populate the data for the table employee:

```
INSERT INTO EMPLOYEE_INFO
(FIRST_NAME, LAST_NAME, JOB_TITLE, DEPARTMENT, SALARY)
VALUES
('RAVI', 'SONI', 'AUTHOR', 'TECHNOLOGY', 5000);
```

The following figure shows the created table with the data inserted:

	id integer	first_name character varying(30)	last_name character varying(30)	job_title character varying(100)	department character varying(100)	salary integer
1	1	RAVI	SONI	AUTHOR	TECHNOLOGY	5000

Integrating Hibernate

To integrate Hibernate, we need to perform these steps:

1.   Download the Hibernate JAR and include them into the classpath. Download (.zip file for Windows) the latest version of Hibernate from http://www. hibernate.org/downloads. Once you unzip the downloaded ZIP file, the directory structure will appear as shown in the following screenshot:

Name	Date modified	Type	Size
documentation	23-Oct-14 4:11 PM	File folder	
lib	23-Oct-14 4:01 PM	File folder	
project	23-Oct-14 4:19 PM	File folder	
changelog.txt	23-Oct-14 4:01 PM	Text Document	343 KB
hibernate_logo.gif	23-Oct-14 4:01 PM	GIF image	2 KB
lgpl.txt	23-Oct-14 4:01 PM	Text Document	26 KB

2.   Inside the lib directory, there will be a lot of directories that contain Hibernate-related JARs, as shown in the following screenshot. The required folder contains all the JARs you need to create a basic Java application.

Name	Date modified	Type	Size
envers	23-Oct-14 4:01 PM	File folder	
jpa	23-Oct-14 4:01 PM	File folder	
jpa-metamodel-generator	23-Oct-14 4:01 PM	File folder	
optional	23-Oct-14 4:01 PM	File folder	
osgi	23-Oct-14 4:01 PM	File folder	
required	23-Oct-14 4:01 PM	File folder	

Once you have downloaded the Hibernate libraries, you can create a new Spring project and add Hibernate libraries to this project using Java Build Path.

Required JARs for the Spring-Hibernate project

We need to add the JARs required to create our Spring-Hibernate projects. These are shown in the following screenshot:

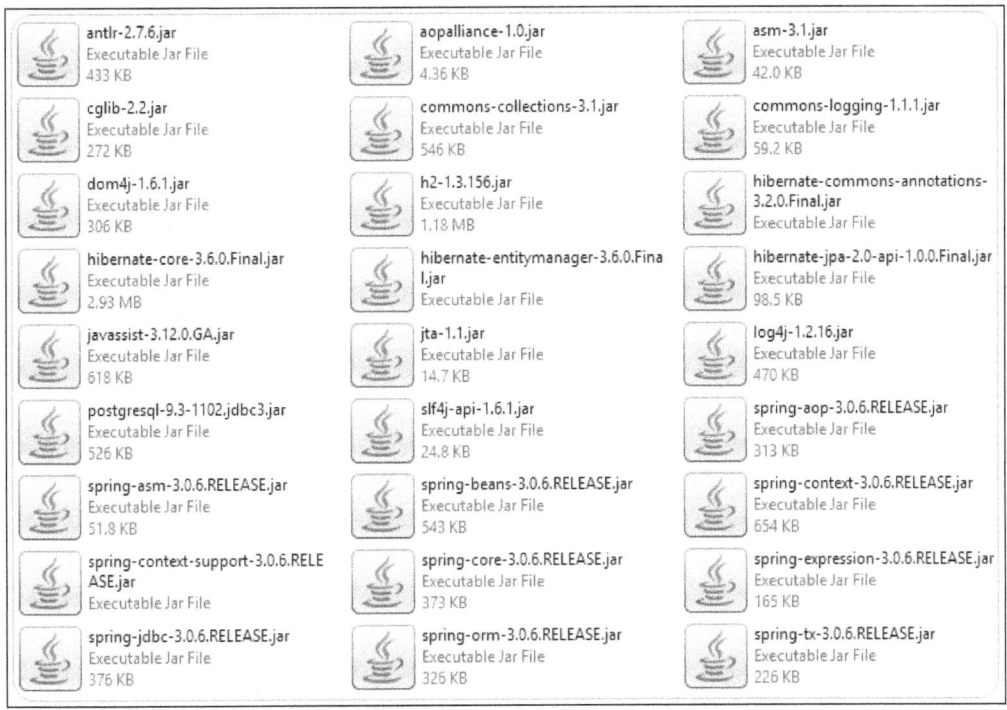

Configuring Hibernate SessionFactory in Spring

The Spring Framework lets us define resources such as JDBC `DataSource` or Hibernate `SessionFactory` as a Spring bean in an application context, which prevents the need for hardcoded resource lookups for application objects. This defined Spring bean references are used by application objects that need to access resources to receive the predefined instances.

The `Session` interface in the Hibernate API provides methods to find, save, and delete objects in a relational database. The Hibernate session is created by first creating the `SessionFactory`. The Spring Framework provides a number of classes to configure Hibernate `SessionFactory` as a Spring bean containing the desired properties.

For session creation, the Spring API provides the implementation of the `AbstractSessionFactoryBean` subclass: the `LocalSessionFactoryBean` class and the `AnnotationSessionFactoryBean` class. Since we will be using annotation style, we will use the `AnnotationSessionFactoryBean` class, which supports annotation metadata for mappings. `AnnotationSessionFactoryBean` extends the `LocalSessionFactoryBean` class, so it has all the basic properties of Hibernate integration.

In the configuration file, we have to declare the `sessionFactory` bean and set `dataSource`, `packagesToScan` or `annotatedClasses`, and `hibernateProperties`. Let's take a look at these in detail:

- The `dataSource` property sets the name of the data source to be accessed by the underlying application.

- The `packagesToScan` property instructs Hibernate to scan the domain object with the ORM annotation under the specified package. The `annotatedClasses` property instructs Hibernate to for the ORM-annotated class.

- The `hibernateProperties` property sets the configuration details for Hibernate. We have defined only a few important properties out of many configuration parameters that should be provided for every application.

The following table describes these properties:

Property	Description
hibernate.dialect	Hibernate uses this property to generate the appropriate SQL optimized for the chosen relational database. Hibernate supports SQL dialects for many databases, and the major dialects include PostgreSQLDialect, MySQLDialect, H2Dialect, Oracle10gDialect, and so on.
hibernate.max_fetch_depth	This property is used to set the maximum depth for the outer join when the mapping object is associated with other mapped objects. This property is used to determine the number of associations Hibernate will traverse by join when fetching data. The recommended value lies between 0 and 3.
hibernate.jdbc.fetch_size	This property is used to set the total number of rows that can be retrieved by each JDBC fetch.
hibernate.show_sql	This property file is used to output all SQL to the log file or console, which is an alternative to set log to debug and troubleshooting process. It can be set to either True or False.

Refer to the Hibernate reference manual for the full list of Hibernate properties at http://docs.jboss.org/hibernate/core/3.6/reference/en-US/html/session-configuration.html.

XML Spring configuration for Hibernate

Spring beans, the data source, a SessionFactory, and a transaction manager bean are configured in the app-context.xml file. You should adapt your Hibernate beans according to the project requirements.

Here is an implementation of app-context.xml. In the following configuration file, we have declared several beans to support the Hibernate SessionFactory:

```
<?xml version="1.0" encoding="UTF-8"?>
<beans xmlns="http://www.springframework.org/schema/beans"
    xmlns:xsi="http://www.w3.org/2001/XMLSchema-instance"
xmlns:context="http://www.springframework.org/schema/context"
    xmlns:tx="http://www.springframework.org/schema/tx"
xmlns:jdbc="http://www.springframework.org/schema/jdbc"
    xsi:schemaLocation="
```

```
        http://www.springframework.org/schema/jdbc
http://www.springframework.org/schema/jdbc/spring-jdbc-3.0.xsd
        http://www.springframework.org/schema/beans
http://www.springframework.org/schema/beans/spring-beans-3.0.xsd
        http://www.springframework.org/schema/tx
http://www.springframework.org/schema/tx/spring-tx-3.0.xsd
        http://www.springframework.org/schema/context
http://www.springframework.org/schema/context/spring-context-
3.0.xsd">
```

In the following code snippet, we have instructed Spring to scan the component under the package `org.packt.spring.chapter6.hibernate` using `component-scan`:

```
<context:annotation-config />
<context:component-scan base-
package="org.packt.spring.chapter6.hibernate" />
```

The `property-placeholder` will refer to the `hibernate.properties` file, as shown in the following code snippet:

```
<context:property-placeholder
        location="classpath:/META-
INF/spring/hibernate.properties" />
```

In the following code snippet, the `dataSource` bean is declared to provide database connection details to Hibernate:

```
<bean id="dataSource"
class="org.springframework.jdbc.datasource.
DriverManagerDataSource">
        <property name="driverClassName"
value="${jdbc.driverClassName}" />
        <property name="url" value="${jdbc.url}" />
        <property name="username" value="${jdbc.username}" />
        <property name="password" value="${jdbc.password}" />
</bean>
```

The `sessionFactory` bean is declared in the following code snippet. The Hibernate `sessionFactory` bean is the most important part. We have used `AnnotationSessionFactoryBean` to support the Hibernate annotation. We have injected the `dataSource` bean into `sessionFactory`. We have instructed Hibernate to scan for the ORM annotated object. And then we have provided the configuration details for Hibernate using `hibernateProperties`, as shown here:

```
<bean id="sessionFactory"
class="org.springframework.orm.hibernate3.
annotation.AnnotationSessionFactoryBean">
        <property name="dataSource" ref="dataSource" />
        <property name="annotatedClasses"
    value="org.packt.spring.chapter6.hibernate.model.Employee" />
        <property name="hibernateProperties">
            <props>
                <prop
key="hibernate.dialect">${hibernate.dialect}</prop>
                <prop
key="hibernate.show_sql">${hibernate.show_sql}</prop>
            </props>
        </property>
</bean>
```

In the following code snippet, we have declared the `transactionManager` bean. To access transactional data, `SessionFactory` requires a transaction manager. The transaction manager provided by Spring specifically for Hibernate 3 is `org.springframework.orm.hibernate3.HibernateTransactionManager`:

```
<bean id="transactionManager"
class="org.springframework.orm.hibernate3.
HibernateTransactionManager">
        <property name="sessionFactory" ref="sessionFactory" />
</bean>
```

The `<tx:annotation-driven>` is declared in the following code snippet to support transaction demarcation requirements using annotations:

```
<tx:annotation-driven transaction-manager=
"transactionManager" />
</beans>
```

hibernate.properties

The Hibernate- and JDBC-specific properties are stored in a `hibernate.properties` file, as follows:

```
# JDBC Properties
jdbc.driverClassName=org.postgresql.Driver
jdbc.url=jdbc:postgresql://localhost:5432/ehrpayroll_db
jdbc.username=postgres
```

```
jdbc.password=sa

# Hibernate Properties
hibernate.dialect=org.hibernate.dialect.PostgreSQLDialect
hibernate.show_sql=true
```

Annotated domain model class

The Java persistent model establishes the static relationships of the persistence model by defining the entity component. The API defines the entity class as the object tier of a table in the database tier. An entity instance is defined as the object tier equivalent of a row in a database table.

The following is a table that maps Object Tier elements to Database Tier elements:

Object Tier element	Database Tier element
Entity class	Database table
Field of entity class	Database table column
Entity instance	Database table row

Hibernate annotation provides the metadata for object and relational table mapping. This metadata is clubbed into a POJO file that helps users understand the code inside POJO as well as the table structure simultaneously while developing. Hibernate provides JPA implementation, which allows the user to use JPA annotation in model beans. The JPA annotations are explained in the following table:

JPA annotation	Description
`@Entity`	The `javax.persistence.Entity` annotation declares a class as an entity bean that can be persisted by Hibernate, since Hibernate provides JPA implementation.
`@Table`	The `javax.persistence.Table` annotation can be used to define table mapping. It provides four attributes that allows us to override the table name, its catalogue, and its schema.
`@Id`	The `javax.persistence.Id` annotation is used to define the primary key, and it will automatically determine the appropriate primary key generation strategy to be used.

JPA annotation	Description
@GeneratedValue	• The `javax.persistence.GeneratedValue` annotation is used to define that the field will be autogenerated • It takes two parameters, strategy and generator • The `GenerationType.IDENTITY` strategy is used so that the generated id value is mapped to the bean and can be retrieved by the Java program
@Column	• The `javax.persistence.Column` annotation is used to map the field with the table column • We can also specify length, nullable, and uniqueness for the bean properties

Now it's time to write `Employee.java`. This class will be mapped to the Employee table in the database using Hibernate. The `Employee` class fields are annotated with JPA annotations so that we don't need to provide mapping in a separate XML file. It should be noted that Hibernate puts emphasis on overriding the `equals()` and `hashCode()` methods of a persistent class when used in collections (such as a list or set) because internally Hibernate works with the objects in the session and cache. It is recommended to implement the `equals()` and `hashCode()` methods using a real-world key, which is a key that would identify the instance in the real world, as shown here:

```
package org.packt.spring.chapter6.hibernate.model;

import javax.persistence.Column;
import javax.persistence.Entity;
import javax.persistence.GeneratedValue;
import javax.persistence.GenerationType;
import javax.persistence.Id;
import javax.persistence.Table;

@Entity
@Table(name = "EMPLOYEE_INFO")
public class Employee  {

    @Id
    @Column(name = "ID")
    @GeneratedValue(strategy = GenerationType.IDENTITY)
    private Integer id;
```

```
@Column(name = "FIRST_NAME")
private String firstName;

@Column(name = "LAST_NAME")
private String lastName;

@Column(name = "JOB_TITLE")
private String jobTitle;

@Column(name = "DEPARTMENT")
private String department;

@Column(name = "SALARY")
private int salary;

// constructor and setter and getter

@Override
public boolean equals(Object obj) {
      if (this == obj) {
            return true;
       }
       if (!(obj instanceof Employee)) {
            return false;
       }
       Employee employee = (Employee) obj;
       if (firstName != null ?
!firstName.equals(employee.firstName)
                    : employee.firstName != null) {
            return false;
       } else {
            return true;
       }
   }

@Override
public int hashCode() {
      return firstName != null ? firstName.hashCode() : 0;
   }

@Override
public String toString() {
      return "Employee [id=" + id + ", name=" + firstName + " "
+ lastName
```

```
                            + ", jobTitle=" + jobTitle + " department="
    + department
                            + " salary=" + salary + "]";
        }
    }
```

In the preceding code snippet:

- The `Employee` class is annotated with the `@Entity` annotation, which will define this class as a mapped entity class. The `Employee` class is also annotated with the `@Table` annotation that defines the table name in the database with which this entity class will map.

- The ID is annotated with the `@ID` annotation, which represents that ID is the primary key of the object. Hibernate will generate the ID value based on the `@GeneratedValue` annotation. The `GenerationType.IDENTITY` strategy reflects that the ID will be generated by the backend (the ID column of the `EMPLOYEE_INFO` table is the primary key with `SERIAL` specified, which means the value of ID will be generated and assigned by the database during the insert operation) during insert.

- The name and e-mail are annotated with the `@Column` annotation.

- If the type and attribute names are exactly the same as the name of table and column, then we can skip the name of the table and column from the annotation.

The Hibernate sessions

The `Session` interface is an important interface that is required while interacting with a database in Hibernate. The `Session` interface is obtained from `SessionFactory`. The `Session` object is light weight and can be used to attain a physical connection with a database. It is initiated each time an interaction needs to happen with a database. Also, persistent objects are saved and retrieved through a `Session` object. It is not usually thread safe, so avoid keeping it open for a long time. They should be created and destroyed as needed. The `Session` interface offers create, delete, and read operations for instances of mapped entity classes.

Instances may exist in one of the following three states at a given point in time:

- **Transient**: This state represents a new instance of persistence class that has no representation in a database and is not associated with `Session`.

- **Persistent**: This state represents that the instance of a persistence class has a representation in the database.

- **Detached**: In this state, the persistent object will be detached from the database. This state will be reached once the Hibernate Session will be closed.

The Session interface methods

The Session interface provides a numbers of method such as beginTransaction(), createCriteria(), save(), delete(), and so on, which you can read about at http://www.tutorialspoint.com/hibernate/hibernate_sessions.htm.

Persistence layer – implement DAOs

The persistence layer will have the DAO. Let's create DAO classes that will interact with the database using the Hibernate SessionFactory. The SessionFactory implementation will be injected into the reference variable at runtime using Spring's **Inversion of Control (IoC)** feature.

The EmployeeDao interface

The EmployeeDao interface declares two methods named getAllEmployees() and insertEmployee(), as shown here:

```
package org.packt.spring.chapter6.hibernate.dao;

import java.util.List;
import org.packt.spring.chapter6.hibernate.model.Employee;

public interface EmployeeDao {

    // to get all employees
    public List<Employee> getAllEmployees();

    // to insert new employee
    public void insertEmployee(Employee employee);
}
```

The EmployeeDaoImpl class

The EmployeeDaoImpl class is annotated with @Repository, which indicates that this class is a DAO. It also has the @Transactional(readOnly = true) annotation, which configures this class and all its methods for read-only access:

```
package org.packt.spring.chapter6.hibernate.dao;

import java.util.List;
import org.hibernate.Session;
import org.hibernate.SessionFactory;
import org.packt.spring.chapter6.hibernate.model.Employee;
import org.springframework.beans.factory.annotation.Autowired;
import org.springframework.stereotype.Repository;

@Repository
@Transactional(readOnly = true)
public class EmployeeDaoImpl implements EmployeeDao {

    @Autowired
    private SessionFactory sessionFactory;

    @SuppressWarnings("unchecked")
    public List<Employee> getAllEmployees() {
        Session session = sessionFactory.openSession();
        String hql = "FROM Employee";
        Query query = session.createQuery(hql);
        List<Employee> emList = query.list();
        return emList;
    }

    @Transactional(readOnly = false)
    public void insertEmployee(Employee employee) {
        Session session = sessionFactory.openSession();
        session.save(employee);
    }
}
```

To get a `SessionFactory`, we declare a member variable named `sessionFactory` of type `SessionFactory` and annotated with the `@Autowired` annotation that automatically initializes the `SessionFactory`. The next step is to get the session from the `sessionFactory`.

In order to use Hibernate in the `getAllEmployees()` and `insertEmployees()` method, we use a `session` object. The `session` object is obtained from a `SessionFactory`. Using this `session` object, we can use the `createQuery` method to create queries and run them.

When we are finished with the session, we should close it. We needn't close it by ourselves; the Spring Framework will do this for us.

Let's understand the methods defined in EmployeeDaoImpl class in more detail:

- Querying the database – getAllEmployees(): The method getAllEmployees() will fetch all the employee details from the Employee table in the database and return the list of employees.

  This method will get Hibernate Session (Session is the main runtime interface between Java application and Hibernate) from sessionFactory using the openSession() method of the SessionFactory class. This session will use the query object to call the list() method that will fetch employees.

- Inserting new record – insertEmployee(): The method insertEmployee() will insert a new record to the Employee table. This method will use the save() method defined in the Hibernate Session to perform the INSERT operation.

  Annotate this method with @Transactional(readOnly = false), which will allow us to perform the INSERT operation.

Service layer – implement services

We have defined the Service layer, which seems redundant in this demo due to the lack of complexity. This layer will simply take a call from the controller (in Spring MVC) or from the main method and pass this call to the DAOs layer.

The EmployeeService interface

The EmployeeService interface declares two methods named getAllEmployees() and insertEmployee(), as shown here:

```
package org.packt.spring.chapter6.hibernate.service;

import java.util.List;
import org.packt.spring.chapter6.hibernate.model.Employee;

public interface EmployeeService {
public List<Employee> getAllEmployees();
public void insertEmployee(Employee employee);
}
```

The EmployeeServiceImpl class

The `EmployeeServiceImpl` class will implement the `EmployeeService` interface and provide a definition for the methods declared in the interface. This class has declared a member variable named `EmployeeDAO` and annotated it with the `@Autowired` annotation. This class is annotated with the `@Service` annotation, which makes this class a service class:

```java
package org.packt.spring.chapter6.hibernate.service;

import java.util.List;

import org.packt.spring.chapter6.hibernate.dao.EmployeeDao;
import org.packt.spring.chapter6.hibernate.model.Employee;
import org.springframework.beans.factory.annotation.Autowired;
import org.springframework.stereotype.Service;

@Service
public class EmployeeServiceImpl implements EmployeeService {

    @Autowired
    private EmployeeDao employeeDao;

    public List<Employee> getAllEmployees() {
        List<Employee> emList = employeeDao.getAllEmployees();
        return emList;
    }

    public void insertEmployee(Employee employee) {
        employeeDao.insertEmployee(employee);
    }
}
```

Directory structure of the application

The final directory structure of the application is as follows:

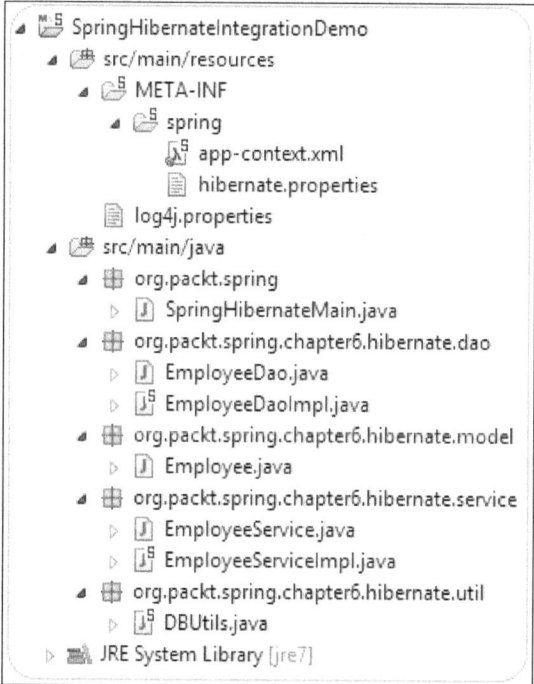

Running the application

Once we are done with the preceding configuration, we can write a main method to store values from the Employee object to the database.

The DBUtils class

We have created a DBUtils class annotated with the @Component annotation to register this class to the Spring container as a bean. This class defined a method named initialize() and annotated it with the @PostConstruct annotation.

The @PostConstruct annotation does not belong to Spring, it's located in the J2EE library: common-annotations.jar. The @PostConstruct annotation is a shared annotation that is part of a JSR for basic annotations. It comes with Java SE 6 or newer versions. The commons-annotations.jar is the final product of the JSR API. The @PostConstruct annotation defines a method that will be called after a bean has been fully initialized. In other words, it will be called after bean construction and the injection of all dependencies.

The `initialize()` method will get the database connection and create a table `EMPLOYEE` and insert dummy data to this table. This class has been used in this project to prevent exceptions in case we miss out on creating a table in the database. In a real-world application, we don't need this class:

```
package org.packt.spring.chapter6.hibernate.util;

import java.sql.Connection;
import java.sql.SQLException;
import java.sql.Statement;

import javax.annotation.PostConstruct;
import javax.sql.DataSource;

import org.springframework.beans.factory.annotation.Autowired;
import org.springframework.stereotype.Component;

@Component
public class DBUtils {

    @Autowired
    private DataSource dataSource;

    @PostConstruct
    public void initialize() {
        try {
            Connection connection =
dataSource.getConnection();
            Statement statement =
connection.createStatement();

            statement.execute("DROP TABLE IF EXISTS
EMPLOYEE_INFO");

            statement.executeUpdate("CREATE TABLE
EMPLOYEE_INFO(" +
                "ID serial NOT NULL Primary key, " +
                "FIRST_NAME varchar(30) not null, " +
                "LAST_NAME varchar(30) not null, " +
                "JOB_TITLE varchar(100) not null, " +
                "DEPARTMENT varchar(100) not null, " +
                "SALARY INTEGER)";

            statement.executeUpdate("INSERT INTO EMPLOYEE_INFO
"
```

```
                              + "(FIRST_NAME, LAST_NAME, JOB_TITLE,
        DEPARTMENT, SALARY) "
                              + "VALUES " + "('RAVI', 'SONI', 'AUTHOR',
        'TECHNOLOGY', 5000)";

                    statement.close();
                    connection.close();
              } catch (SQLException e) {
                    e.printStackTrace();
              }
          }
      }
```

The SpringHibernateMain class

The SpringHibernateMain class contains the main method. The ApplicationContext will initialize the container with the app-context.xml file we defined:

```
package org.packt.spring;

import org.packt.spring.chapter6.hibernate.model.Employee;
import org.packt.spring.chapter6.hibernate.service.EmployeeService;
import org.springframework.context.ApplicationContext;
import org.springframework.context.support.ClassPathXmlApplication
Context;

public class SpringHibernateMain {

    public static void main(String[] args) {

            ApplicationContext context = new
    ClassPathXmlApplicationContext(
                        "/META-INF/spring/app-context.xml");

            EmployeeService employeeService = context.getBean(
                        "employeeServiceImpl",
    EmployeeService.class);

            // insert employee
            Employee emp = new Employee();
            emp.setFirstName("Shree");
            emp.setLastName("Kant");
            emp.setJobTitle("Software Engineer");
            emp.setDepartment("Technology");
```

```
        emp.setSalary(3000);
        employeeService.insertEmployee(emp);

        // fetch all employee
        for (Employee employee :
employeeService.getAllEmployees())
                System.out.println(employee);
    }
}
```

Output to console

Once you run the application, the following output will be expected:

```
Hibernate: insert into EMPLOYEE_INFO (DEPARTMENT, FIRST_NAME,
JOB_TITLE, LAST_NAME, SALARY) values (?, ?, ?, ?, ?)

Hibernate: select employee0_.ID as ID0_, employee0_.DEPARTMENT as
DEPARTMENT0_, employee0_.FIRST_NAME as FIRST3_0_, employee0_.JOB_TITLE
as JOB4_0_, employee0_.LAST_NAME as LAST5_0_,
employee0_.SALARY as SALARY0_ from EMPLOYEE_INFO employee0_

Employee [id=1, name=RAVI SONI, jobTitle=AUTHOR
department=TECHNOLOGY salary=5000]

Employee [id=2, name=Shree Kant, jobTitle=Software Engineer
department=Technology salary=3000]
```

Populated data in the Employee table

Once the application has been run successfully, the updated Employee table with all the data will be as shown here:

	id integer	first_name character varying(30)	last_name character varying(30)	job_title character varying(100)	department character varying(100)	salary integer
1	1	RAVI	SONI	AUTHOR	TECHNOLOGY	5000
2	2	Shree	Kant	Software Engineer	Technology	3000

In the previous sections, we discussed mapping persistent objects using Hibernate. In the next section, we will understand HQL. Hibernate is engineered around the object model and provides a powerful query language named HQL to define our queries so we don't need to construct SQL to interact with the database. HQL is similar to SQL except that we will use objects instead of table names.

Hibernate Query Language

Hibernate Query Language is an object-oriented query language that works on persistence objects and their properties instead of operating on tables and columns. Hibernate will translate HQL queries into conventional SQL queries during the interaction with a database.

Even though you can use SQL queries using native SQL directly with Hibernate, it is recommended that you use HQL to get the benefits of Hibernate's SQL generation and caching strategies.

In HQL, keywords such as SELECT, FROM, WHERE, GROUP BY, and so on are not case sensitive but properties such as table and column names are case sensitive. So org.packt.spring.chapter6.hibernate.model.Employee is not same as org.packt.spring.chapter6.hibernate.model.EMPLOYEE, whereas SELECT is similar to Select.

The Query interface

To use HQL, we need to use Query object. The Query interface is an object-oriented representation of HQL. The Query object can be obtained by calling the createQuery() method of the Session interface. The Query interface provides a number of methods such as executeUpdate(), list(), setFirstResult(), setMaxResult(), and so on. The following code snippet uses HQL to get all records:

```
@Transactional
    public List<Employee> getAllEmployees() {
            Session session = sessionFactory.openSession();

            String hql = "FROM Employee";
            Query query = session.createQuery(hql);

            <Employee> emList =  query.list();
            return emList;
    }
```

Database operation using HQL

HQL supports clauses to perform database operation. Let's have a look at a few clauses.

The FROM clause

The FROM clause is used to load complete persistence objects into memory. The FROM clause is the same as the SELECT clause in SQL, as shown in the following table:

HQL	SQL
FROM Employee	SELECT * from Employee

The syntax to use the FROM clause is as follows:

```
String hql = "FROM Employee";
Query query = session.createQuery(hql);
List results = query.list();
```

We can specify the package and class name if needed to fully qualify the class name, as follows:

```
String hql = "FROM org.packt.spring.chapter6.hibernate.model.
Employee";
Query query = session.createQuery(hql);
List results = query.list();
```

The expected output to the console is:

```
Hibernate: select employee0_.ID as ID0_, employee0_.DEPARTMENT as
DEPARTMENT0_, employee0_.FIRST_NAME as FIRST3_0_,
employee0_.JOB_TITLE as JOB4_0_, employee0_.LAST_NAME as LAST5_0_,
employee0_.SALARY as SALARY0_ from EMPLOYEE_INFO employee0_

Employee [id=1, name=RAVI SONI, jobTitle=AUTHOR
department=TECHNOLOGY salary=5000]

Employee [id=2, name=Shree Kant, jobTitle=Software Engineer
department=Technology salary=3000]
```

The AS clause

In HQL, the AS clause is used to assign aliases to the classes when you have long queries. The syntax to use the AS clause is:

```
String hql = "FROM Employee AS E";
Query query = session.createQuery(hql);
List results = query.list();
```

The AS clause is optional, so you can also specify the alias directly after the class name as follows:

```
String hql = "FROM Employee E";
Query query = session.createQuery(hql);
List results = query.list();
```

The SELECT clause

The SELECT clause gives more control over the result set than the FROM clause. In order to get some specific properties of the object instead of the complete objects, go for the SELECT clause.

The syntax of the SELECT clause is as shown here, where it is just trying to get the name field of the Employee object:

```
String hql = "SELECT E.firstName FROM Employee E";
Query query = session.createQuery(hql);
return query.list();
```

In this code snippet, E.firstName is the property of the Employee object rather than a field of the Employee table.

The WHERE clause

The WHERE clause is used to narrow the specific objects that are returned from the storage. The syntax of the WHERE clause is:

```
String hql = "FROM Employee E WHERE E.firstName='RAVI'";
Query query = session.createQuery(hql);
List results = query.list();
```

The expected output will be as follows:

```
Hibernate: select employee0_.ID as ID0_, employee0_.DEPARTMENT as
DEPARTMENT0_, employee0_.FIRST_NAME as FIRST3_0_,
employee0_.JOB_TITLE as JOB4_0_, employee0_.LAST_NAME as LAST5_0_,
employee0_.SALARY as SALARY0_ from EMPLOYEE_INFO employee0_ where
employee0_.FIRST_NAME='RAVI'

Employee [id=1, name=RAVI SONI, jobTitle=AUTHOR
department=TECHNOLOGY salary=5000]
```

The ORDER BY clause

The ORDER BY clause can be used to sort the results from a HQL query by any property of the objects in the result set, either in the ascending (ASC) or the descending (DESC) order.

The syntax of the ORDER BY clause is as follows:

```
String hql = "FROM Employee E ORDER BY E.firstName DESC";
Query query = session.createQuery(hql);
List results = query.list();
```

The expected output will be as follows:

```
Hibernate: select employee0_.ID as ID0_, employee0_.DEPARTMENT as
DEPARTMENT0_, employee0_.FIRST_NAME as FIRST3_0_,
employee0_.JOB_TITLE as JOB4_0_, employee0_.LAST_NAME as LAST5_0_,
employee0_.SALARY as SALARY0_ from EMPLOYEE_INFO employee0_ order
by employee0_.FIRST_NAME DESC

Employee [id=2, name=Shree Kant, jobTitle=Software Engineer
department=Technology salary=3000]

Employee [id=1, name=RAVI SONI, jobTitle=AUTHOR
department=TECHNOLOGY salary=5000]
```

Whenever we need to sort by more than one property in the result set, just add those additional properties to the end of the ORDER BY clause, separated by commas, as follows:

```
String hql = "FROM Employee E ORDER BY E.firstName DESC, E.id
DESC";
Query query = session.createQuery(hql);
List results = query.list();
```

The expected output will be as follows:

```
Hibernate: select employee0_.ID as ID0_, employee0_.DEPARTMENT as
DEPARTMENT0_, employee0_.FIRST_NAME as FIRST3_0_,
employee0_.JOB_TITLE as JOB4_0_, employee0_.LAST_NAME as LAST5_0_,
employee0_.SALARY as SALARY0_ from EMPLOYEE_INFO employee0_ order
by employee0_.FIRST_NAME DESC, employee0_.ID DESC

Employee [id=2, name=Shree Kant, jobTitle=Software Engineer
department=Technology salary=3000]

Employee [id=1, name=RAVI SONI, jobTitle=AUTHOR
department=TECHNOLOGY salary=5000]
```

The GROUP BY clause

Hibernate uses the GROUP BY clause to pull information from the database and group them based on the value of the attribute and use the result to include an aggregate value.

HQL supports aggregate functions such as count (*), count (distinct x), max (), min (), avg (), and sum (). A few are listed here with descriptions:

Function	Description
avg (property name)	This function calculates the average of a property's value
count (property name or *)	This function counts the number of times a given property occurs in the results
max (property name)	This function returns the maximum value from the group
min (property name)	This function returns the minimum value from the group
sum (property name)	This function returns the sum total of the property value

The syntax of the GROUP BY clause is as follows:

```
Session session = sessionFactory.openSession();
String hql = "SELECT SUM(E.salary) FROM Employee E GROUP BY
E.firstName";
Query query = session.createQuery(hql);
List<Long> groupList = query.list();
```

The expected output will be as follows:

```
Hibernate: select sum(employee0_.SALARY) as col_0_0_ from
EMPLOYEE_INFO employee0_ group by employee0_.FIRST_NAME

Salary: 3000

Salary: 5000
```

Using the named parameter

Hibernate supports named parameters in HQL queries to accept input from users and you don't have to defend against SQL injection attacks.

The syntax to use named parameters is as shown here:

```
Session session = sessionFactory.openSession();
String hql = "FROM Employee E WHERE E.firstName =
```

```
:employee_firstName";
Query query = session.createQuery(hql);
query.setParameter("employee_firstName", "Shree");
return query.list();
```

The expected output will be as follows:

```
Hibernate: select employee0_.ID as ID0_, employee0_.DEPARTMENT as
DEPARTMENT0_, employee0_.FIRST_NAME as FIRST3_0_,
employee0_.JOB_TITLE as JOB4_0_, employee0_.LAST_NAME as LAST5_0_,
employee0_.SALARY as SALARY0_ from EMPLOYEE_INFO employee0_ where
employee0_.FIRST_NAME=?

Employee [id=2, name=Shree Kant, jobTitle=Software Engineer
department=Technology salary=3000]
```

The UPDATE clause

Hibernate supports bulk updates. The Query interface contains a method named executeUpdate() to execute the HQL UPDATE or DELETE statement. The UPDATE clause can be used to update one or more object's properties.

The syntax of the UPDATE clause is as shown here:

```
String hql = "UPDATE Employee E set E.firstName = :name WHERE id =
:employee_id";
Query query = session.createQuery(hql);
query.setParameter("name", "Shashi");
query.setParameter("employee_id", 2);
int result = query.executeUpdate();
System.out.println("Row affected: " + result);
```

The expected output will be as follows:

```
Hibernate: update EMPLOYEE_INFO set FIRST_NAME=? where ID=?

Row affected: 1
```

The DELETE clause

To delete one or more objects, you can use the DELETE clause. The syntax of the DELETE clause is as shown here:

```
String hql = "DELETE from Employee E WHERE E.id = :employee_id";
Query query = session.createQuery(hql);
query.setParameter("employee_id", 2);
```

```
int result = query.executeUpdate();
System.out.println("Row affected: " + result);
```

The expected output will be as follows:

```
Hibernate: delete from EMPLOYEE_INFO where ID=?

Row affected: 1
```

Pagination using Query

HQL supports pagination, where we can construct a paging component in our application. The Query interface supports two methods for pagination:

Method	Description
Query setFirstResult(int startPosition)	This method takes an argument of type int, which represents the result to be retrieved. The row in the result set starts with 0.
Query setMaxResults(int maxResult)	This method takes an argument of type int, and is used to set a limit on the maximum number of objects to be retrieved.

The following code snippet will fetch one row at a time:

```
String hql = "FROM Employee";
Query query = session.createQuery(hql);
query.setFirstResult(0);
query.setMaxResults(1);
return query.list();
```

The expected output will be as follows:

```
Hibernate: select employee0_.ID as ID0_, employee0_.DEPARTMENT as
DEPARTMENT0_, employee0_.FIRST_NAME as FIRST3_0_,
employee0_.JOB_TITLE as JOB4_0_, employee0_.LAST_NAME as LAST5_0_,
employee0_.SALARY as SALARY0_ from EMPLOYEE_INFO employee0_ limit
?

Employee [id=1, name=RAVI SONI, jobTitle=AUTHOR
department=TECHNOLOGY salary=5000]
```

Hibernate Criteria Query Language

There is an alternative way provided by Hibernate to manipulate objects and in turn the data available in an RDBMS table. A Java programmer might feel it is easier to use **Hibernate Criteria Query Language (HCQL)** as it supports methods to add criteria on a query.

The Criteria interface

We can build a criteria object using the `Criteria` interface, where we can apply logical conditions and filtration rules. The Session interface of Hibernate provides the `createCriteria()` method to create a `Criteria` object that returns an instance of a persistence object's class when your application executes a criteria query.

The following is a list of commonly used methods from the `Criteria` interface:

Method	Description
`public Criteria add(Criterion c)`	This method is used to add restrictions
`public Criteria addOrder(Order o)`	This method is used to specify ordering
`public Criteria setFirstResult(int firstResult)`	This method is used to specify the first number of record to be retrieved
`public Criteria setMaxResult(int totalResult)`	This method is used to specify the total number of records to be retrieved
`public List list()`	This method returns the list containing the object
`public Criteria setProjection(Projection projection)`	This method is used to specify the projection

The following code snippet retrieves all the objects that correspond to the `Employee` class using the `criteria` query:

```
public List<Employee> getAllEmployees() {
Session session = sessionFactory.openSession();
Criteria criteria = session.createCriteria(Employee.class);
List<Employee> emList = criteria.list();
return emList;
}
```

The expected output will be as follows:

```
Hibernate: select this_.ID as ID0_0_, this_.DEPARTMENT as
DEPARTMENT0_0_, this_.FIRST_NAME as FIRST3_0_0_, this_.JOB_TITLE
as JOB4_0_0_, this_.LAST_NAME as LAST5_0_0_, this_.SALARY as
SALARY0_0_ from EMPLOYEE_INFO this_

Employee [id=1, name=RAVI SONI, jobTitle=AUTHOR
department=TECHNOLOGY salary=5000]

Employee [id=2, name=Shree Kant, jobTitle=Software Engineer
department=Technology salary=3000]
```

Restrictions with Criteria

Restrictive classes provide methods that we can use as Criteria. Let's have a look at a few of them.

The eq method

The eq method will set the equal constraint to a given property.

The syntax of this method is:

```
public static SimpleExpression eq(String propertyName,Object
value)
```

The following code snippet shows the use of the eq method retrieving all the records of the Employee table whose salary is equal to 5000:

```
Session session = sessionFactory.openSession();
Criteria criteria = session.createCriteria(Employee.class);
criteria.add(Restrictions.eq("salary", 5000));
List<Employee> emList = criteria.list();
```

The expected output will be as follows:

```
Hibernate: select this_.ID as ID0_0_, this_.DEPARTMENT as
DEPARTMENT0_0_, this_.FIRST_NAME as FIRST3_0_0_, this_.JOB_TITLE
as JOB4_0_0_, this_.LAST_NAME as LAST5_0_0_, this_.SALARY as
SALARY0_0_ from EMPLOYEE_INFO this_ where this_.SALARY=?

Employee [id=1, name=RAVI SONI, jobTitle=AUTHOR
department=TECHNOLOGY salary=5000]
```

The gt method

This method sets the greater than constraint to a given property. The syntax of this method is:

```
public static SimpleExpression gt(String propertyName,Object
value)
```

The following code snippet shows the use of the gt method retrieving all the records of the Employee table whose ID is greater than 1:

```
Session session = sessionFactory.openSession();
Criteria criteria = session.createCriteria(Employee.class);
criteria.add(Restrictions.gt("id", 1));
List<Employee> emList = criteria.list();
```

The expected output will be as follows:

```
Hibernate: select this_.ID as ID0_0_, this_.DEPARTMENT as
DEPARTMENT0_0_, this_.FIRST_NAME as FIRST3_0_0_, this_.JOB_TITLE
as JOB4_0_0_, this_.LAST_NAME as LAST5_0_0_, this_.SALARY as
SALARY0_0_ from EMPLOYEE_INFO this_ where this_.ID>?

Employee [id=2, name=Shree Kant, jobTitle=Software Engineer
department=Technology salary=3000]
```

The lt method

This method sets the less than constraint to a given property. The syntax of this method is:

```
public static SimpleExpression lt(String propertyName,Object
value)
```

The following code snippet shows the use of the lt method retrieving all the records of the Employee table whose id is lesser than 3:

```
Session session = sessionFactory.openSession();
Criteria criteria = session.createCriteria(Employee.class);
criteria.add(Restrictions.lt("id", 2));
List<Employee> emList = criteria.list();
```

The expected output will be as follows:

```
Hibernate: select this_.ID as ID0_0_, this_.DEPARTMENT as
DEPARTMENT0_0_, this_.FIRST_NAME as FIRST3_0_0_, this_.JOB_TITLE
as JOB4_0_0_, this_.LAST_NAME as LAST5_0_0_, this_.SALARY as
SALARY0_0_ from EMPLOYEE_INFO this_ where this_.ID<?

Employee [id=1, name=RAVI SONI, jobTitle=AUTHOR
department=TECHNOLOGY salary=5000]
```

The like method

This method sets the `like` constraint to a given property. The syntax of this method is:

```
public static SimpleExpression like(String propertyName, Object
value)
```

The following code snippet shows the use of the `like` method retrieving all the records of the Employee table whose `firstName` property is like RAVI:

```
Session session = sessionFactory.openSession();
Criteria criteria = session.createCriteria(Employee.class);
criteria.add(Restrictions.like("firstName", "RAVI"));
List<Employee> emList = criteria.list();
```

The expected output will be as follows:

```
Hibernate: select this_.ID as ID0_0_, this_.DEPARTMENT as
DEPARTMENT0_0_, this_.FIRST_NAME as FIRST3_0_0_, this_.JOB_TITLE
as JOB4_0_0_, this_.LAST_NAME as LAST5_0_0_, this_.SALARY as
SALARY0_0_ from EMPLOYEE_INFO this_ where this_.FIRST_NAME like ?

Employee [id=1, name=RAVI SONI, jobTitle=AUTHOR
department=TECHNOLOGY salary=5000]
```

The ilike method

This method sets the `ilike` constraint to the given property and is case sensitive. The syntax of this method is:

```
public static SimpleExpression ilike(String propertyName, Object
value)
```

The following code snippet shows the use of the `ilike` method retrieving all the records of the Employee table whose `firstName` property is like RAVI:

```
Session session = sessionFactory.openSession();
Criteria criteria = session.createCriteria(Employee.class);
criteria.add(Restrictions.ilike("firstName", "RAVI"));
List<Employee> emList = criteria.list();
```

The expected output will be as follows:

```
Hibernate: select this_.ID as ID0_0_, this_.DEPARTMENT as
DEPARTMENT0_0_, this_.FIRST_NAME as FIRST3_0_0_, this_.JOB_TITLE
as JOB4_0_0_, this_.LAST_NAME as LAST5_0_0_, this_.SALARY as
SALARY0_0_ from EMPLOYEE_INFO this_ where this_.FIRST_NAME ilike ?

Employee [id=1, name=RAVI SONI, jobTitle=AUTHOR
department=TECHNOLOGY salary=5000]
```

The between method

This method sets the between constraint. The syntax of this method is:

```
public static Criterion between(String propertyName, Object low,
Object high)
```

The following code snippet shows the use of the between method retrieving all the records of the Employee table whose salary is between 4000 and 5000:

```
Session session = sessionFactory.openSession();
Criteria criteria = session.createCriteria(Employee.class);
criteria.add(Restrictions.between("salary", 4000,5000));
List<Employee> emList = criteria.list();
```

The expected output will be as follows:

```
Hibernate: select this_.ID as ID0_0_, this_.DEPARTMENT as
DEPARTMENT0_0_, this_.FIRST_NAME as FIRST3_0_0_, this_.JOB_TITLE
as JOB4_0_0_, this_.LAST_NAME as LAST5_0_0_, this_.SALARY as
SALARY0_0_ from EMPLOYEE_INFO this_ where this_.SALARY between ? and ?

Employee [id=1, name=RAVI SONI, jobTitle=AUTHOR
department=TECHNOLOGY salary=5000]
```

The isNull method

This method sets the isNull constraint to the given property. The syntax of this method is:

```
public static Criterion isNull(String propertyName)
```

The following code snippet shows the use of the isNull method retrieving all the records of the Employee table whose salary is null:

```
Session session = sessionFactory.openSession();
Criteria criteria = session.createCriteria(Employee.class);
criteria.add(Restrictions.isNull("salary"));
List<Employee> emList = criteria.list();
```

The expected output will be as follows:

```
Hibernate: select this_.ID as ID0_0_, this_.DEPARTMENT as
DEPARTMENT0_0_, this_.FIRST_NAME as FIRST3_0_0_, this_.JOB_TITLE
as JOB4_0_0_, this_.LAST_NAME as LAST5_0_0_, this_.SALARY as
SALARY0_0_ from EMPLOYEE_INFO this_ where this_.SALARY is null
```

The isNotNull method

This method sets the isNotNull constraint to the given property. The syntax of this method is:

```
public static Criterion isNotNUll(String propertyName)
```

The following code snippet shows the use of the isNotNull method retrieving all the records of the Employee table whose salary is not null:

```
Session session = sessionFactory.openSession();
Criteria criteria = session.createCriteria(Employee.class);
criteria.add(Restrictions.isNotNull("salary"));
List<Employee> emList = criteria.list();
```

The expected output will be as follows:

```
Hibernate: select this_.ID as ID0_0_, this_.DEPARTMENT as
DEPARTMENT0_0_, this_.FIRST_NAME as FIRST3_0_0_, this_.JOB_TITLE
as JOB4_0_0_, this_.LAST_NAME as LAST5_0_0_, this_.SALARY as
SALARY0_0_ from EMPLOYEE_INFO this_ where this_.SALARY is not null

Employee [id=1, name=RAVI SONI, jobTitle=AUTHOR
department=TECHNOLOGY salary=5000]


Employee [id=2, name=Shree Kant, jobTitle=Software Engineer
department=Technology salary=3000]
```

The And or OR condition

LogicalExpression restrictions can be used to create AND or OR conditions as discussed in the following section.

Restrictions.and

The following code snippet shows the and condition:

```
Session session = sessionFactory.openSession();
Criteria criteria = session.createCriteria(Employee.class);
Criterion salary = Restrictions.eq("salary", 5000);
```

```
Criterion firstName = Restrictions.like("firstName", "RAVI");
LogicalExpression andExp = Restrictions.and(salary, firstName);
criteria.add(andExp);
List<Employee> emList = criteria.list();
```

The expected output will be as follows:

```
Hibernate: select this_.ID as ID0_0_, this_.DEPARTMENT as
DEPARTMENT0_0_, this_.FIRST_NAME as FIRST3_0_0_, this_.JOB_TITLE
as JOB4_0_0_, this_.LAST_NAME as LAST5_0_0_, this_.SALARY as
SALARY0_0_ from EMPLOYEE_INFO this_ where (this_.SALARY=? and
this_.FIRST_NAME like ?)

Employee [id=1, name=RAVI SONI, jobTitle=AUTHOR
department=TECHNOLOGY salary=5000]
```

Restrictions.or

The following code snippet shows the or condition:

```
Session session = sessionFactory.openSession();
Criteria criteria = session.createCriteria(Employee.class);
Criterion jobTitle = Restrictions.eq("jobTitle", "AUTHOR");
Criterion firstName = Restrictions.like("lastName", "Kant");
LogicalExpression orExp = Restrictions.or(jobTitle, firstName);
criteria.add(orExp);
List<Employee> emList = criteria.list();
```

The expected output will be as follows:

```
Hibernate: select this_.ID as ID0_0_, this_.DEPARTMENT as
DEPARTMENT0_0_, this_.FIRST_NAME as FIRST3_0_0_, this_.JOB_TITLE
as JOB4_0_0_, this_.LAST_NAME as LAST5_0_0_, this_.SALARY as
SALARY0_0_ from EMPLOYEE_INFO this_ where (this_.JOB_TITLE=? or
this_.LAST_NAME like ?)

Employee [id=1, name=RAVI SONI, jobTitle=AUTHOR
department=TECHNOLOGY salary=5000]

Employee [id=2, name=Shree Kant, jobTitle=Software Engineer
department=Technology salary=3000]
```

Pagination using Criteria

HCQL supports pagination, where we can construct a paging component in our application. The `Criteria` interface supports two methods for pagination:

Method	Description
`Public Criteria setFirstResult(int startPosition)`	This method takes an argument of type `int`, which represents the result to be retrieved. The row in the result set starts with 0.
`Public Criteria setMaxResults(int maxResult)`	This method takes an argument of type `int`, and is used to set a limit on the maximum number of objects to be retrieved.

The following code snippet will fetch two rows at a time:

```
Session session = sessionFactory.openSession();
Criteria criteria = session.createCriteria(Employee.class);
criteria.setFirstResult(0);
criteria.setMaxResults(2);
List<Employee> emList = criteria.list();
```

Sorting the results

The `org.hibernate.criterion.Order` class of the `Criteria` API can be used to sort your results in either ascending or descending order, according to one of the objects' properties.

- `public static Order asc(String propertyName)`: This method applies the ascending order based on a given property
- `public static Order desc(String propertyName)`: This method applies the descending order based on a given property

The following code snippet will order the result by ID in descending order:

```
Session session = sessionFactory.openSession();
Criteria criteria = session.createCriteria(Employee.class);
criteria.addOrder(Order.desc("id"));
List<Employee> emList = criteria.list();
```

The expected output will be as follows:

```
Hibernate: select this_.ID as ID0_0_, this_.DEPARTMENT as
DEPARTMENT0_0_, this_.FIRST_NAME as FIRST3_0_0_, this_.JOB_TITLE
as JOB4_0_0_, this_.LAST_NAME as LAST5_0_0_, this_.SALARY as
SALARY0_0_ from EMPLOYEE_INFO this_ order by this_.ID desc
```

```
Employee [id=2, name=Shree Kant, jobTitle=Software Engineer
department=Technology salary=3000]

Employee [id=1, name=RAVI SONI, jobTitle=AUTHOR department=TECHNOLOGY
salary=5000]
```

Exercise

Q1. What is ORM?

Q2. Explain the basic elements of the Hibernate architecture.

Q3. What is HQL?

 The answers to these are provided in *Appendix A, Solution to Exercises.*

Summary

In this chapter, you learned about ORM and understood the various properties of Hibernate in detail. Then we discussed the important elements of the Hibernate architecture. We have successfully configured Hibernate with the Spring application. We have covered a few pieces of Hibernate functionalities and its features. For better understanding of Hibernate, refer to the Hibernate documentation at `http://hibernate.org/`.

You also learned how to use HQL and HCQL to query persistent objects. HQL is the most powerful query language to retrieve objects using different conditions. HCQL provides an object-oriented manner to retrieve persistent objects.

In the next chapter, you will look at Spring MVC. You will learn how to implement the web tier and the Spring services provided to implement the Web Tier.

5
Spring Web MVC Framework

The presentation layer in an enterprise application is the front door to your application. It provides users a visual view of the information as well as allowing them to perform business functions provided and managed by the application. The development of the presentation layer is a challenging task these days because of the rise of cloud computing and different kinds of devices that people are using. Many technologies and frameworks have evolved to develop enterprise web applications, such as Spring Web MVC, Java Server Faces (JSF), Struts, Google Web Toolkit (GWT), and jQuery. These provide rich component libraries that can help develop interactive web frontends. Many frameworks also provide widget libraries and tools targeting mobile devices, including tables and smartphones.

The Spring Web **Model View Controller** (**MVC**) framework supports web application development by providing comprehensive and intensive support. The framework is flexible, robust, and well-designed and is used to develop web applications. It is designed in such a way that development of a web application is highly configurable into Model, View, and Controller. In the MVC design pattern, Model represents the information (data) of a web application; View represents the User Interface (UI) components, such as checkbox, textbox, and so forth that are used to display web pages; and Controller processes the user request.

The Spring MVC framework helps in integrating other frameworks, such as Struts and WebWork, with a Spring application. This framework also supports the integration of other view technologies such as Java Server Pages (JSP), FreeMarker, Tiles, and Velocity in a Spring web application.

The Spring MVC module provides the MVC framework to develop web applications. In this chapter, we will cover the following topics:

- **Spring MVC**: We will introduce Spring MVC architecture and discuss how we can use the powerful features provided by Spring MVC to develop well-performing web applications. We will also write our first Spring Web MVC application.

- **Spring MVC and Hibernate ORM framework**: We will integrate the Hibernate ORM framework with Spring MVC to fetch data from the database.

- **Exception handling**: We will discuss how to configure exception handling in Spring that will be supported by all controllers and error pages to display custom messages to the user.

- **i18n (internationalization)**: We will discuss how to use Spring MVC to develop a web application that supports common web application requirements, including i18n (internationalization).

- **Handling form with controller**: We will develop a Spring MVC application that will handle the Spring form and allow the user to submit the form.

In this chapter, we will first briefly introduce MVC as a pattern in web applications and its architecture. Then, we will discuss the Front Controller Design Pattern, which is a prerequisite to understanding Spring MVC. Next, we will look into the high-level view of Spring MVC and its architecture. Finally, we will create our first Spring MVC application.

The list of topics covered in this chapter is as follows:

- MVC architecture and separation of concern
- Front Controller Design Pattern
- Understanding Spring MVC
- Developing a simple Spring MVC application
- Dispatcher servlet in Spring MVC
- Spring configuration: `SpringDispatcher-servlet.xml`
- Controller in Spring MVC
- Model in Spring MVC
- Spring MVC with Hibernate integration
- Exceptional handling using `@ControllerAdvice`
- Spring MVC internationalization (i18n)
- Handling form with controller

The MVC architecture and separation of concern

Separation of concern is the process of splitting functionality into distinct features as little as possible. MVC is an architectural pattern used in the development of web applications; it provides separation of concern in the architecture of an application and separates it into three software modules that communicate with each other using a relatively simple interface. The model holds the business entities that can be passed to the View via Controller to expose them to the end user. The View is independent of the Model and Controller; it represents the presentation form of an application. The Controller is independent of the Model and View with the sole purpose of handling requests and performing business logic. Thus, the model (business entities), controllers (business logic), and views (presentation logic) lie in logical/physical layers, independent of each other.

The presentation layer of an application is commonly implemented using the MVC pattern. MVC offers more organized and maintainable code. It is popularly known as a software design pattern used to develop web applications. The three components of MVC are:

- **Model**: The Model represents the business entity on which the application's data is stored. It is the conceptualization of the objects that the user works with and the mapping of those concepts into data structures: the user model and data model.

- **View**: The View is responsible for preparing the presentation for the client based on the outcome of the request processing, without including any business logic. It renders the model data into the client's user interface type.

- **Controller**: The Controller is responsible for controlling the flow request to response flow in the middleware. It invokes backend services for businesses after receiving a request from the user, and updates the model. It prepares models for the View to present. It is also responsible for determining which view should be rendered.

The following figure illustrates **Model**, **View**, and **Controller**:

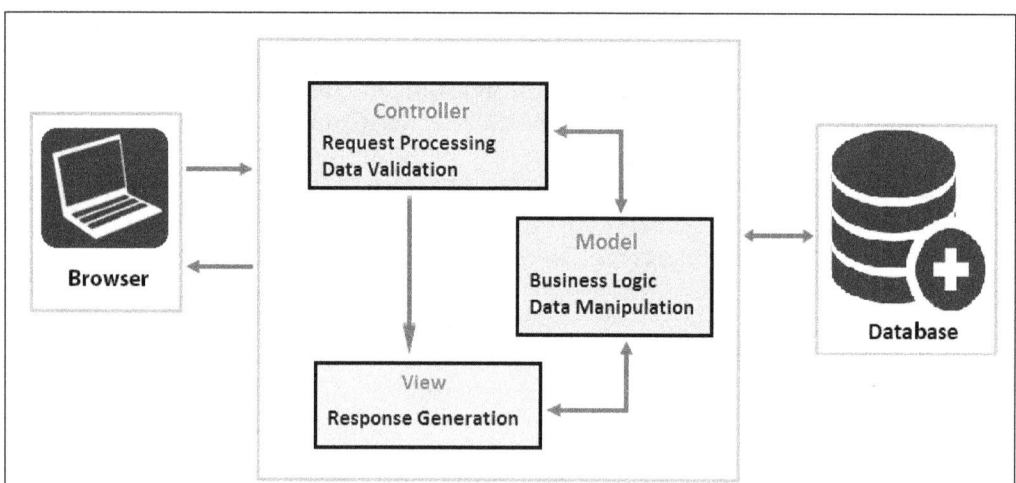

The preceding figure shows MVC in a web application. The **Controller** is typically used to process requests from the client and forward requests for changes to the **Model**. The **View** code accesses the **Model** to render the response to the client.

Front Controller Design Pattern

A pattern represents the strategies that allow programmers to share their knowledge about recurring problems and their solutions. As we have seen in the previous section, the MVC pattern separates the user interface logic from the business logic of web applications. When we want to achieve reusability and flexibility while avoiding duplication and decentralization, we should structure the controller for a very complex web application in the best possible manner.

The Front Controller is used at the initial point of contact to handle all **Hyper Text Transfer Protocol (HTTP)** requests; it enables us to centralize logic to avoid duplicate code, and manages the key HTTP request-handling activities, such as navigation and routing, dispatch, and context transformation. The front controller design pattern enables centralizing the handling of all HTTP requests without limiting the number of handlers in the system.

The **Front Controller** does not just capture HTTP requests; it also initializes some of the very important components of the framework to run, as shown in the following figure. It helps in loading the map of URLs and the components that need to be invoked when a request lands with the URLs. It can also load some of the other components, such as views.

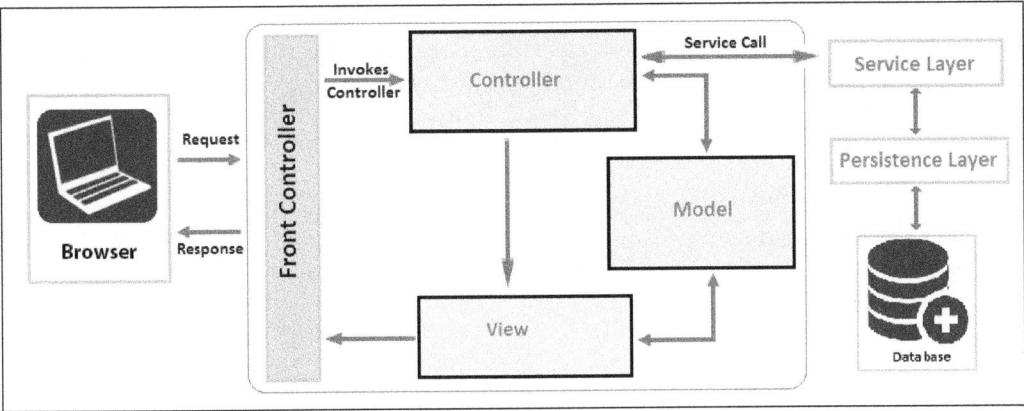

The preceding figure illustrates the front controller design pattern in web applications. The user/browser will interact with only one controller, which is the front controller. The front controller intercepts the user request, performs common functionality, and dispatches the request to the respective controller based on web application configuration and HTTP request information. The controller then interacts with the service layer to perform business logic and persistence logic. Then it updates the model, and the view renders the model data to generate presentation view and return the view to the user. The front controller responds to the client in the form of a view.

In Spring MVC, the Dispatcher Servlet acts as a front controller. As we have discussed about the MVC and the front controller, which are the important to understand the Spring MVC framework, starting with Spring MVC framework followed by its architecture and its elements.

Understanding Spring MVC

A web application developed using the Spring MVC framework is easier to develop, understand, and maintain. Spring MVC is an open source framework; it allows us to download the source code and modify it to support user extensions according to requirements. Its code is exposed to the developer and this enables fast development and maintenance cycle. As a result, we can expect a quick result from the Spring team in fixing the bugs and responding to new requirements in the market.

The Spring MVC framework is implemented using standard Java technologies such as Java, Servlet, and JSP. Thus, we are allowed to host Spring MVC projects on any Java enterprise web server just by including the Spring JAR files into the lib of our web application/project.

The Spring MVC module in the Spring Framework provides comprehensive support for the MVC design for features such as i18n, theming, validation, and so on, to ease the implementation of the presentation layer.

The Spring MVC framework is designed around a `DispatcherServlet`. The `DispatcherServlet` dispatches the HTTP request to the handler, which is a very simple `Controller` interface. Spring MVC allows us to use any form object or command object. Struts built around required base classes such as `Action` class and `ActionForm` class; however, the Spring MVC application doesn't need to implement a framework-specific interface or base class.

Features of the Spring MVC framework

The Spring MVC framework provides a set of the following web support features:

- Powerful configuration of framework and application classes: The Spring Web MVC framework provides straightforward and powerful configuration of the framework as well as of application classes such as JavaBeans.

- It allows easier testing. Most of the Spring classes are designed as JavaBeans, which enables you to inject the test data using the setter method of these JavaBeans classes. The Spring MVC framework also provides classes to handle HTTP requests, which make the unit testing of the web application much simpler.

- It allows separation of roles. Each component of a Spring MVC framework performs a different role during request handling. A request is handled by components such as the `Controller`, `Validator`, `Model Object`, `View Resolver`, and `HandlerMapping` interfaces. The whole task is dependent on these components and provides a clear separation of roles.

- No need for the duplication of code. In the Spring MVC framework, we can use the existing business code in any component of the Spring MVC application. Therefore, no duplicity of the code arises in a Spring MVC application.

- It allows specific validation and binding. Validation errors are displayed when any mismatched data is entered in a form.

Flow of request handling in Spring MVC

The DispatcherServlet is the front controller for the Spring MVC application, providing centralized access to the application for various requests and collaborating with various other objects to complete the request handling and present the response to the client. In Spring MVC, the DispatcherServlet receives requests and dispatches requests to the appropriate controller. There can be any number of DispatcherServlet in a Spring application to handle user interface requests or Restful-WS requests, as shown in the following figure. Each DispatcherServlet uses its own WebApplicationContext configuration to locate the various objects registered in the Spring container, such as the controller, handler mapping, view resolving, i18n, theming, type conversion and formatting, validation, and so on.

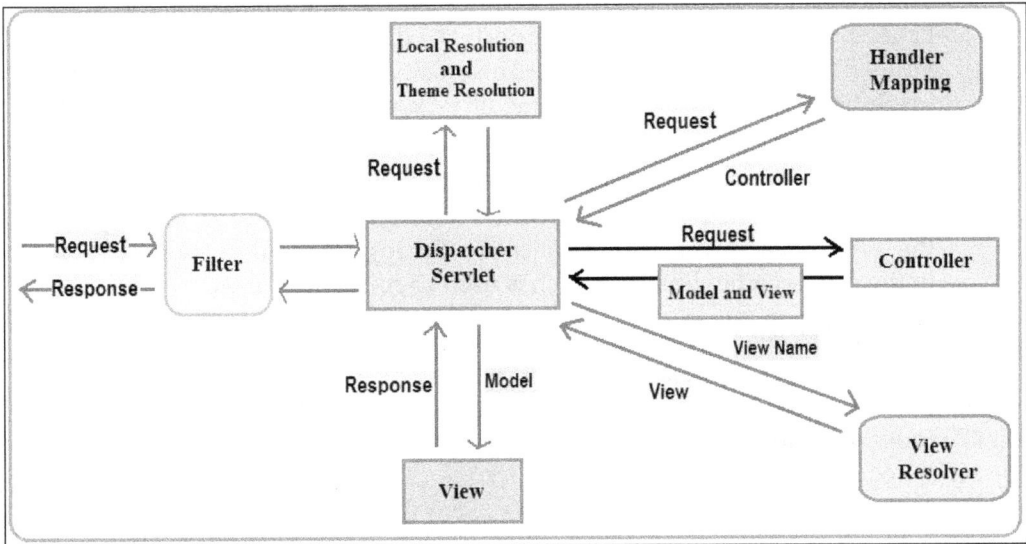

The preceding figure shows the flow of request handling in Spring MVC, along with its components. They are explained as follows:

- **Filter**: The Filter component applies to every HTTP request. In the preceding sections, we will describe the commonly used filters and their purposes.

- **DispatcherServlet**: The Servlet intercepts and analyzes the incoming HTTP request and dispatches them to the appropriate controller to be processed. It is configured in the web.xml file of any web application.

- **Local resolution and theme resolution**: The configuration of i18n and themes is defined in `DispatcherServlet` file's `WebApplicationContext`. It provides support to every request.

- **Handler mapping**: This maps the HTTP request to the handler, that is, a method within a Spring MVC controller class, based on the HTTP paths expressed through the `@RequestMapping` annotation at the method or type level within the controller class.

- **Controller**: The Controller in Spring MVC receives requests from the `DispatcherServlet` class and performs some business logic in accordance with the client.

- **ViewResolver**: The `ViewResolver` interface of Spring MVC supports view resolution based on the view name returned by controller. The `URLBasedViewResolver` class supports the direct resolution of view name to URLs. The `ContentNegotiatingViewResolver` class supports the dynamic resolution of views based on the media type supported by the client, such as PDF, XML, JSON, and so on.

- **View**: In Spring MVC, the View components are user-interface elements, such as textbox items and many others, which are responsible for displaying the output of a Spring MVC application. Spring MVC provides a set of tags in the form of a tag library, which is used to construct views.

Whenever an HTTP request from a browser comes to a Spring MVC application, it is first intercepted by `DispatcherServlet`, which acts like the front controller for a Spring MVC application. The `DispatcherServlet` class intercepts the incoming HTTP request and determines which controller handles the request, and then sends the HTTP request to a Spring MVC controller.

The controller implements the behavior of the Spring MVC application. The controller receives the request from the `DispatcherServlet` class and performs some business logic in accordance with the client request. A Spring MVC application may have several controllers, and to decide on the controller to send the request, `DispatcherServlet` takes help from one or more handler mappings. The handler mapping makes its decision based on the URL carried by the request.

After the business logic is performed by controller, some information referred to as the model is generated, that needs to be carried back to the client and display in the browser. But it is not sufficient to send raw information to the client. So the raw information needs to be given to the view, which can be JSP or FreeMarker. The Controller also packages up the model data and identifies the view name that will render the output. Then, it sends the request along with view name and model back to `DispatcherServlet`.

The `DispatcherServlet` class consults the view resolver to map the view name to a specific view implementation, which may or may not be JSP, FreeMarker, JSON, Thymeleaf, and so on. A good point here is that Spring is agnostic of the view technology. So, at this point, the request job is almost over and `DispatcherServlet` knows about the view which will render the result. It delivers the model data to the view component, and the request job is finally done here. This model data will be used by the view to render the output, which will be carried back by the response object to the client.

Developing a simple Spring MVC application

Let's create a simple Spring MVC application. Here, we will create the application in simple steps using **Spring Source Tool (STS)** IDE, which will display **"Hello World!!"** in the browser. The details of MVC components will be discussed later in the following sections. Here, we will create a Maven Project in STS IDE. In a Maven project, we can provide dependencies in `pom.xml`, rather than downloading and adding the JARs to the project. For the first time, an Internet connection is required in order to get JARs downloaded automatically to the `.m2` folder. For more understanding on Maven, please refer to the book *Instant Apache Maven Starter*, *Maurizio Turatti* and *Maurizio Pillitu*, *Packt Publishing*.

Creating a new Maven project

Take a look at the following instructions to create a new Maven project:

1. Navigate to **File** | **Project** | **Maven**.

2. Select **Maven Project**, and hit the **Next** button.

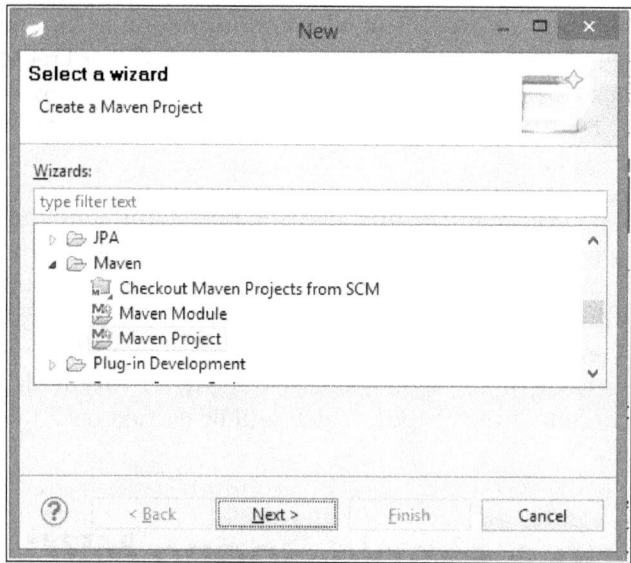

3. Under **Select project name and location**, the **Create a simple project (skip archetype selection)** option should be unchecked. Click on the **Next** button to continue with default values.

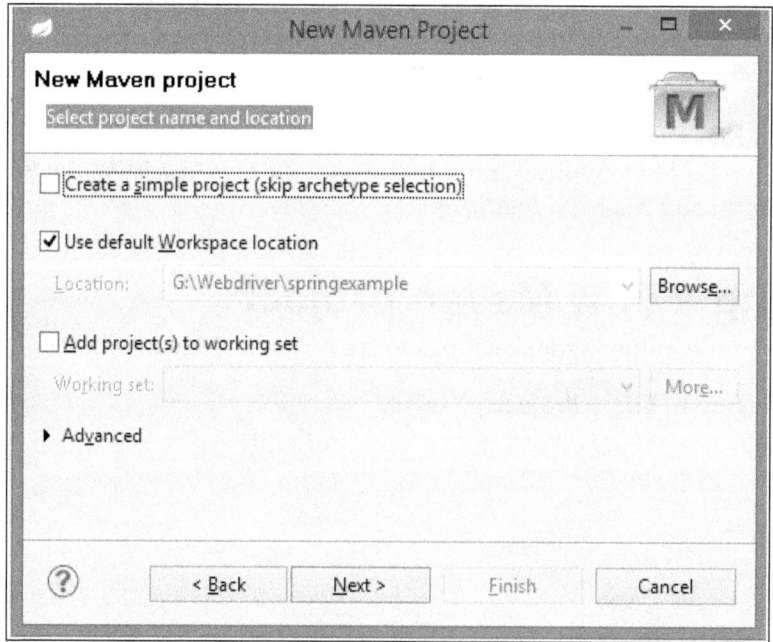

4. Now we need to add Maven archetype to create a web application. To add the archetype, click on **Add Archetype** and set **Archetype Group Id** to org.apache.maven.archetypes and **Archetype Artifact Id** to maven-archetype-webapp. Set **Archetype Version** to 1.0. Then, click on **OK** to continue.

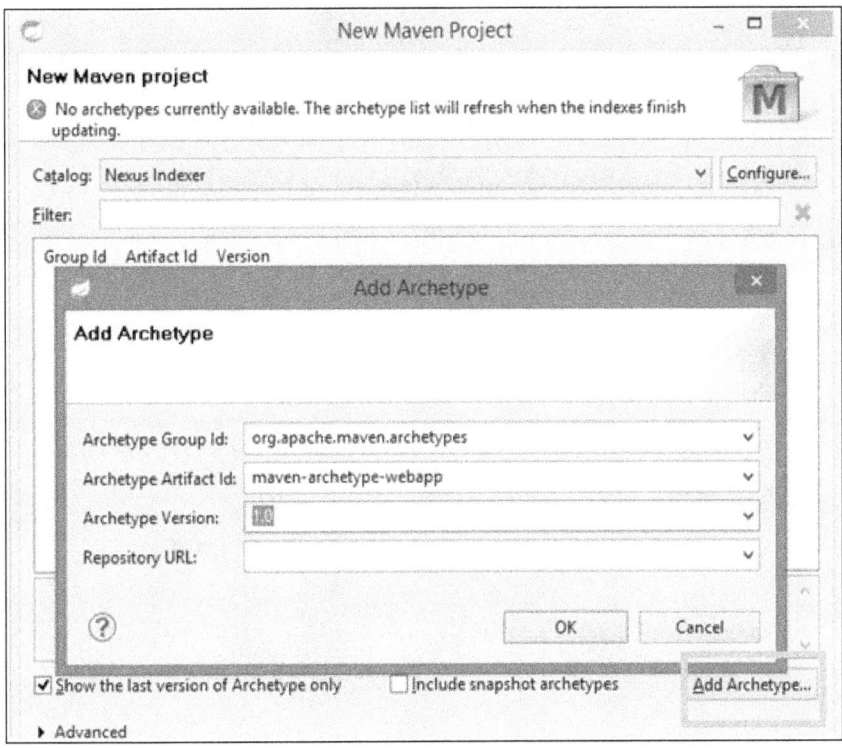

5. On the **Specify Archetype parameter** page wizard, we can define the main package of project. Set the **Group Id** to `org.packt.Spring.chapter7.springmvc` and the **Artifact Id** to `SpringMVCPayrollSystem`. Click on the **Finish** button to exit the wizard and to create the project.

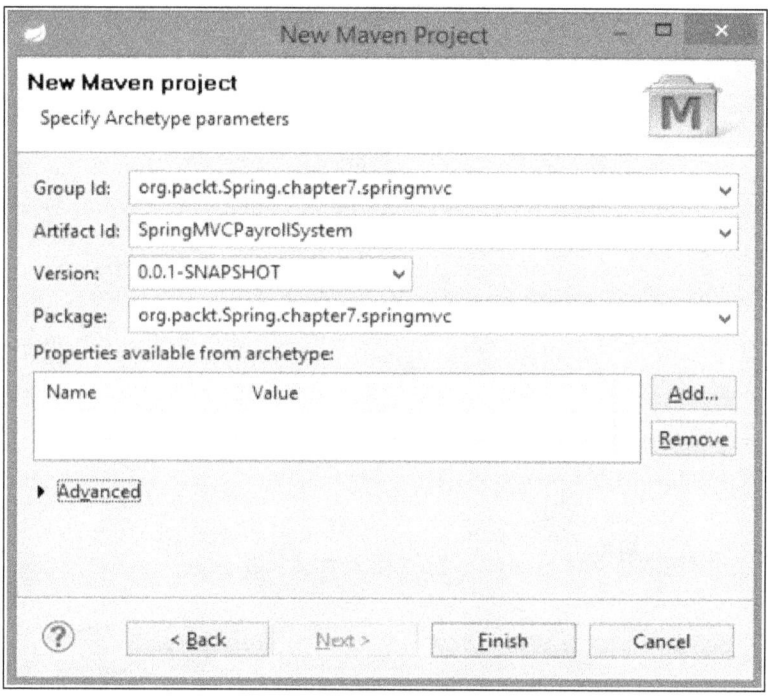

Finally, the Maven project will be created as shown in the following screenshot:

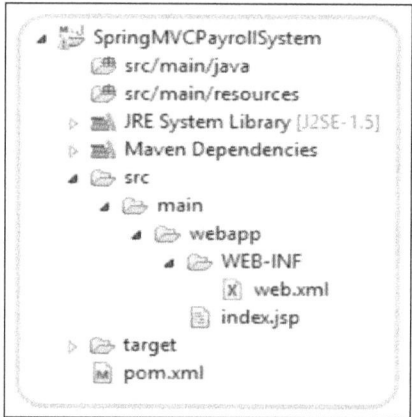

As seen in the preceding screenshot, the `SpringMVCPayrollSystem` project contains:

- `/src/main/java`: This folder contains the project's source files
- `/src/main/resources`: This folder contains the configuration files
- `/target`: This folder contains compiled and packaged deliverables
- `/src/main/webapp/WEB-INF`: This folder contains the web application's deployment descriptors
- `pom.xml`: This is the **Project Object Model (POM)** file; it is the single file that contains all project-related configurations

Adding Spring MVC dependencies to pom.xml

To add the Spring MVC dependencies to Maven's `pom.xml` file, edit the `pom.xml` page of the POM editor, and add the dependencies needed for the MVC, that is, `spring-webmvc` package, as shown in the following code:

```
<project xmlns="http://maven.apache.org/POM/4.0.0" xmlns:xsi="http://
www.w3.org/2001/XMLSchema-instance"
    xsi:schemaLocation="http://maven.apache.org/POM/4.0.0
http://maven.apache.org/maven-v4_0_0.xsd">
    <modelVersion>4.0.0</modelVersion>
    <groupId>org.packt.Spring.chapter7.springmvc</groupId>
    <artifactId>SpringMVCPayrollSystem</artifactId>
    <packaging>war</packaging>
    <version>0.0.1-SNAPSHOT</version>
    <name>SpringMVCPayrollSystem Maven Webapp</name>
    <url>http://maven.apache.org</url>

    <properties>
        <spring.version>4.0.2.RELEASE</spring.version>
    </properties>

    <dependencies>
        <dependency>
            <groupId>junit</groupId>
            <artifactId>junit</artifactId>
            <version>3.8.1</version>
            <scope>test</scope>
        </dependency>
        <dependency>
            <groupId>org.springframework</groupId>
            <artifactId>spring-core</artifactId>
```

```
                <version>${spring.version}</version>
        </dependency>
        <dependency>
                <groupId>org.springframework</groupId>
                <artifactId>spring-webmvc</artifactId>
                <version>${spring.version}</version>
        </dependency>
    </dependencies>

    <build>
        <finalName>SpringMVCPayrollSystem</finalName>
    </build>
</project>
```

Once the build has been completed, the JARs will be downloaded to the `.m2` folder (provided an Internet connection is available), as shown in the following screenshot. We can also refer to *Resolved Dependencies in Dependency Hierarchy* in the POM editor.

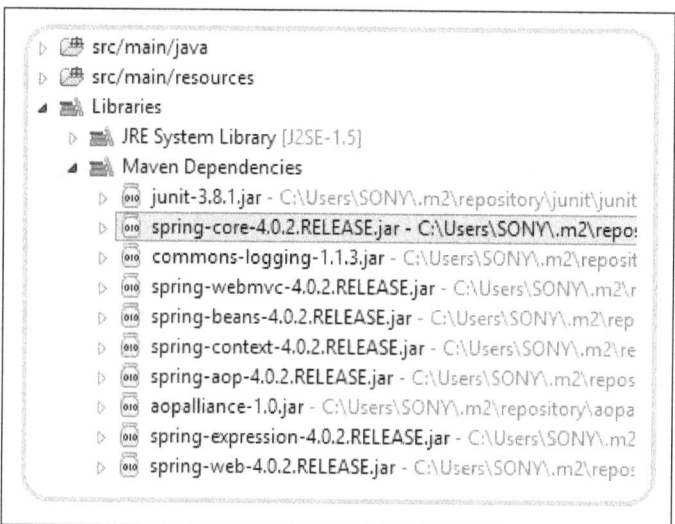

Configuring the application

Now we need to configure the Spring MVC application using the `web.xml` and `SpringDispatcher-servlet.xml` files.

The /WEB-INF/web.xml file

The /WEB-INF/web.xml file represents the deployment descriptor of a web application, which defines the application that a server needs to know, such as Servlet and other components:

```xml
<?xml version="1.0" encoding="UTF-8"?>
<web-app xmlns:xsi="http://www.w3.org/2001/XMLSchema-instance"
    xmlns="http://java.sun.com/xml/ns/javaee"
    xmlns:web="http://java.sun.com/xml/ns/javaee/web-app_2_5.xsd"
    xsi:schemaLocation="http://java.sun.com/xml/ns/javaee
    http://java.sun.com/xml/ns/javaee/web-app_3_0.xsd"
    id="WebApp_ID" version="3.0">
    <display-name>Archetype Created Web Application</display-name>

    <servlet>
            <servlet-name>SpringDispatcher</servlet-name>
            <servlet-class>
                    org.springframework.web.servlet.DispatcherServlet
</servlet-class>
            <load-on-startup>1</load-on-startup>
    </servlet>

    <servlet-mapping>
            <servlet-name>SpringDispatcher</servlet-name>
            <url-pattern>/</url-pattern>
    </servlet-mapping>
</web-app>
```

In the preceding code snippet, the Servlet name has been specified as SpringDispatcher and Servlet class as DispatcherServlet. We have defined URL mapping as /, which will map to all request URLs. We will understand this in more detail in the upcoming sections.

The /WEB-INF/SpringDispatcher-servlet.xml file

Since we have defined the Servlet name as SpringDispatcher in web.xml, so we need to define SpringDispatcher-servlet.xml in the /WEF-INF/ folder. Follow these steps to create this file:

1. Right-click on **WEB-INF** and go to **New | Other**.

2. Then, create a new Spring bean configuration file by selecting **Spring Bean Configuration File** from the `Spring` folder and clicking on **Next**.

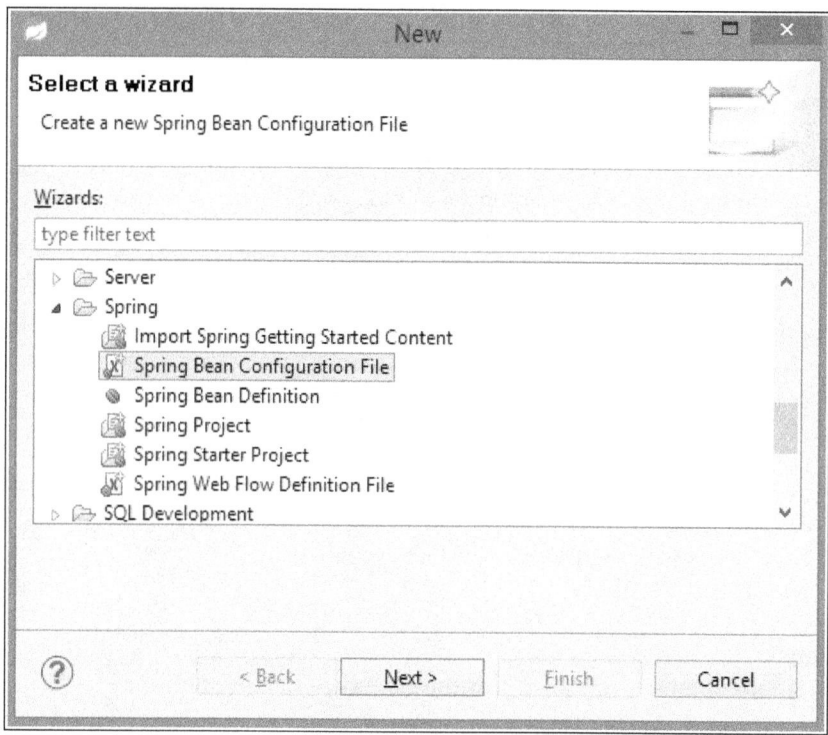

3. Now, set the **File name** option as `SpringDispatcher-servlet.xml` and click on **Next**.

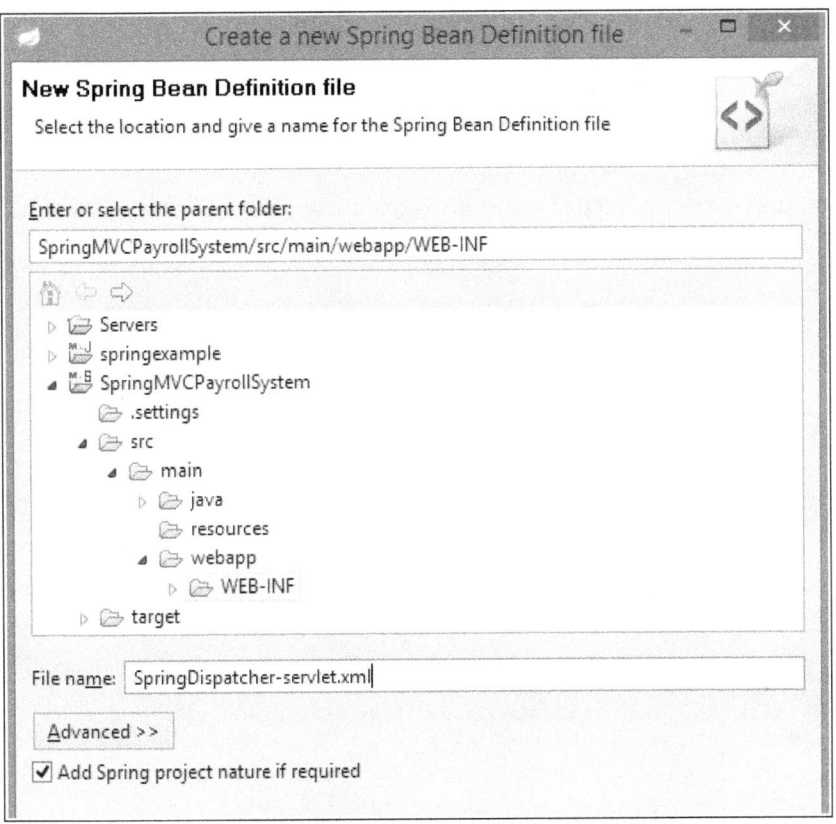

4. Select the desired XSD namespace to use with the new Spring bean definition, such as beans, context, and mvc. Then, click on **Finish**.

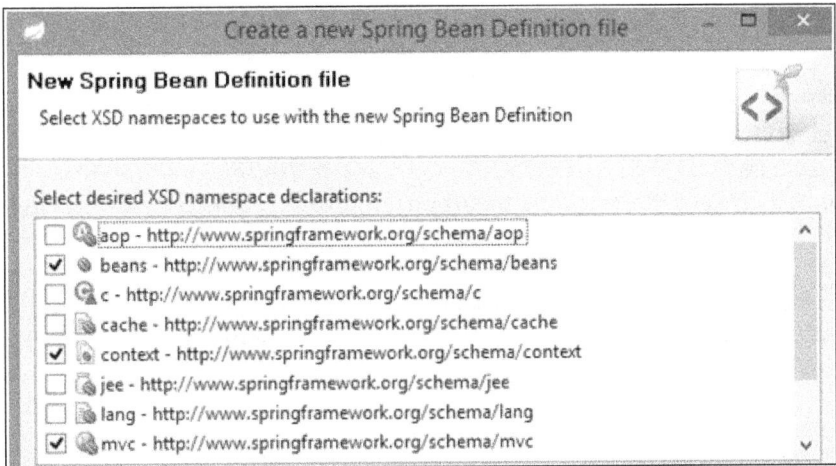

Then, we will have `SpringDispatcher-servlet.xml`, where we need to define a few beans:

```xml
<?xml version="1.0" encoding="UTF-8"?>
<beans xmlns="http://www.springframework.org/schema/beans"
    xmlns:xsi="http://www.w3.org/2001/XMLSchema-instance"
    xmlns:context="http://www.springframework.org/schema/context"
    xmlns:mvc="http://www.springframework.org/schema/mvc"
    xsi:schemaLocation="http://www.springframework.org/schema/beans
        http://www.springframework.org/schema/beans/spring-
beans.xsd
        http://www.springframework.org/schema/context
        http://www.springframework.org/schema/context/spring-
context-4.0.xsd
        http://www.springframework.org/schema/mvc
        http://www.springframework.org/schema/mvc/spring-mvc-
4.0.xsd">

    <context:component-scan base-package="org.packt.Spring.chapter7.
springmvc" />

    <bean
    class="org.springframework.web.servlet.view.
InternalResourceViewResolver">
        <property name="prefix">
            <value>/WEB-INF/views/</value>
        </property>
        <property name="suffix">
            <value>.jsp</value>
        </property>
    </bean>


</beans>
```

In the preceding code snippet, we have declared `<context:component-scan>` with the base package `org.packt.Spring.chapter7.springmvc`, so that the annotated class of this package or subpackage gets scanned by the Spring container. We have also defined the `org.springframework.web.servlet.view.InternalResourceViewResolver` bean as the internal resource view resolver, with the values of the properties prefix and suffix as `/WEB-INF/views/` and `.jsp` respectively. So this `InternalResourceViewResolver` will find the `.jsp` file in the `WebContent/WEB-INF/views/` folder.

When this Spring configuration file is created in this project, this project will become a Spring project, as seen in the following screenshot:

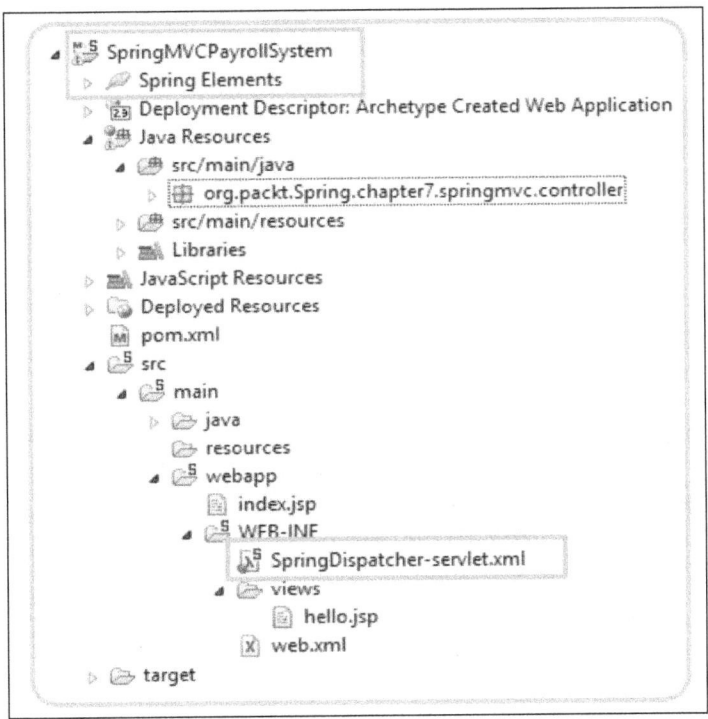

Since we are done with setting up the environment for the Spring MVC application, we can now create the controller and view. First, let's create the EmployeeController controller class.

Creating the controller – EmployeeController

We will create the EmployeeController class within the org.packt.Spring. chapter7.springmvc.controller package:

```
package org.packt.Spring.chapter7.springmvc.controller;

import org.springframework.stereotype.Controller;
import org.springframework.ui.ModelMap;
import org.springframework.web.bind.annotation.RequestMapping;
import org.springframework.web.bind.annotation.RequestMethod;

@Controller
@RequestMapping("/employee")
```

```
public class EmployeeController {

    @RequestMapping(method = RequestMethod.GET)
    public String welcomeEmployee(ModelMap model) {

            model.addAttribute("name", "Hello World!");
            model.addAttribute("greetings",
                    "Welcome to Packt Publishing - Spring MVC
!!!");
            return "hello";
    }
}
```

In the preceding code snippet, we have annotated the `EmployeeController` class with the `@Controller` stereotype annotation, and the `@RequestMapping("/employee")` annotation that will map the URL to the entire class, and handler methods within the class. The `welcomeEmployee(ModelMap model)` method will handle the GET request from `DispatcherServlet`. The `org.springframework.ui.ModelMap` is used to hold the model. The `name` and `greetings` attributes have been set with values `Hello World!` and `Welcome to Packt Publishing - Spring MVC !!!` respectively.

As we are done with creating the controller class for the Spring MVC application, we now need to create the view page `hello.jsp`.

Creating the view – hello.jsp

Here, we will create the view page `hello.jsp` within the `/WEB-INF/views/` folder:

```
<%@ page language="java" contentType="text/html; charset=ISO-8859-1"
    pageEncoding="ISO-8859-1"%>
<!DOCTYPE html PUBLIC "-//W3C//DTD HTML 4.01
Transitional//EN""http://www.w3.org/TR/html4/loose.dtd">
<html>
<head>
<meta http-equiv="Content-Type" content="text/html;
charset=ISO-8859-1">
<title>Chapter-7 Spring MVC</title>
</head>
<body>

    <h1 style="color: green; text-align: center;">${name}</h1>
    <h3 style="color: orange; text-align:
center;">${greetings}</h3>
```

```
</body>
</html>
```

In the preceding code snippet, the view renders data from the model to prepare the page for the user. Now it's time to run the application to get results in the browser.

Running the application

In order to run this application, we have to follow a few steps. Here, we are using the server named VMware vFabric tc Server Developer Edition v2.9, which is the inbuilt server in STS IDE. We can also use another server, such as Apache Tomcat. Follow these steps to run the application:

1. First, right-click on the SpringMVCPayrollSystem project and go to **Run As | Run On Server**. Then, select the server to be used.

2. Select the server as VMware vFabric tc Server Developer Edition v2.9 (or another server if you wish to), and then click on **Next**, where we need to modify the resources on the server.

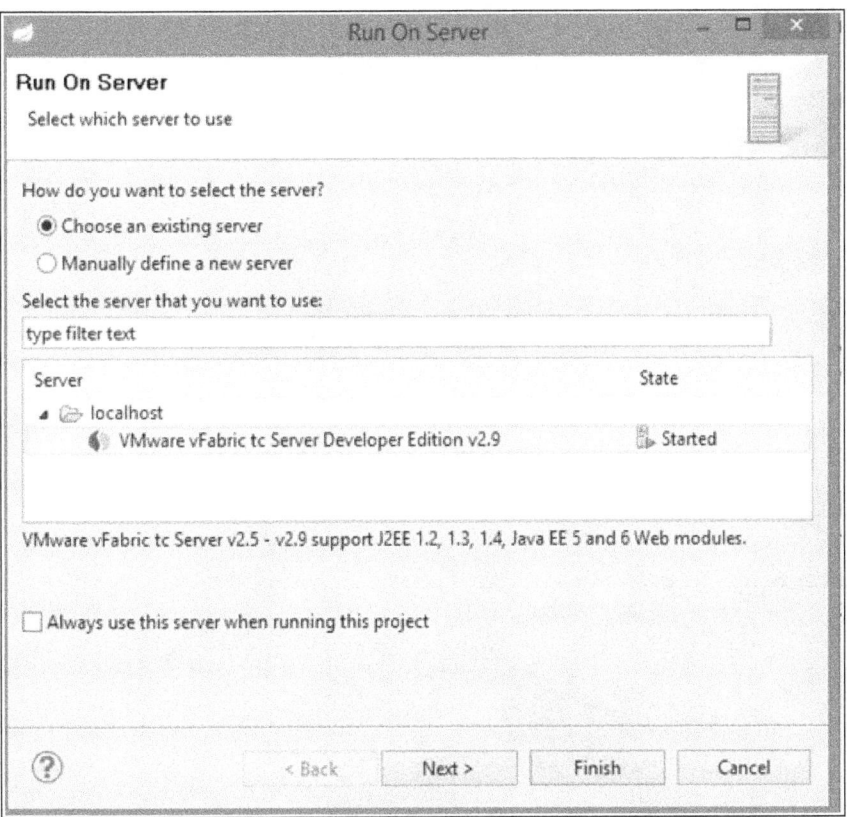

3. We can add or remove resources that will run on the server. The **Available** section on the left-hand side will give the list of resources that can be moved to the right using the **Add** button. The **Configured** section on the right-hand side will give the list of resources that have been configured and will run on server. To remove a resource from the **Configured** section, select the resource and click on **Remove**; to remove all the resources at once, click on **Remove All**. Here, we have the SpringMVCPayrollSystem project in the **Configured** section.

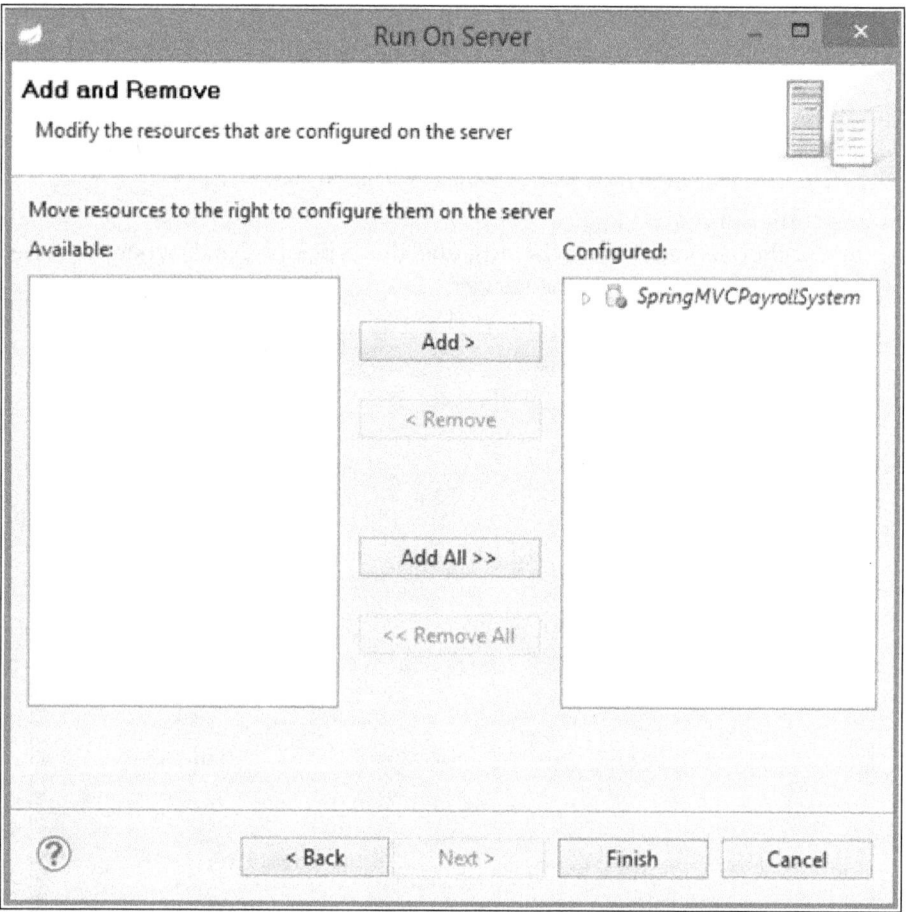

4. Once we move the resource to the **Configured** section and click on **Finish**, the server will start running. By clicking on `http://localhost:8080/SpringMVCPayrollSystem/employee` in the browser, we will see the following result:

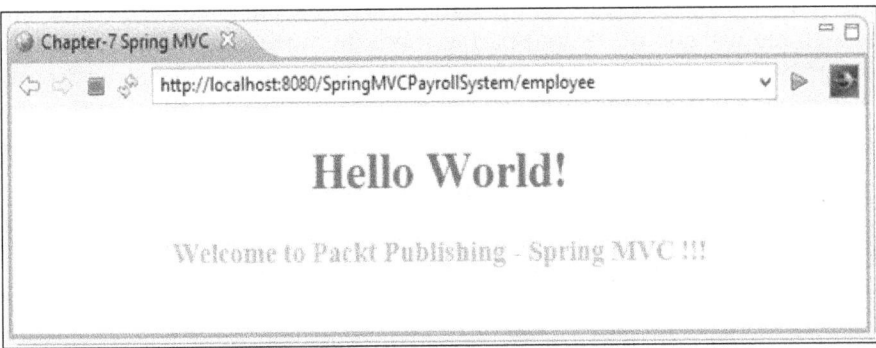

Since we have developed a Spring Web MVC application, we will understand each component in greater detail. Let's start with `DispatcherServlet`.

DispatcherServlet in Spring MVC

The `DispatcherServlet` class of the Spring MVC framework is an implementation of front controller and is a Java Servlet component for Spring MVC applications. It is a front controller class that receives all incoming HTTP client requests for the Spring MVC application. It is also responsible for initializing framework components used to process the request at various stages.

The `DispatcherServlet` class is fully configured with the **Inversion of Control (IoC)** container that allows us to use various Spring features such as Spring context, Spring **Object Relational Mapping (ORM)**, Spring **Data Access Object (DAO)**, and so on. `DispatcherServlet` is a Servlet that handles HTTP requests and is inherited from `HttpServlet` base class.

Configuring `DispatcherServlet` in our Spring web application into the web application deployment descriptor (`web.xml`) is necessary, just like any other servlet. Using URL mapping in the configuration file, the HTTP requests to be handled by `DispatcherServlet` are mapped. A Spring MVC application can have any number of `DispatcherServlet` classes and each `DispatcherServlet` class will have its own `WebApplicationContext`.

DispatcherServlet in deployment descriptor – web.xml

For a Java web application, the web deployment descriptor web.xml is the essential configuration file. In web.xml, we define the Servlet for our web application and how the web request should be mapped to them. In the Spring MVC application, we only have to define a single DispatcherServlet instance, which acts as the front controller for the Spring MVC application, even though we are allowed to define more than one if required.

The following code snippet declares the DispatcherServlet in web.xml:

```
<servlet>
    <servlet-name>SpringDispatcher</servlet-name>
    <servlet-class>
            org.springframework.web.DispatcherServlet
    </servlet-class>
    <load-on-startup>1</load-on-startup>
</servlet>

<servlet-mapping>
    <servlet-name>SpringDispatcher</servlet-name>
    <url-pattern>/**</url-pattern>
</servlet-mapping>
```

In the preceding code snippet, SpringDispatcher is the user-defined name of the DispatcherServlet class, which is enclosed with the <servlet-name> element. When this newly created SpringDispatcher class is loaded in a web application, it loads an ApplicationContext from an XML file.

The next task after creating the SpringDispatcher class is to map this class with the incoming HTTP request that indicates what URLs are handled by the DispatcherServlet class. To map the DispatcherServlet class, we use the <servlet-mapping> element and to handle URLs, we use the <url-pattern> tag in the web.xml file, as seen in the preceding code snippet.

The /** (slash with **) pattern doesn't imply any specific type of response and simply indicates that DispatcherServlet will serve all incoming HTTP requests, including the request for any static content.

Registering Spring MVC configuration file location

As we discussed in the previous section, `DispatcherServlet` loads the `[servlet-name]-servlet.xml` file in the `WEB-INF` folder to compose `WebApplicationContext`. In order to define this file as a random file in a random location, or as a multi-file, we use `<init-param>` under `<servlet>` to define an initialization parameter named `contextConfigLocation`:

```
<init-param>
<param-name>contextConfigLocation</param-name>
<param-value>/config/springmvc/someCommon-servlet.xml,
/config/springmvc/someUser-servlet.xml</param-value>
</init-param>
```

Spring configuration – SpringDispatcher-servlet.xml

By default, when the `DispatcherServlet` class is loaded, it loads the Spring application context from the XML file whose name is based on the name of the Servlet. In the preceding code, as the name of the Servlet has been defined as `SpringDispatcher`, `DispatcherServlet` will try to load the application context from a file named `SpringDispatcher-servlet.xml` located in the application's `WEB-INF` directory.

The `DispatcherServlet` class will use the `SpringDispatcher-servlet.xml` file to create an `ApplicationContext`, which is a standard Spring bean configuration file, as shown here:

```
<beans xmlns="http://www.springframework.org/schema/beans"
   xmlns:context="http://www.springframework.org/schema/context"
   xmlns:mvc="http://www.springframework.org/schema/mvc"
xmlns:xsi="http://www.w3.org/2001/XMLSchema-instance"
   xsi:schemaLocation="
http://www.springframework.org/schema/beans
http://www.springframework.org/schema/beans/spring-beans-3.0.xsd
http://www.springframework.org/schema/context
        http://www.springframework.org/schema/context/spring-
context-3.0.xsd http://www.springframework.org/schema/mvc
http://www.springframework.org/schema/mvc/spring-mvc-3.0.xsd">

    <mvc:annotation-driven />
```

```
<context:component-scan base-
package="org.packt.Spring.chapter7.springmvc" />

<bean
class="org.springframework.web.servlet.
view.InternalResourceViewResolver">
        <property name="prefix" value="/WEB-INF/views/" />
        <property name="suffix" value=".jsp" />
</bean>
</beans>
```

Let's take a look at some of the MVC features used in the preceding code snippet:

- `<mvc:annotation-driven/>`: This tells the Spring Framework to support annotations like `@Controller`, `@RequestMapping`, and others, all of which simplify the writing and configuration of controllers.

- `InternalResourceViewResolver`: The Spring MVC framework supports different types of views for presentation technologies, including JSPs, HTML, PDF, JSON, and so on. When the `DispatcherServlet` class defined in the application's `web.xml` file receives a view name returned from the handler, it resolves the logical view name into a view implementation for rendering.

- In the preceding code snippet, we have configured the `InternalResourceViewResolver` bean to resolve the bean into JSP files in the `/WEB-INF/views/` directory.

- `<context:component-scan>`: This tells Spring to automatically detect annotations. It takes the value of the base package, which corresponds to the one used in the Spring MVC controller.

Controllers in Spring MVC

The `DispatcherServlet` class delegates the incoming HTTP client request to the controllers to execute the functionality specific to it. The controller interprets user input and transforms this input into a specific model which will be represented by the view to the user.

While developing web functionality, we will develop resource-oriented controllers. Rather than each use case having one controller in the web application, we will have a single controller for each resource that the Spring web application serves. An abstract implementation method is provided by Spring for the user to develop the controller without being dependent on a specific API. We do not need to inherit any specific interface or class while developing a controller based on Spring MVC using the `@Controller` annotation.

The @Controller annotation to define a controller

The @Controller annotation is used to define a class as a controller class without inheriting any interface or class. The following code snippet defines the EmployeeController class as a controller using the @Controller annotation:

```
package org.packt.Spring.chapter7.springmvc.controller;

import org.springframework.stereotype.Controller;

@Controller
public class EmployeeController {
    // ...
}
```

The @Controller annotation indicates the role to the annotated class. Such an annotated class is scanned by the dispatcher for mapped methods and detects the @RequestMapping annotation, which we will discuss in next section. This defined controller can be automatically registered in the Spring container by adding <context:component-scan/> in SpringDispatcher-servlet.xml file.

```
<?xml version="1.0" encoding="UTF-8"?>
<beans xmlns="http://www.springframework.org/schema/beans"
    xmlns:xsi="http://www.w3.org/2001/XMLSchema-instance"
    xmlns:p="http://www.springframework.org/schema/p"
    xmlns:context="http://www.springframework.org/schema/context"
    xsi:schemaLocation="
        http://www.springframework.org/schema/beans
        http://www.springframework.org/schema/beans/spring-beans.xsd
        http://www.springframework.org/schema/context
        http://www.springframework.org/schema/context/spring-context.
xsd">

<context:component-scan base-package="org.packt.Spring.chapter7.
springmvc"/>

<!-- ... -->

</beans>
```

The @RequestMapping annotation to map requests

The web request in Spring MVC is mapped to handlers by one or more `@RequestMapping` annotations declared in the controller class. The handler mapping is used to match the URL as per its path relative to the `ApplicationContext` interface's deployment path and the path that is mapped to `DispatcherServlet`. For example, in the URL `http://localhost:8080/SpringMVCPayrollSystem/employee` the path to match is `/employee` as the context path is `/SpringMVCPayrollSystem`.

Let's take an example:

```java
package org.packt.Spring.chapter7.springmvc.controller;

import org.springframework.stereotype.Controller;
import org.springframework.ui.Model;
import org.springframework.web.bind.annotation.RequestMapping;

@Controller
@RequestMapping("/employee")
public class EmployeeController {

    @Autowired
    private EmployeeService employeeService;

    @RequestMapping(method = RequestMethod.GET)
    public String getEmployeeName(@RequestParam("employeeId") int
employeeId,
            Model model) throws Exception {

        Model.addAttribute("employeeName", employeeService.
getEmployeeName(employeeId))

        return "employeeList";
    }
}
```

In the preceding code snippet, since we have activated annotation scanning on the `org.packt.Spring.chapter7.springmvc` package declared inside `SpringDispatcher.xml` file, the annotation will be detected upon deployment for this controller class.

The @Controller annotation will defines this class the Spring MVC controller class. The @RequestMapping at the class level take the value /employee that means any HTTP request received on /employee URI is attended by the EmployeeController class. Once the controller class attends to the HTTP request, it delegates this (initial request) call to the default HTTP GET method which is a handler method, declared in the controller. The @RequestMapping(method = RequestMethod.GET) annotation is used to decorate the getEmployeeName method as controller's default HTTP GET handler method.

The method returns the view named employeeList. In the next section, we will explore the views to which the Spring MVC controller's handler methods delegate their result.

The @RequestMapping annotation can be applied to a class level where the mapping strategy will be to map specific URI pattern to the controller class, or applied to method level where mapping strategy will be to map particular HTTP method to each controller handler method. The scope of request URL can also be reduced by adding HTTP method or request parameter, other than defining URL path in @RequestMapping.

Mapping requests at the class level

The @RequestMapping annotation can be used to decorate the Spring MVC controller class that allows handler method to fine grained URLs with their own @RequestMapping annotation, as shown in the following code snippet:

```
@Controller
@RequestMapping(value = "/employee")
public class EmployeeController {

@Autowired
    private EmployeeService employeeService;

    @RequestMapping("/add")
    public String addEmployee (Model model) {
            model.addAttribute("employee", new Employee());
            model.addAttribute("empList", employeeService.list());
            return "employeeList";
    }
}
```

```
    @RequestMapping(value = {"/remove", "/delete"}", method =
RequestMethod.GET)
    public String removeEmployee ((@RequestParam("employeeId") int
employeeId){
        employeeService.removeEmployee(employeeId);
        return "redirect:";
    }


    @RequestMapping(value = "/{employeeId}", method =
RequestMethod.GET)
    public String getEmployee (@PathVariable("employeeId")Integer
employeeId, Model model){

        //...
        return "employeeList";
    }
}
```

The @RequestMapping annotation at class level uses a URI /employee, which delegates all requests under the /employee URI to the controller's handler methods.

The first two controller's handler methods make use of only the @RequestMapping annotation. The handler method addEmployee() is invoked when an HTTP GET request is made on the /employee/add URL. The handler method removeEmployee() is called when an HTTP GET method is made on either the /employee/remove URL or the /employee/delete URL.

The third controller's handler method uses one more annotation @PathVariable to specify the @RequestMapping value, which will pass the value present in URL as input in the handler method. The handler method declares @PathVariable("employeeId") Integer employeeId . If the HTTP request is in the form of /employee/10121, the handler method will have access to the employeeId variable with the 10121 value.

We can also define some utility methods without using the @RequestMapping annotation for the class without influencing Spring MVC.

Mapping requests at the method level

To decorate the handler method directly is the simplest strategy to use the @RequestMapping annotation, which allows us to map requests at the method level in a controller class. In order to use this strategy, we need to declare each handler method in the controller class with the @RequestMapping annotation containing the URL pattern. The DispatcherServlet class will dispatch the request to the handler annotated with @RequestMapping to handle the request.

Let's say, if we define @RequestMapping("/employee") at the class level, and @RequestMapping("/add") at the method level, then the URL path that the method defined as @RequestMapping("/add") will be interpreted as "/employee/add". The style and path pattern is also supported by @RequestMapping, for example, as "/employee/*".

Let's take an example of the following code snippet, where both values, which is the URL route and the default HTTP GET handler method, are defined in the @RequestMapping annotation at the method level:

```java
@Controller
public class EmployeeController {

@Autowired
    private EmployeeService employeeService;

    @RequestMapping(value = "/employee", method =
RequestMethod.GET)
    public String getEmployeeName(@RequestParam("employeeId") int
employeeId, Model model){
        //...
        return "employeeList";
    }

    @RequestMapping("/employee/add")
    public String addEmployee (Model model){
        //...
        return "employeeList";
    }

    @RequestMapping(value = {"/employee/remove",
"/employee/delete"}", method = RequestMethod.GET)
```

```
        public String removeEmployee ((@RequestParam("employeeId") int
employeeId){
            //...
            return "redirect:";
    }
}
```

It is important to note that the Spring MVC controller should have at minimum a URL route and a default HTTP GET handler method; otherwise a ServletException is thrown.

Properties information in @RequestMapping

The scope of the HTTP request URL to be handled can be limited by applying the following properties information in @RequestMapping. The @RequestMapping annotation has the following properties that can be configured:

- **Value**: The value specifies the value of the mapping. The format of the URL value is value="/getEmployee"; for example, @RequestMapping(value="/ getEmployee").

  It indicates that the incoming "/employee" request is mapped to the controller class. If the value is used at the class level, it serves as primary mapping; if it is used at the method level, then it is relative to primary mapping.

  The value can take more than one URL path, for example, @RequestMapping(value={"/addEmployee", "/updateEmployee"}). Here, both "/addEmployee" and "/updateEmployee" URLs will be handled.

- **Method**: The method enables you to specify the type of HTTP request, such as GET, POST, PUT, DELETE, and so on. The DispatcherServlet class invokes the handler method based on the HTTP request it receives.

  The value is provided as enumeration of org.springframework. web.bind.annotation.RequestMethod, for example, @RequestMapping(method = RequestMethod.GET') or @RequestMapping(method = RequestMethod.POST).

- **Params**: This specifies the request parameters that come along with the HTTP request. It can be represented in various forms, such as name = value pairs; for example, params={"params1=apple","params2","!myparam"}.

It is used to narrow down the mapping functionality. Let's take an example:

`@RequestMapping(params={"params1=apple","params2","!myparam"})`

The particular method or controller is invoked only if the incoming request has a parameter `params1` and `params2` and if the value of `params1` is `apple` and `myparam` is not present in the HTTP request.

- **Headers**: The header specifies the HTTP header as `name=value` pairs. It is used to narrow down the mapping functionality; for example, `@RequestMapping(value="/employee.do", header="content-type=text/*")`.

The particular method or controller is invoked only if the incoming request has an HTTP header called `content-type` whose value matches `text/html` or `text/plain` in the HTTP request.

Method parameters of @RequestMapping

The `@RequestMapping` annotation can be applied to methods with signatures. These methods can accept any parameters. The parameters of the method that are annotated with `@RequestMapping` are listed in the following table:

Parameter	Description
`ServletRequest/ HttpServletRequest`	This helps to access the request collection
`java.util.Local`	This specifies the request locale
`HttpSession`	This helps to work with the HTTP session

`@PathVariable`	This helps to access the variable in the request path; for example, if the request path is `/employee/{employeeId}`, the `employeeId` variable in the path is accessed by annotating the method argument using `@PathVariable`:
	
	 `@RequestMapping("/employee/{empl oyeeId}")`
	 `    public String getEmployee(@PathVariable("emplo yeeId") int employeeId{ })`

Parameter	Description
@RequestParam	This helps to bind the HTTP request parameter to the argument of the controller method; its functionality is similar to ServletRequest. getParameter(java.lang.String); for example: ```@RequestMapping("/employee.do")\n public String\n getEmployee(@RequestParam("emplo\nyeeId") int employeeId{ })```
@ModelAttribute	This represents a command or model object
Model, Map, or ModelMap	This specifies the collection to which more information can be added; this is passed on to the view page
Errors/BindingResult	This holds the results of validating a command or model object
Session Status	This helps to end a conversational session
@RequestHeader	This specifies the access to an HTTP header
@RequestBody	This helps to access the content of the incoming request

@RequestParam

The @RequestParam annotation binds request parameters to method parameters. It can be used to bind the HTTP request parameter to the argument of the controller method. Its functionality is similar to ServletRequest.getParameter(java.lang. String). Let's take an example of the @RequestParam annotation, as seen in the following code snippet:

```
@RequestMapping("/employee.do")
    public String getEmployee(@RequestParam("employeeId") int
employeeId,ModelMap model) {
        Employee employee =
this.employeeService.getEmployee(employeeId);
        model.addAttribute("employee",employee);
        return "/listEmployee.do";
    }
```

It should be noted that the parameter that applies to `@RequestParam` should exist in the HTTP request; otherwise an exception `org.springframework.web.bind.` `MissingServletRequestParameterException` will be thrown:

```
org.springframework.web.bind.MissingServletRequestParameterException:
Required java.lang.Integer parameter 'employeeId' is not present
```

We can also specify parameters to be optional just by setting the `@RequestParam` required attribute to `false`:

```
(@RequestParam(value = "employeeId", required = false))
```

Return values in @RequestMapping annotated methods

The `@RequestMapping` annotated methods can have return values, some of which have been described in the following table (for the entire list, visit `http://` `docs.spring.io/spring/docs/4.1.x/spring-framework-reference/` `htmlsingle/#mvc-ann-return-types`):

Return type	Description
ModelAndView	This holds Model and View information
String	This represents the View name
View	This represents the View object
Model/Map	This contains data exposed by a view; view is determined implicitly by the `RequestToViewNameTranslator` class
Void	This specifies that a view can be handled by the invoked method internally or can be determined implicitly by the `RequestToViewNameTranslator` class

ViewResolver in Spring MVC

The controller class handler methods return different values that denote the logical view names. The views can represent Java Server Pages (JSP), FreeMarker, Portable Document Format (PDF), Excel, and Extensible Stylesheet Language (XSL) pages. The control will be delegated to view template from `DispatcherServlet`.

The view name returned by the method is resolved to the actual physical source by the `ViewResolver` beans declared in the context of the web application. Spring provides a number of `ViewResolver` classes that are configured in the XML files.

All `ViewResolvers` implement the `org.springframework.web.servlet.`
`ViewResolver` interface. The `ViewResolver` interface maps the view names with
the implementations of the `org.springframework.web.servlet.ViewResolver`
interface. Here is list of few `ViewResolvers` provided by the Spring Framework:

ViewResolver	Description
`org.springframework.web.servlet.view.` `ResourceBundleViewResolver`	This configures view names in property files; the default resource bundle is properties
`org.springframework.web.servlet.view.` `InternalResourceViewResolver`	This refers to a convenient `ViewResolver` class that uses suffix and prefix properties for the view name and `RequestDispatcher` to transfer the control
`org.springframework.web.servlet.view.` `Freemarker.FreeMarkerViewResolver`	This maps the view name with the `FreemarkerView` class, which is used for the FreeMarker template engine
`org.springframework.web.servlet.view.` `velocity.VelocityViewResolver`	This maps the view name with the `VelocityView` class, which is used for the Velocity template engine

The `ViewResolver` should be chosen according to the view technology used in the
web application.

We are not going to cover all `ViewResolvers` in this book. Here, we will cover
only `InternalResourceViewResolver` to configure the view resolver for JSP
as view technology.

Configuring ViewResolver for JSP as view technology

`InternalResourceViewResolver` resolves the logical view name into a `View` object,
which delegates rendering responsibility to a template, such as JSP, located in the
context of the web application.

`ViewResolver` can be configured in the `/WEB-INF/SpringDispatcher-servlet.xml` configuration file to resolve the view. Let's consider an example of configuring `InternalResourceViewResolver`:

```
<bean class="org.springframework.web.servlet.view.
InternalResourceViewResolver">
<property name="prefix" value="/WEB-INF/view/" />
<property name="suffix" value=".jsp" />
</bean>
```

In the preceding code snippet, we have used `InternalResourceViewResolver` with the prefix `WEB-INF/view/` and suffix `.jsp` to the view name.

The `DispatcherServlet` class interacts with `InternalResourceViewResolver` to resolve logical view. It resolves the view name by taking prefixes such as `/WEB-INF/views/`, and appending it with a logical view name, and adds suffixes (`.jsp`) such as `/WEB-INF/views/welcome.jsp`. The `InternalResourceViewResolver` hands over the path to view the object which will dispatch the request to JSP page.

Model in Spring MVC

The form values that a user enters in a page can be configured to be collected in a container or model object and given to the controller for processing. Instead of accessing the request parameters individually, they can be bound to an instance and accessed.

In Spring, the objects that hold form value are known as command objects. Command objects are **Plain Old Java Objects (POJO)** created with variables and getter/setter properties. If the variable name matches the request parameter name, the request parameter value is set into the variable.

Command objects in Spring can be configured to be accessed in a view using the `org.springframework.web.bind.annotation.ModelAttribute` annotation. The `@ModelAttribute` annotation can be used for methods or method parameters. It has a value property that can be used to set the name of the model attribute.

Let's consider an example: `@ModelAttribute(value="employeeform")` specifies the model attribute name as `employeeform`. If it is not specified, then the name of the attribute is derived from the type of parameters or the return value of the method. If the parameter type is `org.packt.Spring.chapter7.springmvc.model.Employee`, then the name of the model attribute is `employee`. The model can accessed from the view using the request collection.

Spring MVC with Hibernate integration

In this section, we will develop an end-to-end web application using Spring MVC, which acts as frontend technology, and Hibernate, which acts as backend ORM technology. You already learned how to integrate Spring and Hibernate and developed a simple application in an earlier chapter. In this section, we will move forward and integrate Spring MVC and Hibernate in a web application. For more understanding of Spring and Hibernate integration along with PostgreSQL as database to persist the data.

> It is recommended that you go through *Chapter 4,*
> *Hibernate with Spring,* before you start this section.

In this section, our goal is to create a simple Spring MVC application named eHrPayrollSystem in the Spring **Source Tool Suite** (**STS**) IDE along with Hibernate as ORM framework, and connect it to PostgreSQL as the database to persist the data. Here, this web application will just fetch the list of employees from the database and display them to the user on the view page. We will perform the CRUD operation in our web application in a later section of this chapter.

Application architecture

The following figure shows the layered architecture of the eHrPayrollSystem web application. The **Data Access Layer**, also called the DAO layer, which will access data from the database. The DAO layer will use the Hibernate ORM framework API to interact with the database. The **service layer** will invoke this DAO layer. In our eHrPayrollSystem web application, we have EmployeeDao as a DAO interface and EmployeeService as service interface.

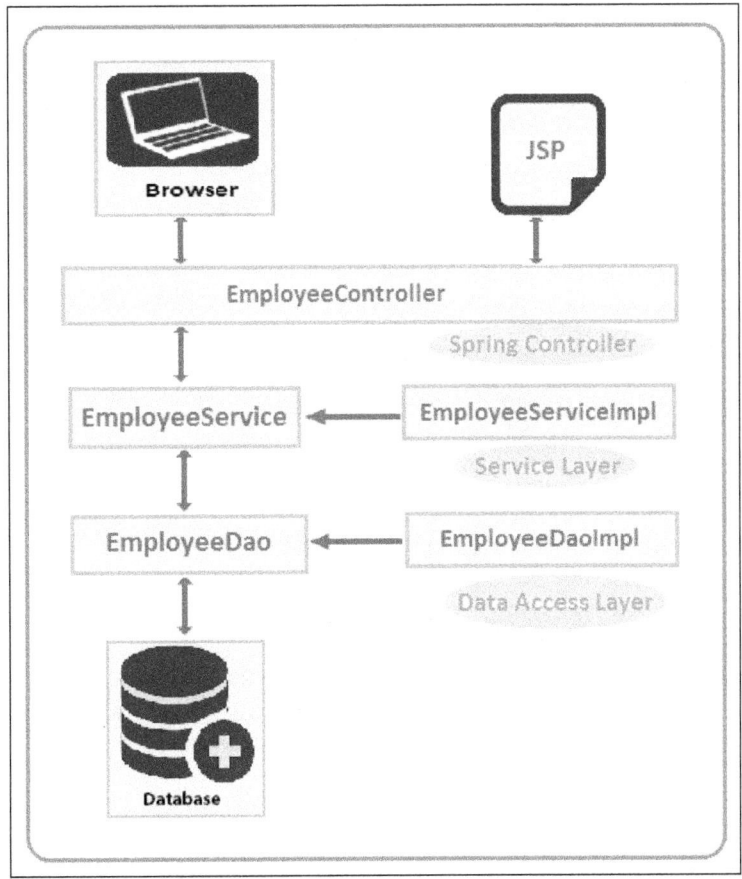

Sample data model for example code

For the eHrPayrollSystem web application, we will be using PostgreSQL as the database (for more details, refer to *Chapter 4, Hibernate with Spring*). Let's first create a database for our project in the PostgreSQL database and then create a table.

Script to create database named ehrpayroll_db:

```
CREATE DATABASE ehrpayroll_db
```

Script to create EMPLOYEE_INFO table:

```
CREATE TABLE EMPLOYEE_INFO(
ID serial NOT NULL Primary key,
FIRST_NAME varchar(30) not null,
LAST_NAME varchar(30) not null,
JOB_TITLE varchar(100) not null,
DEPARTMENT varchar(100) not null,
SALARY INTEGER
);
```

Script to populate data for employee_info table:

```
INSERT INTO EMPLOYEE_INFO
(FIRST_NAME, LAST_NAME, JOB_TITLE, DEPARTMENT, SALARY)
VALUES
('RAVI', 'SONI', 'AUTHOR', 'TECHNOLOGY', 5000);
INSERT INTO EMPLOYEE_INFO
(FIRST_NAME, LAST_NAME, JOB_TITLE, DEPARTMENT, SALARY)
VALUES
('Shree', 'Kant', 'Software Engineer', 'TECHNOLOGY', 3000);
```

Project structure

The screenshot of the final structure of the eHrPayrollSystem project is as follows:

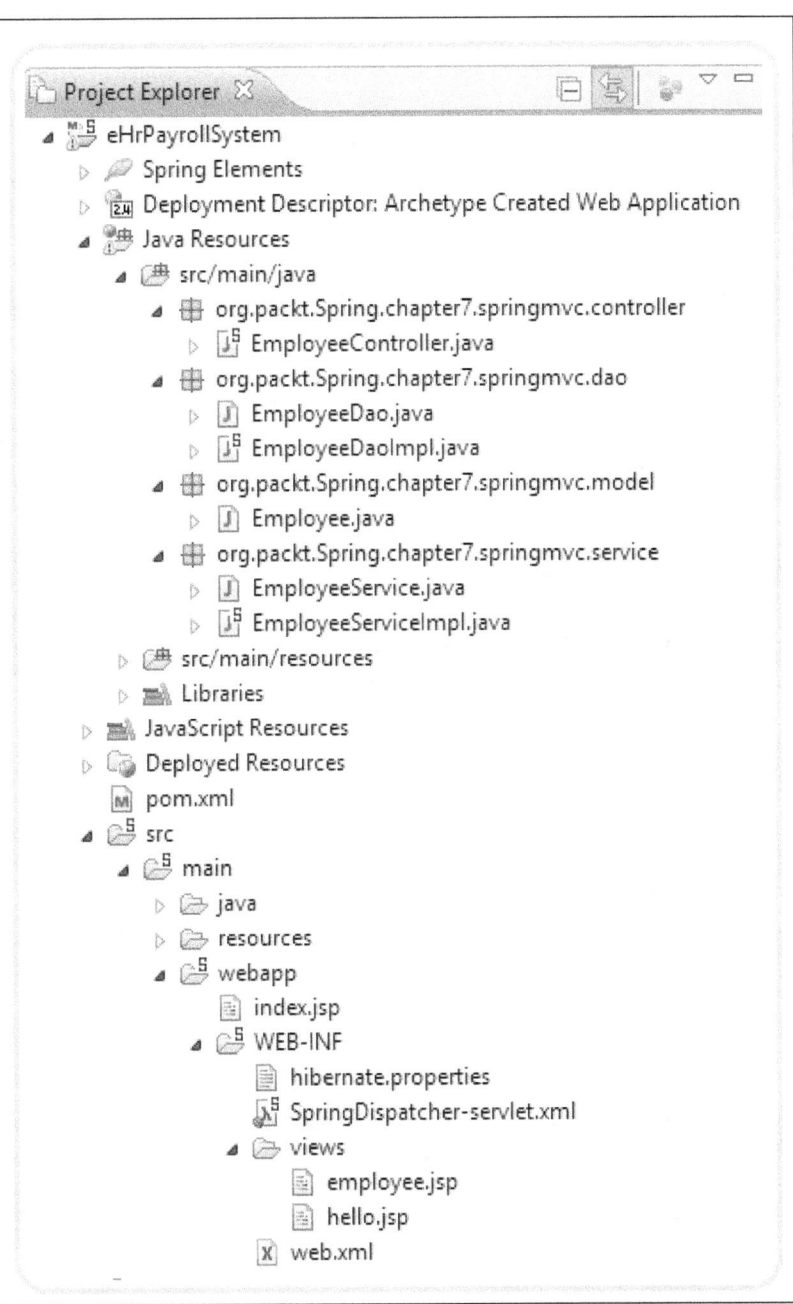

We have created packages for Java resources, as described here, under the `src/main/java` folder:

- `org.packt.Spring.chapter7.springmvc.controller`: Spring controller classes will be defined to this package for the `eHrPayrollSystem` web application. We will create an `EmployeeController` class in this package.

- `org.packt.Spring.chapter7.springmvc.dao`: This represents the DAO layer for the `eHrPayrollSystem` web application. The `EmployeeDao` interface and `EmployeeDaoImpl` class will be created in this package. The DAO layer will interact with the database using Hibernate API.

- `org.packt.Spring.chapter7.springmvc.model`: The entity class will go into this package. Employee is an entity class defined within this package with different attributes and annotations.

- `org.packt.Spring.chapter7.springmvc.service`: This represents the Service layer for the `eHrPayrollSystem` web application. The `EmployeeService` interface and `EmployeeServiceImpl` class will be created within this package.

The pom.xml file

In an earlier section of this chapter, we developed our web application as a Maven project by providing dependencies specific to the Spring Framework. Now we have to add other dependencies related to Servlet, JSTL, JDBC connection pooling, Hibernate ORM framework, PostgreSQL database, and so on:

```
<project xmlns="http://maven.apache.org/POM/4.0.0" xmlns:xsi="http://
www.w3.org/2001/XMLSchema-instance"
   xsi:schemaLocation="http://maven.apache.org/POM/4.0.0
http://maven.apache.org/maven-v4_0_0.xsd">
   <modelVersion>4.0.0</modelVersion>
   <groupId>org.packt.Spring.chapter7.springmvc</groupId>
   <artifactId>SpringMVCPayrollSystem</artifactId>
   <packaging>war</packaging>
   <version>0.0.1-SNAPSHOT</version>
   <name>SpringMVCPayrollSystem Maven Webapp</name>
   <url>http://maven.apache.org</url>
   <!-- Declare versions for Spring framework, Hibernate framework
and AspectJ -->
   <properties>
       <spring.version>4.0.2.RELEASE</spring.version>
       <hibernate.version>4.3.5.Final</hibernate.version>
```

```xml
        <org.aspectj-version>1.7.4</org.aspectj-version>
</properties>
<dependencies>
    <!-- jUnit dependencies -->
    <dependency>
        <groupId>junit</groupId>
        <artifactId>junit</artifactId>
        <version>3.8.1</version>
        <scope>test</scope>
    </dependency>
    <!-- Spring Core dependencies -->
    <dependency>
        <groupId>org.springframework</groupId>
        <artifactId>spring-core</artifactId>
        <version>${spring.version}</version>
    </dependency>
    <!-- Spring webmvc dependencies -->
    <dependency>
        <groupId>org.springframework</groupId>
        <artifactId>spring-webmvc</artifactId>
        <version>${spring.version}</version>
    </dependency>
    <!-- Spring transaction dependencies -->
    <dependency>
        <groupId>org.springframework</groupId>
        <artifactId>spring-tx</artifactId>
        <version>${spring.version}</version>
    </dependency>
    <!-- Spring ORM dependencies -->
    <dependency>
        <groupId>org.springframework</groupId>
        <artifactId>spring-orm</artifactId>
        <version>${spring.version}</version>
    </dependency>
    <!-- AspectJ dependencies -->
    <dependency>
        <groupId>org.aspectj</groupId>
        <artifactId>aspectjrt</artifactId>
        <version>${org.aspectj-version}</version>
    </dependency>
    <!-- Hibernate ORM framework dependencies -->
    <dependency>
        <groupId>org.hibernate</groupId>
```

```xml
        <artifactId>hibernate-core</artifactId>
        <version>${hibernate.version}</version>
    </dependency>
    <!-- Hibernate entity manager dependencies -->
    <dependency>
        <groupId>org.hibernate</groupId>
        <artifactId>hibernate-entitymanager</artifactId>
        <version>${hibernate.version}</version>
    </dependency>
    <!-- Java Servlet and JSP dependencies -->
    <dependency>
        <groupId>javax.servlet</groupId>
        <artifactId>servlet-api</artifactId>
        <version>2.5</version>
        <scope>provided</scope>
    </dependency>
    <dependency>
        <groupId>javax.servlet.jsp</groupId>
        <artifactId>jsp-api</artifactId>
        <version>2.1</version>
        <scope>provided</scope>
    </dependency>
    <!-- JSTL dependency -->
    <dependency>
        <groupId>jstl</groupId>
        <artifactId>jstl</artifactId>
        <version>1.2</version>
    </dependency>
    <!-- Apache Commons DBCP dependency (for database connection
pooling) -->
    <dependency>
        <groupId>commons-dbcp</groupId>
        <artifactId>commons-dbcp</artifactId>
        <version>1.4</version>
    </dependency>
    <!-- Postgresql Connector Java dependency (JDBC driver for
Postgresql) -->
    <dependency>
        <groupId>postgresql</groupId>
        <artifactId>postgresql</artifactId>
        <version>9.0-801.jdbc4</version>
    </dependency>
    <!--logging dependencies -->
    <dependency>
```

```
            <groupId>org.slf4j</groupId>
            <artifactId>slf4j-log4j12</artifactId>
            <version>1.4.2</version>
        </dependency>
        <dependency>
            <groupId>log4j</groupId>
            <artifactId>log4j</artifactId>
            <version>1.2.14</version>
        </dependency>
    </dependencies>
    <build>
        <finalName>SpringMVCPayrollSystem</finalName>
    </build>
</project>
```

 For more information on `web.xml`, you can refer to the *Developing a simple Spring MVC application* section earlier in this chapter.

The hibernate.properties file

The `hibernate.properties` file in the `/src/main/webapp/WEB-INF` folder contains database connection information, such as driver class name, database URL, username, password, and so on.

Refer to the `/src/main/webapp/WEB-INF/hibernate.properties` file. You can check the same in the following code snippet:

```
# JDBC Properties
jdbc.driverClassName=org.postgresql.Driver
jdbc.url=jdbc:postgresql://localhost:5432/ehrpayroll_db
jdbc.username=postgres
jdbc.password=sa


# Hibernate Properties
hibernate.dialect=org.hibernate.dialect.PostgreSQLDialect
hibernate.show_sql=true
```

The SpringDispatcher-servlet.xml file

The `SpringDispatcher-servlet.xml` file contains the `dataSource` bean, `sessionFactory` bean, `transactionManager` bean, and `InternalResourceViewResolver` bean.

Refer to `/src/main/webapp/WEB-INF/SpringDispatcher-servlet.xml` or take a look at the following code snippet:

```xml
<?xml version="1.0" encoding="UTF-8"?>
<beans xmlns="http://www.springframework.org/schema/beans"
    xmlns:xsi="http://www.w3.org/2001/XMLSchema-instance"
xmlns:context="http://www.springframework.org/schema/context"
    xmlns:jdbc="http://www.springframework.org/schema/jdbc"
xmlns:tx="http://www.springframework.org/schema/tx"
    xsi:schemaLocation="http://www.springframework.org/schema/beans
http://www.springframework.org/schema/beans/spring-beans.xsd
    http://www.springframework.org/schema/context
http://www.springframework.org/schema/context/spring-context-
3.0.xsd
    http://www.springframework.org/schema/jdbc
http://www.springframework.org/schema/jdbc/spring-jdbc-3.0.xsd
    http://www.springframework.org/schema/tx
http://www.springframework.org/schema/tx/spring-tx-3.0.xsd">
    <context:component-scan base-
package="org.packt.Spring.chapter7.springmvc" />
    <context:property-placeholder location="/WEB-
INF/hibernate.properties" />
    <bean id="dataSource"
        class="org.springframework.jdbc.datasource.
DriverManagerDataSource
">
        <property name="driverClassName"
value="${jdbc.driverClassName}" />
        <property name="url" value="${jdbc.url}" />
        <property name="username" value="${jdbc.username}" />
        <property name="password" value="${jdbc.password}" />
    </bean>
    <bean id="sessionFactory"
        class="org.springframework.orm.hibernate4.
LocalSessionFactoryBean">
        <property name="dataSource" ref="dataSource" />
        <property name="annotatedClasses"
            value="org.packt.Spring.chapter7.springmvc.model.Employee" />
        <property name="hibernateProperties">
            <props>
                <prop
key="hibernate.dialect">${hibernate.dialect}</prop>
                <prop key="hibernate.show_sql">${hibernate.show_sql}</
prop>
            </props>
```

```
        </property>
    </bean>
    <bean id="transactionManager"
        class="org.springframework.orm.hibernate4.
HibernateTransactionMana
ger">
        <property name="sessionFactory" ref="sessionFactory" />
    </bean>
    <tx:annotation-driven transaction-manager="transactionManager"
/>
    <bean
        class="org.springframework.web.servlet.view.InternalResource
ViewResolver">
        <property name="prefix">
            <value>/WEB-INF/views/</value>
        </property>
        <property name="suffix">
            <value>.jsp</value>
        </property>
    </bean>
</beans>
```

Hibernate model class – entity class

Employee has been defined as an entity class to store employee information. It will be linked to EMPLOYEE_INFO table in the database (for more information, please refer to *Chapter 4, Hibernate with Spring*).

Refer to `src/main/java/org/packt/Spring/chapter7/springmvc/model/Employee.java`. You can also take a look at the following code snippet for a preview:

```java
package org.packt.Spring.chapter7.springmvc.model;

import javax.persistence.Column;
import javax.persistence.Entity;
import javax.persistence.GeneratedValue;
import javax.persistence.GenerationType;
import javax.persistence.Id;
import javax.persistence.Table;

@Entity
@Table(name = "EMPLOYEE_INFO")
public class Employee {
```

```java
@Id
@Column(name = "ID")
@GeneratedValue(strategy = GenerationType.IDENTITY)
private Integer id;

@Column(name = "FIRST_NAME")
private String firstName;

@Column(name = "LAST_NAME")
private String lastName;

@Column(name = "JOB_TITLE")
private String jobTitle;

@Column(name = "DEPARTMENT")
private String department;

@Column(name = "SALARY")
private int salary;

// constructor and setter and getter

@Override
public boolean equals(Object obj) {
    if (this == obj) {
        return true;
    }
    if (!(obj instanceof Employee)) {
        return false;
    }
    Employee employee = (Employee) obj;
     if (firstName != null ?
!firstName.equals(employee.firstName)
                : employee.firstName != null) {
        return false;
    } else {
        return true;
    }
}

@Override
public int hashCode() {
    return firstName != null ? firstName.hashCode() : 0;
```

```
        }

    public String toString() {
            return "Employee [id=" + id + ", name=" + firstName + ""
+ lastName
                        + ", jobTitle=" + jobTitle + " department="
+ department
                        + " salary=" + salary + "]";
    }
}
```

The DAO layer

The **Data Access Object (DAO)** layer of the eHrPayrollSystem application consists of the EmployeeDao interface and its corresponding implementation class, EmployeeDaoImpl.

The EmployeeDao interface

The EmployeeDao interface will have the listEmployee() method declaration to access data from the database.

Take a look at src/main/java/org/packt/Spring/chapter7/springmvc/dao/ EmployeeDao.java. Here's a preview of what you'll find in the file:

```
package org.packt.Spring.chapter7.springmvc.dao;

import java.util.List;

import org.packt.Spring.chapter7.springmvc.model.Employee;

public interface EmployeeDao {

    public List<Employee> listEmployee();

}
```

The EmployeeDao implementation

The EmployeeDaoImpl class is a DAO class that implements the data access interface EmployeeDao annotated with the @Repository annotation (for more details, refer to *Chapter 4, Hibernate with Spring*).

Take a look at `src/main/java/org/packt/Spring/chapter7/springmvc/dao/EmployeeDaoImpl.java`. You can also check out the following code snippet:

```java
package org.packt.Spring.chapter7.springmvc.dao;

import java.util.List;

import org.hibernate.Query;
import org.hibernate.Session;
import org.hibernate.SessionFactory;
import org.packt.Spring.chapter7.springmvc.model.Employee;
import org.slf4j.Logger;
import org.slf4j.LoggerFactory;
import org.springframework.beans.factory.annotation.Autowired;
import org.springframework.stereotype.Repository;

@Repository
public class EmployeeDaoImpl implements EmployeeDao {

    private static final Logger logger = LoggerFactory
                .getLogger(EmployeeDaoImpl.class);

    @Autowired
    private SessionFactory sessionFactory;

    @SuppressWarnings("unchecked")
    public List<Employee> listEmployee() {
            Session session = sessionFactory.openSession();
            String hql = "FROM Employee";
            Query query = session.createQuery(hql);
            List<Employee> empList = query.list();
            logger.info("Person List::" + empList);
            return empList;
    }
}
```

The service layer

The service layer of `eHrPayrollSystem` consists of the `EmployeeService` interface and its corresponding implementation class `EmployeeServiceImpl`.

The EmployeeService interface

The EmployeeService interface will have the listEmployee() method declaration.

You can refer to the src/main/java/org/packt/Spring/chapter7/springmvc/service/EmployeeService.java file or you can take a look at the given code snippet for a preview:

```
package org.packt.Spring.chapter7.springmvc.service;

import java.util.List;

import org.packt.Spring.chapter7.springmvc.model.Employee;

public interface EmployeeService {

    public List<Employee> listEmployee();

}
```

The EmployeeService implementation

The EmployeeServiceImpl class is a service class that implements the interface EmployeeService, annotated with @Service (for more details, refer to *Chapter 4, Hibernate with Spring*).

Take a look at the following code. You'll find the same in the src/main/java/org/packt/Spring/chapter7/springmvc/service/EmployeeServiceImpl.java file:

```
package org.packt.Spring.chapter7.springmvc.service;

import java.util.List;

import org.packt.Spring.chapter7.springmvc.dao.EmployeeDao;
import org.packt.Spring.chapter7.springmvc.model.Employee;
import org.springframework.beans.factory.annotation.Autowired;
import org.springframework.stereotype.Service;

@Service
public class EmployeeServiceImpl implements EmployeeService {

    @Autowired
```

```
private EmployeeDao employeeDao;

public List<Employee> listEmployee() {
    return this.employeeDao.listEmployee();
}
}
```

Spring MVC controller classes

The EmployeeController class is a controller class defined in the org.packt. Spring.chapter7.springmvc.controllerpackage.

Take a look at the /src/main/java/org/packt/Spring/chapter7/springmvc/ controller/EmployeeController.java file for the following code snippet:

```
package org.packt.Spring.chapter7.springmvc.controller;

import org.packt.Spring.chapter7.springmvc.service.EmployeeService;
import org.springframework.beans.factory.annotation.Autowired;
import org.springframework.stereotype.Controller;
import org.springframework.ui.ModelMap;
import org.springframework.web.bind.annotation.RequestMapping;
import org.springframework.web.bind.annotation.RequestMethod;

@Controller
@RequestMapping("/employee")
public class EmployeeController {

    @Autowired
    private EmployeeService employeeService;

    @RequestMapping(method = RequestMethod.GET)
    public String welcomeEmployee(ModelMap model) {
        model.addAttribute("name", "Hello World!");
        model.addAttribute("greetings",
                    "Welcome to Packt Publishing - Spring MVC
!!! @Author: Ravi Kant Soni");
        return "hello";
    }

    @RequestMapping(value = "/listEmployees", method =
RequestMethod.GET)
    public String listEmployees(ModelMap model) {
```

```
        model.addAttribute("employeesList",
employeeService.listEmployee());
        return "employee";
    }
}
```

The `EmployeeController` class defines a `listEmployees()` method. This method uses the `EmployeeService` interface to fetch all the employee details in the `eHrPayrollSystem` web application. The `listEmployees()` method has been mapped to request `"/employee/listEmployees"`, so whenever Spring encounters this URL request, it will call this method. This method returns the view named employee which will be resolved to `employee.jsp` by the view resolver.

Another method is `welcomeEmployee()`, which will be called by Spring when it encounters the URL `"/employee"`. This method will return a view named hello, which will be resolved as `hello.jsp` name.

The View page

Finally, we need to add JSP files to the folder `/WEB-INF/views`.

The hello.jsp page

This JSP page contains an anchor tag with the URL `"employee/listEmployees"`.

Check out the `/WEB-INF/views/hello.jsp` file for the following code snippet:

```
<body>
    <h1 style="color: green; text-align: center;">${name}</h1>
    <h3 style="color: orange; text-align:
center;">${greetings}</h3>
    <table align="center" cellspacing="10">
            <tr style="color: blue; font-style: italic; font-size:
14pt">
                    <td align="left">Click Here</td>
                    <td align="right" bgcolor="lightgreen"><a
href="employee/listEmployees">List
                                Of Employees</a></td>
            </tr>
    </table>
</body>
```

The employee.jsp page

This JSP will iterate the `employeeList` model data and display employee information. We will discuss the tags in a later section of this chapter.

Check out the `/WEB-INF/views/employee.jsp` file for the following code snippet:

```jsp
<%@ taglib uri="http://java.sun.com/jsp/jstl/core" prefix="c"%>
<html>
    <head>
        <meta http-equiv="Content-Type" content="text/html;
charset=ISO-8859-1">
        <title>Employee List</title>
    </head>
    <body>
        <div align="center">
            <h1 style="background-color: lightgreen; color:
darkgreen">Employee
                List
            </h1>
            <table cellspacing="0" cellpadding="6" border="1">
                <tr bgcolor="grey" style="color: white">
                    <th>No</th>
                    <th>First Name</th>
                    <th>Last Name</th>
                    <th>Job Title</th>
                    <th>Department</th>
                    <th>Salary</th>
                </tr>
                <c:forEach var="employee" items="${employeesList}"
varStatus="status">
                    <tr bgcolor="lightyellow">
                        <td><b>${status.index + 1}</b></td>
                        <td>${employee.firstName}</td>
                        <td>${employee.lastName}</td>
                        <td>${employee.jobTitle}</td>
                        <td>${employee.department}</td>
                        <td>${employee.salary}</td>
                    </tr>
                </c:forEach>
            </table>
        </div>
    </body>
</html>
```

The index.jsp page

This is the first page that will be executed when we start web application for the URL `http://localhost:8080/eHrPayrollSystem`. The `<%response.sendRedirect("employee");%>` will redirect this page to the URL `http://localhost:8080/eHrPayrollSyste/employee`.

Check out the `/src/main/webapp/index.jsp` file for the following code snippet:

```
<html>
<body>
    <%
            response.sendRedirect("employee");
    %>
</body>
</html>
```

Running the application

Congratulations! We have successfully set up the Spring-Hibernate environment and are done with coding. Now, it's time to compile and execute the `eHrPayrollSystem` application. If everything goes well, we will get the output as seen here at the URL `http://localhost:8080/eHrPayrollSystem/employee`:

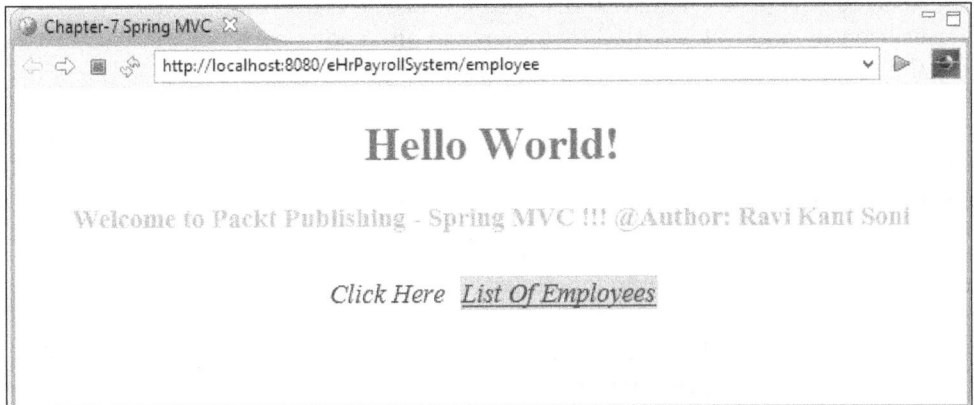

On clicking **List Of Employees** on the page, it will redirected to the URL
`http://localhost:8080/eHrPayrollSystem/employee/listEmployees`:

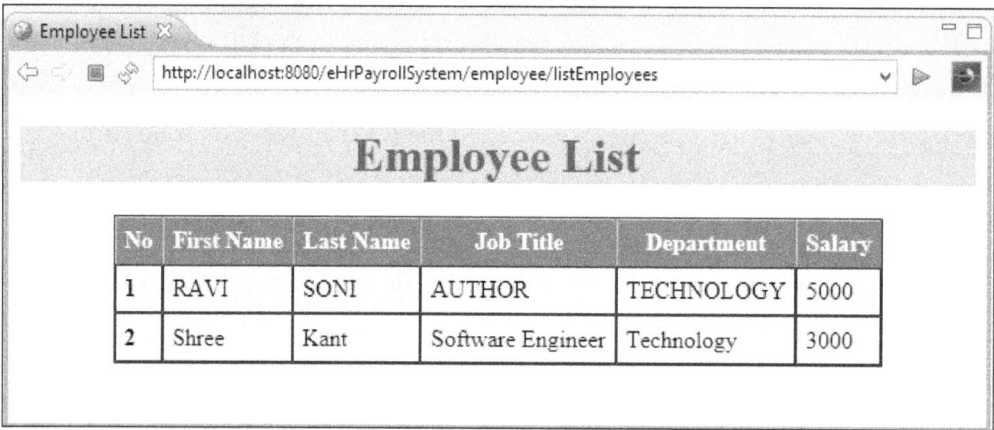

Exception handling using @ControllerAdvice

Usually the evil stack trace appears to the user whenever any unknown exceptions occur to an application. The user will complain to our application as stack traces are not user friendly and not handled by the user at all. And sometimes these stack trace revile the internal method call which can cause security risks.

However, we can configure the web application deployment descriptor `web.xml` to display user-friendly JSP pages in case of class exception or HTTP errors. The Spring MVC provides a way to manage views in case of a class exception.

From Spring 3.2 onwards, we have the `@ControllerAdvice` annotation. This annotation is used to define the global exception handler using the `@ExceptionHandler` annotation. So, any exception thrown by the application will be handled by this class having methods annotated with `@ExceptionHandler`. Thus, if a method is declared with the `@ExceptionHandler` annotation in the `@ControllerAdvice` class, it will be applicable to all controllers in application.

The `@ExceptionHandler` annotation makes it easier to handle exception and errors. This annotation can be used for any method in the controller class with the list of Exception classes as parameters. When a controller method throws an exception, the method annotated with `@ExceptionHandler` is executed only if the thrown exception matches the configured exception classes.

The Spring configuration file `SpringDispatcher-servlet.xml` must define `mvc` namespace in order to have the `@ControllerAdvice` annotation get identified:

```
<mvc:annotation-driven/>
```

It should be noted that if only `<context:annotation-config />` has been defined in this file, then `@ControllerAdvice` will not be loaded and will not work. Let's implement this concept in our `SpringMVCPayrollSystem` project, which we created earlier in this chapter.

The GenericException class

This is a generic exception with custom error code and error description.

Check out the `src/main/java/org/packt/Spring/chapter7/springmvc/exception/GenericException.java` file for the following code snippet:

```java
package org.packt.Spring.chapter7.springmvc.exception;

public class GenericException extends RuntimeException {

    private static final long serialVersionUID = 1L;

    private String exceptionMsg;
    private String exceptionCode;

    public GenericException(String exceptionCode, String
exceptionMsg) {
            this.exceptionCode = exceptionCode;
            this.exceptionMsg = exceptionMsg;
    }

    // getter and setter methods
}
```

The SpringException class

The `SpringException` class is annotated with `@ControllerAdvice` from the `org.springframework.web.bind.annotation` package. It will be applied globally, that is, to all controllers in the application. This class has two methods annotated with the `@ExceptionHandler` annotation, which will be called whenever an exception is thrown and the exception from the controller class matches the configured Exception classes.

Check out the `src/main/java/org/packt/Spring/chapter7/springmvc/` `exception/SpringException.java` file for the following code snippet:

```java
package org.packt.Spring.chapter7.springmvc.exception;

import org.springframework.web.bind.annotation.ControllerAdvice;
import org.springframework.web.bind.annotation.ExceptionHandler;
import org.springframework.web.servlet.ModelAndView;

@ControllerAdvice
public class SpringException {

    @ExceptionHandler(Exception.class)
    public ModelAndView allException(Exception e) {

        ModelAndView modelAndView = new
ModelAndView("error/exception");
        modelAndView.addObject("error",
e.getClass().getSimpleName());
        modelAndView.addObject("message", e.getMessage());

        return modelAndView;
    }


    @ExceptionHandler(GenericException.class)
    public ModelAndView genericException(GenericException ex) {

        ModelAndView modelAndView = new
ModelAndView("error/exception");
        modelAndView.addObject("error",
ex.getClass().getSimpleName());
        modelAndView.addObject("message",
                    ex.getExceptionCode() + " - " +
ex.getExceptionMsg());

        return modelAndView;
    }
}
```

The EmployeeController class

The EmployeeController class has three methods. One is just to render the hello.
jsp page. The other two will throw the following exceptions:

- If the request contains the URL as "/employee/testIOException", then it
  throws IOException and the allException() method will be fired from the
  SpringException class.

- If the request contains the URL as "/employee/testGenericException",
  then it throws GenericException and the genericException() method
  will be fired from the SpringException class.

Check out the src/main/java/org/packt/Spring/chapter7/springmvc/
controller/EmployeeController.java file for the following code snippet:

```java
package org.packt.Spring.chapter7.springmvc.controller;

import java.io.IOException;

import org.packt.Spring.chapter7.springmvc.exception.GenericException;
import org.springframework.stereotype.Controller;
import org.springframework.ui.ModelMap;
import org.springframework.web.bind.annotation.RequestMapping;
import org.springframework.web.bind.annotation.RequestMethod;

@Controller
@RequestMapping("/employee")
public class EmployeeController {

    @RequestMapping(method = RequestMethod.GET)
    public String welcomeEmployee(ModelMap model) {
            model.addAttribute("name", "Hello World!");
            model.addAttribute("greetings",
                        "Welcome to Packt Publishing - Spring MVC
!!!");
            return "hello";
    }


    @RequestMapping("/testIOException")
    public String testIOException(ModelMap model) throws
IOException {
```

```
        if (true) {
                throw new IOException("This is an IO Exception");
        }
        return "hello";
    }


    @RequestMapping("/testGenericException")
    public String testGenericException(ModelMap model) throws
IOException {

        if (true) {
                // add custom code and message that appear to error
page
                throw new GenericException("R333", "This is a
custom message");
        }
        return "hello";
    }
}
```

The hello.jsp page

This view page contains two hyperlinks with the URLs `"employee/testIOException"` and `"employee/testGenericException"` that will be mapped to the controller method.

Check out the `/WEB-INF/views/hello.jsp` file for the following code snippet:

```
<body>
    <h1 style="color: green; text-align: center;">${name}</h1>
    <h2 style="color: orange; text-align: center;">${greetings}</h2>
    <table align="center" border="1" cellspacing="0" cellpadding="10">
        <tr>
            <td rowspan="2" style="color: red; text-align: center;">
               Exception Handling
            </td>
            <td><a href="employee/testIOException">Click here to test
IO
               Exception</a>
            </td>
        </tr>
        <tr>
            <td><a href="employee/testGenericException">Click here to
               test Generic Exception</a>
```

```
        </td>
      </tr>
    </table>
  </body>
```

The exception.jsp page

This page will be executed when an exception is thrown from the controller.

Take a look at the /WEB-INF/views/error/hello.jsp file for the following code snippet:

```
<body>

    <h1 style="color: red">Sorry! Unable to process current Request</
    h1>

    <b>${error}</b>: ${message}

</body>
```

Running the application

Once you compile and run the application successfully, the output will appear in the browser as at the URL http://localhost:8080/SpringMVCWithException/employee:

Once you click on **Click here to test IO Exception**, the page will be redirected to the URL `http://localhost:8080/SpringMVCWithException/employee/testIOException`:

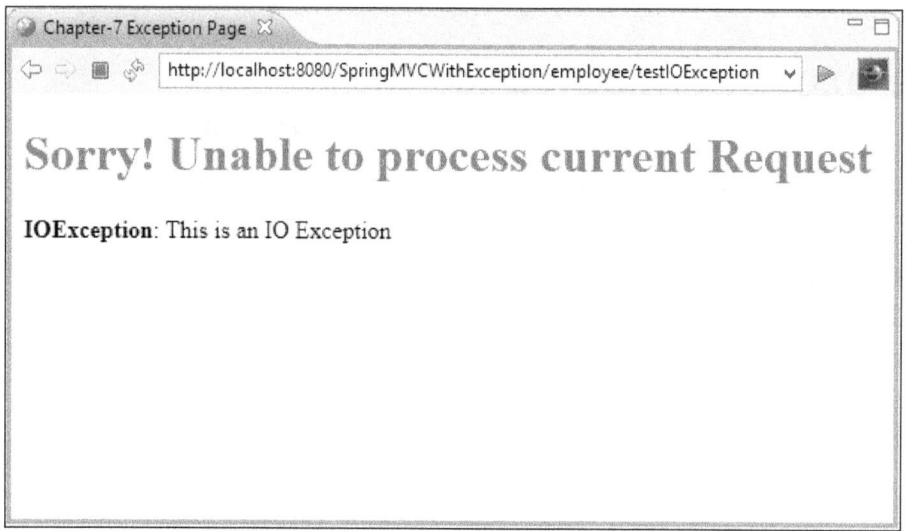

For the URL `http://localhost:8080/SpringMVCWithException/employee/testGenericException`, you'll get the following output:

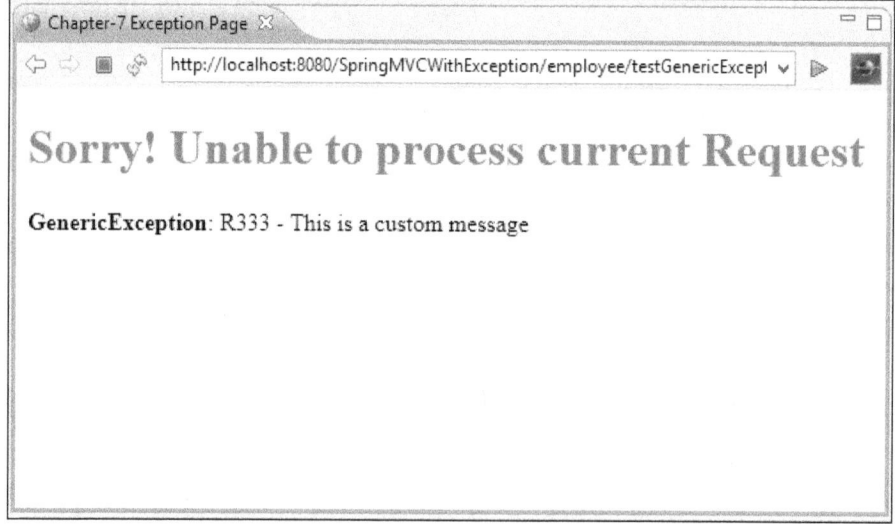

Spring MVC internationalization (i18n)

It is always good practice to use internationalization (i18n) whenever you develop a web application. The goal is to externalize the user messages and text into properties file. It is always good to externalize the language-related settings in the early stage, even though we won't find internationalization (i18n) requirement on first day of application development, but it will be fruitful when our application needs to respond more than one language. The i18n can be enabled very easily with Spring MVC.

The properties file

Let's say that our web application supports two locales: en and fr. This application will consider English as the default locale, and the user will have options to change the locale. The two properties files for these two locales are messages_en.properties and messages_fr.properties:

- `src/main/resources/messages/messages_en.properties`: This file contains the following snippet:

  ```
  # employee
  employee.first.name=First Name
  employee.last.name=Last Name
  ```

- `src/main/resources/messages/messages_fr.properties`: This file contains the following snippet:

  ```
  # employee
  employee.first.name=Pr\u00E9nom
  employee.last.name=Nom
  ```

Spring configuration

We need to configure beans of type ReloadableResourceBundleMessageSource, LocaleChangeInterceptor, and SessionLocaleResolver to support internationalization (i18n) in our web application.

ReloadableResourceBundleMessageSource

In the Spring configuration file SpringDispatcher-servlet.xml, add the org.springframework.context.support.ReloadableResourceBundleMessageSource bean, which will allow the alteration of properties files without restarting the JVM:

```
<!-- Application Message Bundle -->
<bean id="messageSource"
```

```
class="org.springframework.context.support.ReloadableResourceBundleMe
ssageSource">
<property name="basename" value="classpath:messages/messages" />
<property name="defaultEncoding" value="UTF-8"/>
</bean>
```

The `messageSource` bean needs to be configured in the configuration file to enable i18n for our web application. The `basename` property of this bean is used to provide the resource bundle location. The value of this property is `classpath:messages/messages`. This means that properties files are located in the class path under the messages folder and follow the name pattern as `messages_{locale}.properties`. The `defaultEncoding` for the properties file is `UTF-8`, which defines the encoding used for the messages.

LocaleChangeInterceptor

The `LocaleResolver` allows us to change the current locale and is used in combination with `LocaleChangeInterceptor`. It uses the defined parameter in the user request to change the current locale. For example, a request with the URL `http://localhost:8080/eHRPayrollSystem/employeeList?lang=fr` will change the language of the page to French.

```
<mvc:interceptors>
<bean class="org.springframework.web.servlet.i18n.
LocaleChangeIntercepto
r">
<property name="paramName" value="lang" />
</bean>
</mvc:interceptors>
```

SessionLocaleResolver

Using the `localeResolver` object, Spring's `DispatcherServlet` enables us to resolve messages based on the client's locale. The `localeResolver` bean of type `org.springframework.web.servlet.i18n.SessionLocaleResolver` allows us to retrieve locales from the session that might be associated with request from user:

```
<bean id="localeResolver" class="org.springframework.web.servlet.i18n.
SessionLocaleResolver">
<property name="defaultLocale" value="en" />
</bean>
```

If the session is not found, then `defaultLocale` is set to `en`, that is, English.

The hello.jsp page

The `hello.jsp` page contains two hyperlinks, and one click will change the locale. The `spring:message` is used to display the message from the corresponding message's properties file based on the current locale:

```jsp
<%@ page contentType="text/html;charset=UTF-8"%>
<%@ taglib prefix="spring" uri="http://www.springframework.org/tags"%>
<html>
    <head>
        <title>Chapter-7 Spring MVC</title>
    </head>
    <body>
        <h1 style="color: green; text-align: center;">Chapter 7:
Spring
        MVC - internationalization
        </h1>
        <table align="center" border="1">
            <tr>
                <td><b style="color: brown">Language</b></td>
                <td><a href="?lang=en">English</a>|</td>
                <td><a href="?lang=fr">French</a></td>
            </tr>
        </table>
        <h2 style="color: orange; text-align: center;">
            <spring:message code="employee.first.name" text="default
text" />
            : ${firstName}
        </h2>
        <h2 style="color: orange; text-align: center;">
            <spring:message code="employee.last.name" text="default
text" />
            : ${lastName}
        </h2>
    </body>
</html>
```

Running the application

On clicking French, the language will be changed to French or `fr`.

For English locale, go to `http://localhost:8083/`
`SpringMVCInternationalization/employee` or `http://localhost:8083/`
`SpringMVCInternationalization/employee?lang=en`, as shown in the
following screenshot:

For French locale, go to `http://localhost:8083/`
`SpringMVCInternationalization/employee?lang=fr`:

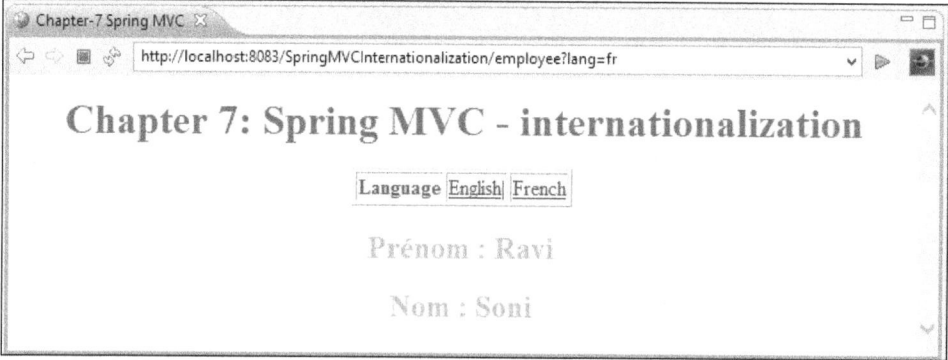

Handling form with the controller

In a web application, we can have a form to add employee information to the system.
A user needs to have a form where he/she can provide employee information, and
when he/she submits the form, a controller needs to accept the form submission. So,
a controller needs to have at least two functions:

- One function to display employee information form to user on HTTP GET
  request

- Another function to handle when the form is submitted using the HTTP POST method, by processing business functionality for data present in the form

Spring MVC handles form submission by using three components, namely controller, model and view:

- **Controller**: The controller in Spring MVC is generally used to handle requests. The controller in Spring MVC can also be used to bind the model object with view and vice versa.
- **Model**: Model is a POJO class. The model class is created to bind form field with properties of the object which will be put into the model.
- **View**: The form tags in Spring MVC are used to render the form field equivalent to HTML. The form tags bind the model's object with the form.

ModelAndView in Spring MVC

The `org.springframework.web.servlet.ModelAndView` in the Spring Framework plays both model and view. `ModelAndView` holds data for both model and view. There are different constructors for `ModelAndView`; the one we have used in our application is:

```
public ModelAndView(String viewName, String modelName,Object
modelObject)
```

The arguments of a `ModelAndView` constructor are:

- `viewName`: This is the name of the page which we are looking for
- `modelName`: This can be any name which represents the model
- `modelObject`: This is a bean that is associated with the form

Let's take an example:

```
ModelAndView("addemployee", "command", new Employee());
```

Here, `addemployee` is `viewname`, `command` is `modelName`, and `new Employee()` will be the `employee` object, which will be associated with the form in the `addemployee.jsp` page in our application.

Spring MVC Controller class

The `EmployeeController` class is designated to handle the request URL `/employee`:

```
@RequestMapping(value = "/employee")
```

@ModelAttribute in the controller class

The `org.springframework.web.bind.annotation.ModelAttribute` in Spring MVC is used to an annotation for the handler method or method arguments in the controller class. The `@ModelAttribute` annotation binds a named model attribute to any arguments in a method or to the method itself. Let's say we have created a `ModelAttribute` with the name `employeeForm`: `@ModelAttribute("employeeForm")`.

ModelMap in the controller class

The `org.springframework.ui.ModelMap` is an implementation of map, and in Spring MVC, it is used whenever working with UI tools. It carries the data that can be viewed.

In Spring MVC, writing handler methods is very flexible, as we have seen earlier in this chapter. We have implemented four methods, namely `listEmployees()`, `addEmployee()`, `updateEmployee()`, `deleteEmployee()`, to handle the GET and POST requests.

Check out the `/src/main/java/org.packt/spring/chapter7/springmvc/ controller/EmployeeController` file for the following code snippet:

```
package org.packt.Spring.chapter7.springmvc.controller;

import org.packt.Spring.chapter7.springmvc.model.Employee;
import org.packt.Spring.chapter7.springmvc.service.EmployeeService;
import org.springframework.beans.factory.annotation.Autowired;
import org.springframework.stereotype.Controller;
import org.springframework.ui.ModelMap;
import org.springframework.web.bind.annotation.ModelAttribute;
import org.springframework.web.bind.annotation.PathVariable;
import org.springframework.web.bind.annotation.RequestMapping;
import org.springframework.web.bind.annotation.RequestMethod;
import org.springframework.web.servlet.ModelAndView;
```

```
@Controller
@RequestMapping("/employee")
public class EmployeeController {

    @Autowired
    private EmployeeService employeeService;

    @RequestMapping(method = RequestMethod.GET)
    public String listEmployees(ModelMap model) {
            model.addAttribute("employeesList",
employeeService.listEmployee());
            return "employee";
    }

    @RequestMapping(value = "/addemployee", method =
RequestMethod.POST
    public ModelAndView addEmployee(ModelMap model) {
            return new ModelAndView("addemployee", "command", new
Employee());
    }

    @RequestMapping(value = "/updatemployee", method =
RequestMethod.POST)
    public String updateEmployee(
                @ModelAttribute("employeeForm") Employee employee,
ModelMap model) {
            this.employeeService.insertEmployee(employee);
             model.addAttribute("employeesList",
employeeService.listEmployee());
            return "employee";
    }

    @RequestMapping(value = "/delete/{empId}", method =
RequestMethod.GET)
    public String deleteEmployee(@PathVariable("empId") Integer
empId,
    ModelMap model) {
            this.employeeService.deleteEmployee(empId);
            model.addAttribute("employeesList",
employeeService.listEmployee());
            return "employee";
    }
}
```

Let's understand each method defined in the `EmployeeController` class as shown in the preceding code snippet in detail:

- `listEmployees()`: In this method, we have `ModelMap`. We have added an attribute to this model with the key `'employeesList'` and the value contains the employee list, which returns from the `employeeService.listEmployee()` method.

- `addEmployee()`: In this method, we have called the `ModelAndView` constructor that takes `addemployee` as view name, `commandName` as command that can be associated with the Spring form `<form:form>` tag, and employee object, which must match the value of the `commandName` attribute of the `<form:form>` tag.

- `updateEmployee()`: The `insertEmployee()` method handles form submission via the `POST` request. Out of all parameters defined in this method, `@ModelAttribute("employeeForm")` is the important parameter. When the form is submitted, the form value can be accessed.

- `deleteEmployee()`: This method will delete employees based on employeeId associated with the URL, for example, `"/delete/{empId}"`. The `(@PathVariable("empId")` integer `empId` is an important attribute of this method that will take the value associated to the URL.

The View page

The `employee.jsp` page uses `EL` expressions to display values of properties of the employee object in the model.

Check out the `/WEB-INF/views/employee.jsp` file for the following code snippet:

```
<%@page contentType="text/html" pageEncoding="UTF-8"%>
<%@ taglib uri="http://java.sun.com/jsp/jstl/core" prefix="c"%>
<html>
    <head>
        <meta http-equiv="Content-Type" content="text/html;
charset=ISO-8859-1">
        <title>Employee List</title>
    </head>
    <body>
        <div align="center">
            <h1 style="background-color: lightgreen; color:
darkgreen">Employee
                Page
            </h1>
```

```
        </div>
        <div align="center">
            <table align="center" width="80%" cellspacing="0"
cellpadding="5">
                <tr>
                    <td align="right"><a href="${pageContext.request.
contextPath}/employee/addemployee"
    style="background-color: lightblue;"> Add Employee </a></td>
                </tr>
                <tr>
                    <td>
                        <table cellspacing="0" cellpadding="6" border="1"
width="100%">
                            <tr>
                                <td colspan="7"
                                    style="background-color: lightblue;
color: darkgreen; font-size: 16pt"
                                    align="center">Employee List</td>
                            </tr>
                            <tr bgcolor="grey" style="color: white">
                                <th>No</th>
                                <th>First Name</th>
                                <th>Last Name</th>
                                <th>Job Title</th>
                                <th>Department</th>
                                <th>Salary</th>
                                <th>Delete</th>
                            </tr>
                            <c:forEach var="employee"
items="${employeesList}"
                                varStatus="status">
                                <tr bgcolor="lightyellow">
                                    <td><b>${status.index + 1}</b></td>
                                    <td>${employee.firstName}</td>
                                    <td>${employee.lastName}</td>
                                    <td>${employee.jobTitle}</td>
                                    <td>${employee.department}</td>
                                    <td>${employee.salary}</td>
                                    <td><a href="${pageContext.request.
contextPath}/employee/delete/${employee.id}">Delete</a></td>
                                </tr>
                            </c:forEach>
                        </table>
                    </td>
```

```
        </tr>
      </table>
    </div>
  </body>
</html>
```

The Spring MVC form

The Spring MVC form provides a tag library to create a form that will be associated with a bean. When we submit this Spring MVC form, the associated bean will automatically be populated, and that bean will be used for further processing.

The JSP page must be created using Spring tags and should not have generic HTML tags. The `<form:form>` tag is very similar to the regular HTML `<form>` tag, and plays a major role in the Spring MVC form. The `commandName` can be added to it to specify the name of the model class object, which will act as backing object for this form.

```
<%@taglib
uri="http://www.springframework.org/tags/form"prefix="form"%>
```

For more reference on Spring form tag, refer to *Appendix C, Spring Form Tag Library*.

Check out the `/WEB-INF/views/addemployee.jsp` file for the following code snippet:

```
<%@taglib uri="http://www.springframework.org/tags/form"
prefix="form"%>
<html>
    <head>
        <meta http-equiv="Content-Type" content="text/html;
charset=ISO-8859-1">
        <title>Add Employee</title>
    </head>
    <body>
        <div align="center">
            <h1 style="background-color: lightgreen; color:
darkgreen">Add
                New Employee Page
            </h1>
        </div>
        <div align="center">
            <table  cellspacing="0" cellpadding="6" border="1"
widht="60%">
```

```
            <tr>
               <td colspan="8"
                   style="background-color: lightblue; color:
darkgreen; font-size: 16pt"
                   align="center">Employee Information</td>
            </tr>
            <tr>
               <td>
                  <form:form method="POST" action="updatemployee">
                     <table widht="100%">
                        <tr>
                           <td>
                              <form:label path="firstName">First
Name</form:label>
                           </td>
                           <td align="left" width="70%">
                              <form:input path="firstName" />
                           </td>
                        </tr>
                        <tr>
                           <td>
                              <form:label path="lastName">Last Name</
form:label>
                           </td>
                           <td align="left">
                              <form:input path="lastName" />
                           </td>
                        </tr>
                        <tr>
                           <td>
                              <form:label path="jobTitle">Job
Title</form:label>
                           </td>
                           <td align="left">
                              <form:input path="jobTitle" />
                           </td>
                        </tr>
                        <tr>
                           <td>
                              <form:label
path="department">Department</form:label>
                           </td>
                           <td align="left">
```

```
                    <form:input path="department" />
                </td>
            </tr>
            <tr>
                <td>
                    <form:label path="salary">Salary</
form:label>
                </td>
                <td align="left">
                    <form:input path="salary" />
                </td>
            </tr>
            <tr>
                <td colspan="2"><input type="submit"
value="Submit" /></td>
            </tr>
        </table>
    </form:form>
</td>
</tr>
</table>
</div>
</body>
</html>
```

Running the application

On compiling and running the application, the expected output will appear URL
`http://localhost:8080/eHRPayrollFormHandling/employee`, as shown in the
following screenshot:

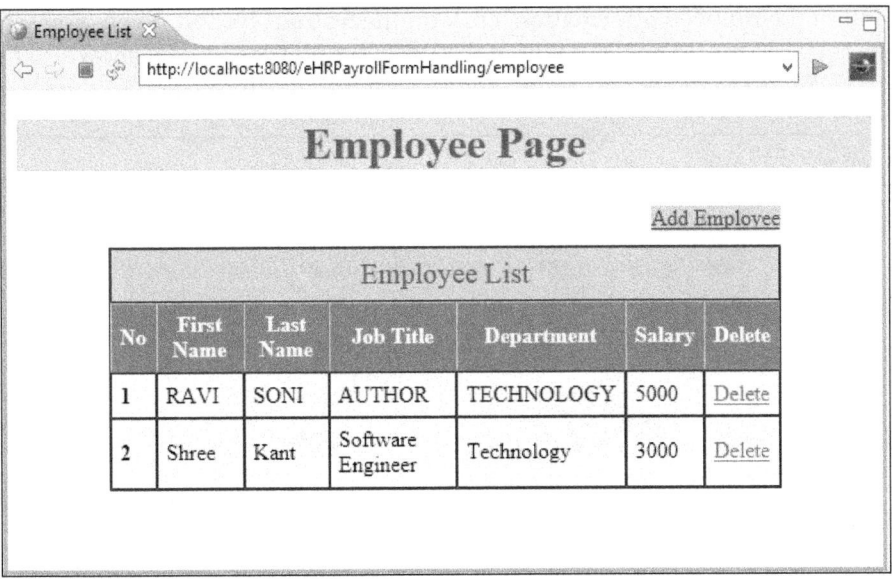

On clicking the **Add Employee** link, you will be directed to **Add New Employee Page**. Enter the employee information into the input box, as shown in the following screenshot. The URL is `http://localhost:8080/eHRPayrollFormHandling/employee/addemployee`:

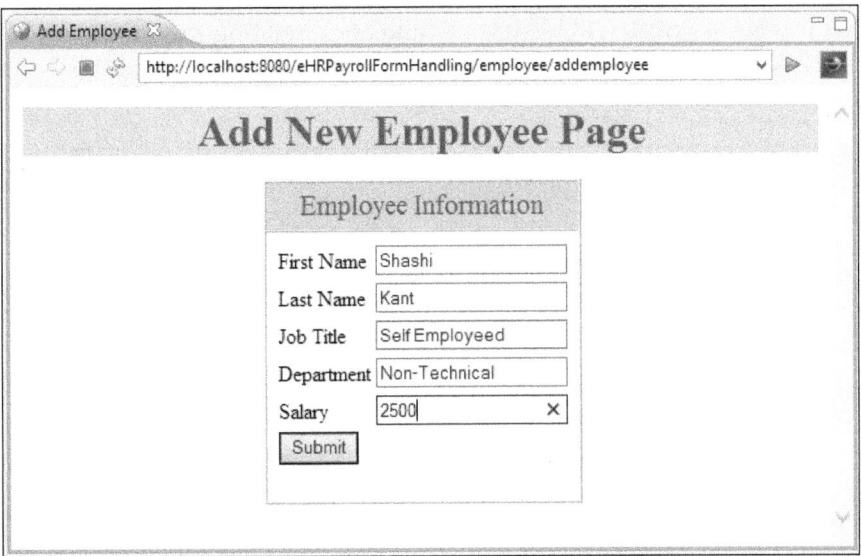

After entering employee information, click on the **Submit** button. Then, you will be brought back to **Employee Page** where the list of employees will be shown to the user. The URL is `http://localhost:8080/eHRPayrollFormHandling/employee`:

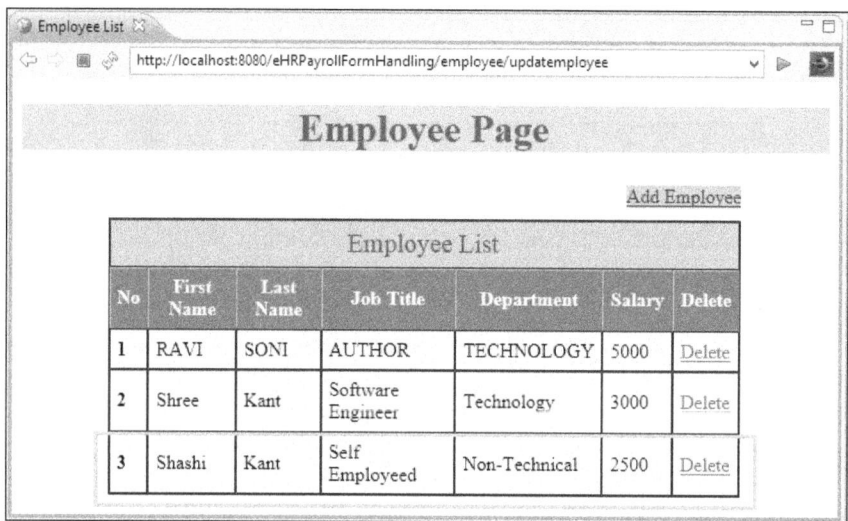

In the preceding screenshot, newly added employee information is visible to the user along with old employees. We can also delete an employee by clicking on the **Delete** link for each employee on the page. Let's say we have clicked the **Delete** link for an employee 1; this employee will be deleted, and after deleting this employee, a new list of employees will be visible to the user. The URL is `http://localhost:8080/eHRPayrollFormHandling/employee/delete/1`:

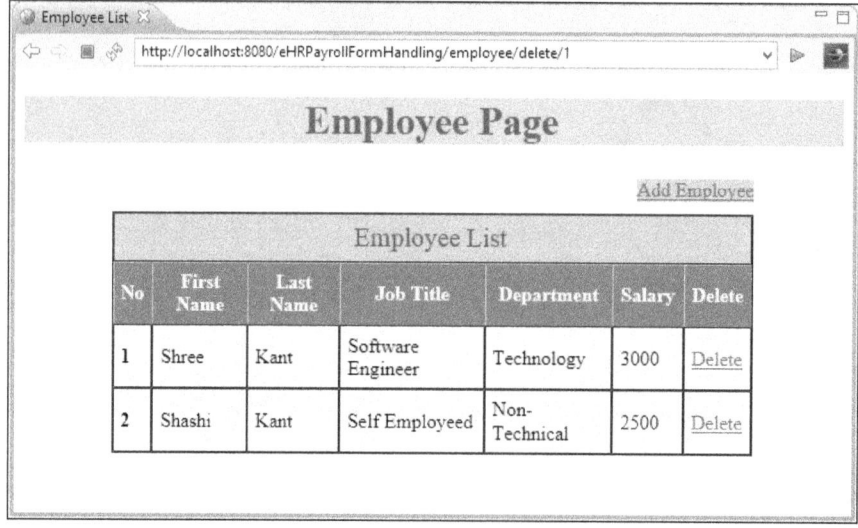

Exercise

Q1. What is Spring Web MVC framework?

Q2. What is DispatcherServlet in Spring MVC framework?

Q3. What is Controller in Spring MVC?

Q4. What is ViewResolver in Spring MVC?

>  The answers to these are provided in *Appendix A, Solution to Exercises.*

Summary

In this chapter, we covered the Spring MVC framework and its components, such as `DispatcherServlet` class and `HandlerMapping`. We developed a Spring Web MVC application by creating a controller, view, and web configuration file. We discovered that `DispatcherServlet` is the central component of a Spring Web MVC application. It accepts requests from the view page and dispatches the control to the controller classes. We also understood that controller classes process requests and send back a view and some data to be displayed in the view. The view components are resolved by the `ViewResolver` class.

We have seen annotation and their uses in Spring MVC: the `@Controller` annotation is used to create controller class, `@ModelAttribute` is used to represent the model or command objects, `@ExceptionHandler` is used to handle exceptions, and `@RequestMapping` is used to map incoming requests to various methods of controller classes. In addition, we have explored handling forms using the controller in Spring MVC. We also developed a Spring MVC application after integration with the Hibernate ORM framework.

In the next chapter, Spring Security, we will first try to understand what Spring Security is. Then, we will look into the dependencies needed for Spring Security. We will take a look at authentication and authorization in Spring Security. We will take a quick review of Servlet filters in web applications and will understand how Spring Security is dependent on this filter mechanism. After that, we will see the two important aspects of Spring Security: the authentication manager and authentication provider.

6
Spring Security

In the previous chapter, you learned about the features of the Spring Web MVC framework. We also understood different components of the Spring MVC framework, such as `DispatcherServlet` and `HandlerMapping`. You also learned how to develop web applications using the Spring MVC framework by creating a controller, view, and web configuration file.

In this chapter, we will first try to understand what Spring Security is. Then, we will look into the dependencies needed for Spring Security. We will take a look at authentication and authorization in Spring Security. Next, we will do a quick review of the Servlet filter in web application and also understand how Spring Security is dependent on this filter mechanism. We will discuss how to secure web applications using filters along with the Spring interceptor and filter concepts in Spring Security. Then, we will see the two important aspects of Spring Security, that is, the authentication manager and authentication provider. We will also see different ways of logging into web applications, such as HTTP basic authentication, form-based login services, anonymous login, and also the Remember Me support in Spring Security. We will also discuss authenticating and authorization against databases. Then, we will implement method-level security.

The list of topics covered in this chapter is as follows:

- Introduction to Spring Security
- Review on Servlet filters
- Security use case
- Spring Security configuration
- Securing web application's URL access
- Logging into web application
- Users authentication

- Method-level security
- Developing an application using Spring MVC, Hibernate, and Security

What is Spring Security?

Security for a web application is nothing but protecting resources and allowing only specific users to access it. Spring Security shouldn't be assumed as a firewall, a proxy server, intrusion detection, JVM security, or anything similar. Spring Security is basically made for the Java EE Enterprise software application and is primarily targeted towards Spring-framework-based web applications.

The Spring Security framework initially started as Acegi Security Framework, which was later adopted by Spring as its subproject Spring Security. The Spring Security framework is a de facto standard to secure Spring-based applications. The Spring Security framework provides security services for enterprise Java software applications by handling authentication and authorization. Spring Security handles authentication and authorization at both the web request level and the method invocation level. Spring Security is a highly customizable and powerful authentication and access control framework.

Major operations

The two major operations provided by Spring Security are authentication and authorization.

- **Authentication**: This is the process of assuring that the user is the one that the user claims to be. Authentication is a combination of identification and verification. Identification can be performed in a number of ways. For example, through a username and password that can be stored in a database, LDAP, or CAS (single sign-on protocol). Spring Security provides a password encoder interface to make sure that the user's password is hashed.

- **Authorization**: This provides access control to an authenticated user. Authorization is the process of assuring that the authenticated user is allowed access only to those resources that they are authorized to use. Let's take an example of the HR Payroll application, where some parts of the application have access to HR and to some other parts all the employees have access. The access rights given to the user of the system will determine the access rules.

In web-based applications, this is often done through URL-based security and is implemented using filters that play a primary role in securing the Spring web application.

Sometimes, URL-based security is not enough for web applications as URLs can be manipulated and have relative pass. Let's take an example of HrPayrollSystem, where the HR and manager are involved, and there is an employees list page. On this employees list page, there is a **Delete** button for each employee. The **Delete** button contains a hyperlink for a delete method call in the controller class. This button appears for HR but it is hidden for managers. Even though the manager doesn't see the **Delete** button, the delete method can be called by altering the URL in the browser. This results in the delete operation by the manager, which shouldn't have happened.

So, Spring Security also provides method-level security. The authorized user will only able to invoke those methods which he is granted for.

Servlet filters review

Spring Security is developed on top of the Spring Framework and uses the filters concept in the Servlet engine. Filters are like Servlet; they come into action when any request comes to Servlet and can decide whether the request should be forwarded to Servlet or not. Spring Security registers a single javax.servlet.Filter, that is, the DelegatingFilterProxy.

Before starting with Spring Security, let's quickly recall what **Servlet** filters are. In the following figure, a user enters the URL in the browser. The request comes to the container and then to **Servlet** after referring to web.xml for Servlet mapping with respecting URL. After processing the request, the request goes back to the user.

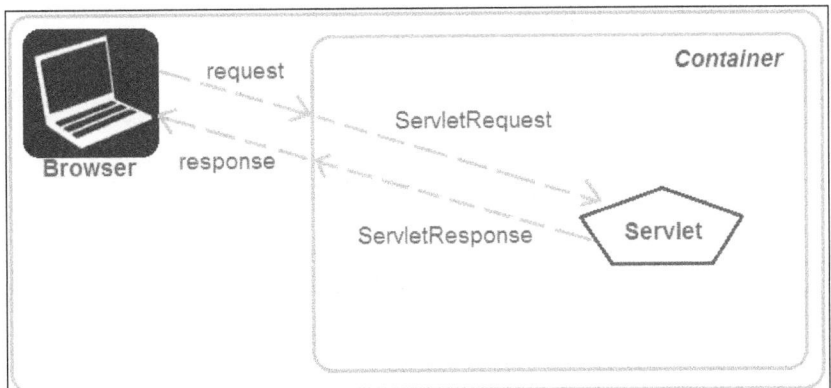

A **Filter** is present between **Servlet** and **Container**. It intercepts the requests and responses to and from Servlet and can pre-process and post-process, as shown in the following diagram:

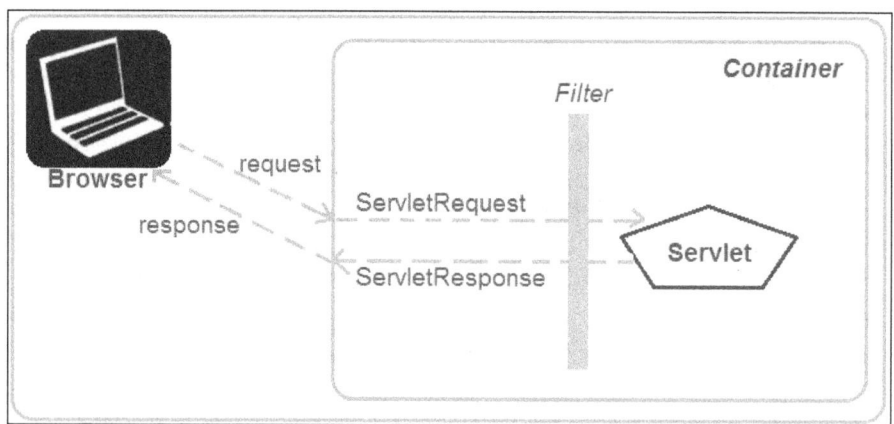

In the web.xml file, you'll find the following code:

```
<filter>
    <filter-name>filterA</filter-name>
    <filter-class>FilterA</filter-class>
</filter>
<filter-mapping>
    <filter-name>filterA</filter-name>
    <url-pattern>/*</url-pattern>
</filter-mapping>
```

In the preceding code snippet, we have mapped filterA to all URLs. Now, in the FilterA.java class, you'll find the following code:

```
public void doFilter(ServletRequest request, ServletResponse
response, FilterChain filterChain)
{
    // do something before filter
    System.out.println("Starting Filter");

    // run rest of the application
    filterChain.doFilter(request, response);

    // cleanup
    System.out.println("Ending Filter");
}
```

Now, we have the code for `FilterA`. First, it invokes a message before the rest of the applications run. Then, it runs the rest of the application. Lastly, it prints a message again. From the following diagram, let's understand how requests gets impacted by this filter:

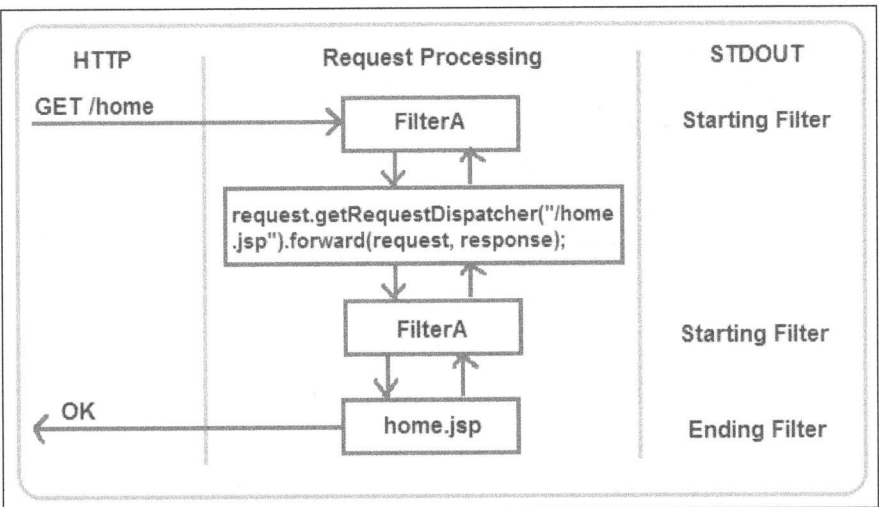

As shown in the preceding diagram, when we make a request to our application using HTTP `GET` /home URL, the Servlet container recognizes the `filterA` intercepts this URL. The container invokes the `doFilter()` method of the `FilterA` class. As soon as the `doFilter()` method is invoked, it prints the message `Starting Filter`. Then, `filterA` invokes the `filterChain`, and then `home.jsp` is invoked. Next, it returns to the `filterChain`.

Filters can be used for the following operations:

- Blocking access to a resource based on user identity or role membership
- Auditing incoming requests
- Comparing the response data stream
- Transforming the response
- Measuring and logging Servlet performance

Spring Security is dependent on this filter mechanism. So, before reaching out to Servlet to perform some business logic, some security can be performed using the filters.

Security use case

The use case we will use for all our examples is as follows:

1. The user reaches the application or homepage of the application and clicks on a secure link (for example, login).

2. The moment the user clicks on the secured link, Spring Security brings the login page.

3. The login page will perform a credential check from the authentication provider; this can be plain-text, database, or similar.

4. An authentication failure happens if wrong credentials are given by the user; otherwise, the user will be allowed to the secured area.

5. When the user clicks on logout, they will be directed to the homepage.

The following diagram illustrates the preceding steps:

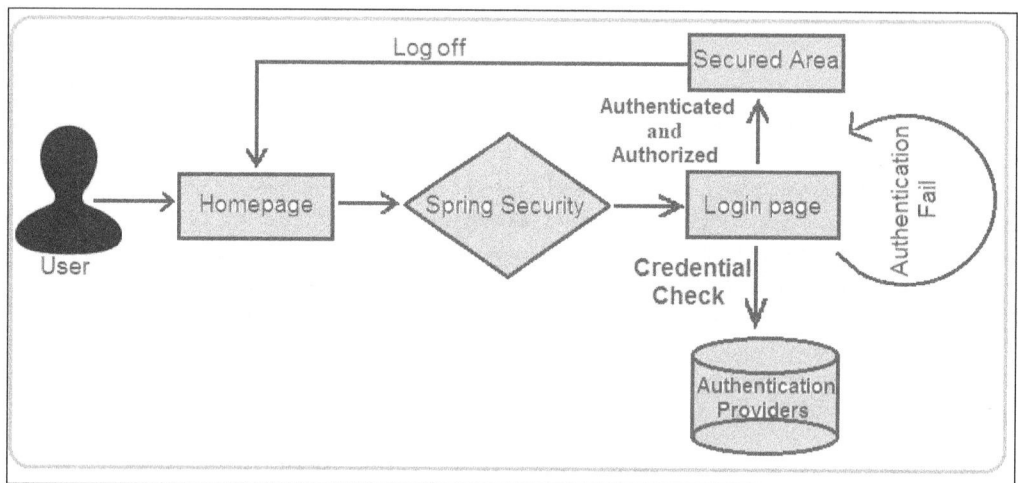

Spring Security configuration

To add Spring Security to our Spring web application, we need to perform a basic Spring Security setup. To do this, follow these steps:

1. Add Spring JARs or Spring Security dependencies.

2. Update `web.xml` with `springSecurityFilterChain`.

3. Create a Spring Security configuration file.

Spring Security setup

We can either download and add Spring Security JARs to classpath or we can provide dependencies to Maven.

Adding JARs to the classpath

There are three important JARs that we need for Spring Security. These can be downloaded from the Spring website and are as follows (the version should match other Spring JARs used in the project):

- `spring-security-config-3.X.X.RELEASE.jars`: This contains support for Spring Security's XML namespace

- `spring-security-core-3.X.X.RELEASE.jars`: This provides the essential Spring Security library

- `spring-security-web-3.X.X.RELEASE.jars`: This provides Spring Security's filter-based web security support

If we have developed a Maven application, then we need to update `pom.xml`.

Spring Security dependencies – pom.xml

Update dependencies to Maven. We have `spring-security-core`, `spring-security-web`, and `spring-security-config`:

```
<properties>
    <spring.security.version>3.1.4.RELEASE</spring.security.version>
</properties>

<!-- Spring Security -->
<dependency>
    <groupId>org.springframework.security</groupId>
    <artifactId>spring-security-core</artifactId>
    <version>${spring.security.version}</version>
</dependency>

<dependency>
    <groupId>org.springframework.security</groupId>
    <artifactId>spring-security-web</artifactId>
    <version>${spring.security.version}</version>
</dependency>

<dependency>
```

```
<groupId>org.springframework.security</groupId>
<artifactId>spring-security-config</artifactId>
<version>${spring.security.version}</version>
</dependency>
```

Namespace configuration

In the Spring configuration file, we need to add one more entry to schema, which is related to Spring Security and the corresponding `schemaLocation` and their `xsd`, which lives in Spring JARs. The security prefixed elements go here.

In the `SpringDispatcher-servlet.xml` file, you'll find the following code:

```
<beans xmlns="http://www.springframework.org/schema/beans"
    xmlns:security="http://www.springframework.org/schema/security"
    xmlns:xsi="http://www.w3.org/2001/XMLSchema-instance"
    xsi:schemaLocation="http://www.springframework.org/schema/beans
    http://www.springframework.org/schema/beans/spring-beans-
3.1.xsd
    http://www.springframework.org/schema/security
    http://www.springframework.org/schema/security/spring-security-
3.1.xsd">
</beans>
```

Securing web application's URL access

`HttpServletRequest` is the starting point of a Java web application. To configure web security, you need to set up a filter that provides various security features. To enable Spring Security, add filter and their mapping in the `web.xml` file.

The first step – web.xml

The first step is to configure `DelegatingFilterProxy` instance in `web.xml` while securing the web application's URL access with Spring Security.

In the `web.xml` file, you'll find the following code:

```
<!--Spring Security -->
<filter>
<filter-name>springSecurityFilterChain</filter-name>
    <filter-class>org.springframework.web.filter.
DelegatingFilterProxy</filter
-class>
</filter>
```

```
<filter-mapping>
<filter-name>springSecurityFilterChain</filter-name>
   <url-pattern>/*</url-pattern>
</filter-mapping>
```

The `DelegatingFilterProxy` filter class, which is a special servlet filter, doesn't do much by itself. It delegates the control to an implementation of `javax.servlet.Filter`, which is registered as a special bean with ID is `springSecurityFilterChain` in Spring application context. In the earlier code snippet, we added `/*`, which will map to all the HTTP requests and go to this `springSecurityFilterChain`.

In the preceding code snippet, we declared the URL pattern `/*`, which requires some level of granted authority and prevents other users without authority from accessing the resources behind those URLs.

Separating security configurations

If we are planning to separate the entire security specific configuration into a separate configuration file named `Spring-Security.xml`, we must change the security namespace to be the primary namespace for that file. Here, there are no security prefixed elements.

In the `Spring-Security.xml` file, you'll find the following code:

```
<beans:beans
xmlns="http://www.springframework.org/schema/security"
xmlns:beans="http://www.springframework.org/schema/beans"
xmlns:xsi="http://www.w3.org/2001/XMLSchema-instance"
xsi:schemaLocation="http://www.springframework.org/schema/beans
http://www.springframework.org/schema/beans/spring-beans-3.1.xsd
http://www.springframework.org/schema/security
http://www.springframework.org/schema/security/spring-security-
3.1.xsd">

    <http auto-config="true">
            <intercept-url pattern='/employeeList'
access='ROLE_USER,ROLE_ADMIN ' />
            <intercept-url pattern='/employeeAdd' access='ROLE_USER'
/>
            <intercept-url pattern='/employeeDelete'
access='ROLE_ADMIN' />

    </http>
```

```
<authentication-manager>
        <authentication-provider>
                <user-service>
                        <user name="admin" password="adminpassword"
authorities="ROLE_ADMIN" />
                        <user name="ravisoni" password="mypassword"
authorities="ROLE_USER" />
                </user-service>
        </authentication-provider>
</authentication-manager>

</beans:beans>
```

The preceding configuration file has been divided into two major sections, as shown in previous code snippet:

- The first section includes `<http>` tag and `<intercept-url>` tag; these define what you want to secure

- The second section includes the `<authentication-manager>`, `<authentication-provider>`, and `<user-service>` tags; these define how you want to secure

Web security is enabled using the `<http>` tag. This tag is the container element for the HTTP security configuration. To define the Spring Security configuration for HTTP requests, we must first define the `<http>` tag, which automatically sets up `FilterChainProxy`. The `auto-config=true` attribute automatically configures the basic Spring Security Services that a web application needs. This can be fine-tuned with the corresponding subelements in it.

The `<intercept-url>` element is defined inside the `<http>` configuration element. It restricts access to specific URLs. The `<intercept-url>` tag defines the URL pattern and set of access attributes that are required to access URLs. It is mandatory to include a wildcard at the end of the URL pattern, and failing to do so will allow a hacker to skip the security check by appending arbitrary request parameter. The access attributes decide if the user can access the URLs. In most cases, access attributes are defined in terms of roles. In the previous code snippet, users with the ROLE_USER role are able to access the /employeeList and /employeeAdd URLs. However, to delete an employee via the /employeeDelete URL, a user must have the ROLE_ADMI role.

The <authentication-manager> tag used to process authentication information. The <authentication-provider> tag is nested inside the <authentication-manager> tag, and used to define credential information and the roles that will be granted to this user. In the preceding code snippet, inside the <authentication-manager> tag, we have provided the <authentication-provider> tag, which specifies a text-based user ID and password.

Logging into web application

Users can log into a web application using multiple ways supported by Spring Security:

- **HTTP basic authentication**: These processes the basic credentials presented in the header of the HTTP request. HTTP basic authentication is generally used with stateless clients which pass their credentials on each request.

- **Form-based login service**: This provides the default login form page for users to log into the web application.

- **Logout service**: This allows users to log out of this application.

- **Anonymous login**: This grants authority to an anonymous user like normal user.

- **Remember Me support**: This remembers a user's identity across multiple browser sessions.

First, we will disable the HTTP autoconfiguration by removing the auto-config attribute from the <http> tag to better understand the different login mechanisms in isolation:

```
<http>
        <intercept-url pattern='/employeeList'
access='ROLE_USER,ROLE_ADMIN ' />
        <intercept-url pattern='/employeeAdd' access='ROLE_USER'
/>
        <intercept-url pattern='/employeeDelete'
access='ROLE_ADMIN' />


</http>
```

HTTP basic authentication

The HTTP basic authentication in Spring Security can be configured by using the `<http-basic/>` element. Here, the browser will display a login dialog for user authentication:

```
<beans:beans
xmlns="http://www.springframework.org/schema/security"
xmlns:beans="http://www.springframework.org/schema/beans"
xmlns:xsi="http://www.w3.org/2001/XMLSchema-instance"
xsi:schemaLocation="http://www.springframework.org/schema/beans
http://www.springframework.org/schema/beans/spring-beans-3.1.xsd
http://www.springframework.org/schema/security
http://www.springframework.org/schema/security/spring-security-
3.1.xsd">

    <http>
            <intercept-url pattern='/employeeList'
access='ROLE_USER,ROLE_ADMIN ' />
            <intercept-url pattern='/employeeAdd' access='ROLE_USER'
/>
            <intercept-url pattern='/employeeDelete'
access='ROLE_ADMIN' />

            <!-- Adds Support for basic authentication -->
            <http-basic/>

    </http>

    <authentication-manager>
            <authentication-provider>
                    <user-service>
                            <user name="admin" password="adminpassword"
authorities="ROLE_ADMIN" />
                            <user name="ravisoni" password="mypassword"
authorities="ROLE_USER" />
                    </user-service>
            </authentication-provider>
    </authentication-manager>

</beans:beans>
```

The interesting thing with HTTP basic authentication is that we don't have to create any login page. The browser will present a login box before the user on our behalf. As each request contains user authentication information that is the same as the HTTP stateless mechanism, we don't need to maintain session.

When we try to access a secured URL in our web application, the browser will open an authentication dialog box automatically for a username and password:

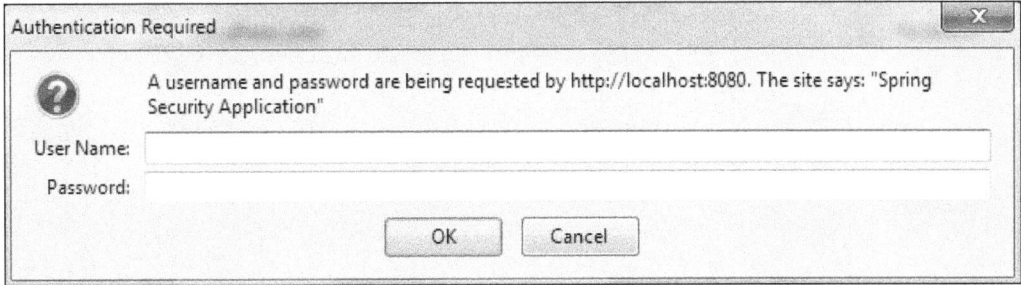

Form-based login service

Spring Security supports form-based login service by providing the default login form page for users to input their login details. The `<form-login>` element defines the support for the login form, as shown in the following code snippet. By default, a login form, which will map to the `/spring_security_login` URL, will automatically be created by Spring Security, as shown here:

```
<http>
    . . .
    <!-- Adds Support for basic authentication -->
        <form-login />
</http>
```

We can also create our own custom login page (`login.jsp`) in the root directory of the web application. This should not go inside `WEB-INF` as it prevents users from accessing it directly. The form action URL in `login.jsp` will take the `j_spring_security_check` value; this is the URL where the form will be posted to trigger the authentication process, and `j_username` is used as the username and `j_password` is used as the password, as shown in the following code snippet:

```
<html>
<head>
<title>Login</title>
</head>

<body>
    <form action="j_spring_security_check" method='POST'>
        <table>
            <tr>
                <td>UserName:</td>
```

```
      <td><input type='text' name='j_username' value=''></td>
   </tr>
   <tr>
      <td>Password:</td>
      <td><input type='password' name='j_password' /></td>
   </tr>
   <tr>
      <td>Remember me:</td>
      <td><input type='checkbox' name='_spring_security_
remember_me' /></td>
   </tr>
   <tr>
      <td><input name="submit" type="submit" value="submit"
/></td>
   </tr>
   </table>
  </form>
</body>
</html>
```

While referring to the custom login page for Spring Security, we need to specify its URL in the `login-page` attribute of `<form-login/>`. As shown in following code snippet, `<form-login login-page="/login" authentication-failure-url="/loginfailed" default-target-url="/employeeList" />` defines that when the login button is clicked, it should be navigated to `/login`. The default target URL is defined as `/employeeList`; this means when a user is authenticated, this URL hits by default. When an authentication failure happens, it should navigate to `/loginfailed`:

```
<http>

    . . .

        <form-login login-page="/login" authentication-failure-
url="/loginfailed" default-target-url="/employeeList" />

</http>
```

Logout service

The logout service handles logout requests and is configured via the `<logout>` element. In Spring Security, by default, it is mapped to the `/j_spring_security_ logout` URL, and it redirects the user to the context path's root when the logout successful:

```
<http>
 . . .
<logout />
</http>
```

We can provide the logout link in our page by referring the URL
`<a href="/j_spring_security_logout"> Logout </a>`.

We can also configure log out so that the user is redirected to another URL after the logout is successful, as shown in the following code snippet:

```
<http>
 . . .
<logout logout-success-url="/login" />
</http>
```

Anonymous login

The `<anonymous>` element is used to configure anonymous login service, where the username and authority of the anonymous user can be configured:

```
<http>
        <intercept-url pattern='/employeeList' access='ROLE_
USER,ROLE_ADMIN,ROLE_GUEST ' />
        <intercept-url pattern='/employeeAdd' access='ROLE_USER'
/>
        <intercept-url pattern='/employeeDelete'
access='ROLE_ADMIN' />


 . . .

        <anonymous username='guest' granted-
authority='ROLE_GUEST' />

</http>
```

Remember Me support

The `<remember-me />` element is used to configure the Remember Me support in Spring Security. By default, it encodes authentication information and the Remember Me expiration time along with private key as a token. It stores this to the user's browser cookie. The next time a user accesses the same application, they can be log in automatically using the token:

```
http>
. . .
<remember-me />
</http>
```

Users authentication

While users log into applications to access secure resources, the user's principle needs to be authenticated and authorized. The authentication provider helps in authenticating users in Spring Security. If a user is successfully authenticated by the authentication provider, then only the user will able to log into the web application, otherwise, the user will not be able to log into the application.

There are multiples of ways supported by Spring Security to authenticate users, such as a built-in provider with a built-in XML element, or authenticate user against a user repository (relational database or LDAP repository) storing user details. Spring Security also supports algorithms (MD5 and SHA) for password encryption.

Users authentication with in-memory definitions

If there are only few users for your application with infrequent modification in their details, then you can define user details in Spring Security's configuration file instead of extracting information from the persistence engine, so that their details are loaded into your application's memory, as shown here:

```
<authentication-manager>
        <authentication-provider>
                <user-service>
                        <user name="admin" password="adminpassword"
authorities="ROLE_ADMIN" />
                        <user name="ravisoni" password="mypassword"
authorities="ROLE_USER" />
                        <user name="user" password="mypassword"
disabled="true" authorities="ROLE_USER" />
```

```
            </user-service>
        </authentication-provider>
    </authentication-manager>
```

The user's details can be defined in `<user-service>` with multiple `` elements. For each user, a username, password, disabled status, and a set of granted authority can be specified, as shown in the previous code snippet. The disabled user indicates that the user cannot log into system anymore.

The user details can also be externalized by keeping them in the properties file (for instance, `/WEB-INF/usersinfo.properties`):

```
<authentication-manager>
        <authentication-provider>
                <user-service properties="/WEB-
INF/usersinfo.properties" />
        </authentication-provider>
    </authentication-manager>
```

Next, we will see the specified properties file containing user details in the form of properties, where each property represents the user's details. In this property file, the key of the property represents the username, while the property value is divided into several parts separated by commas. The first part represents the password and the second part represents the user's enable status (this is optional with the default status is enabled), and the remaining parts represent authority granted to the user.

The `/WEB-INF/usersinfo.properties` file is as follows:

```
admin=adminpassword,ROLE_ADMIN
ravisoni=mypassword,ROLE_USER
user=mypassword,disabled,ROLE_USER
```

Users authentication against database

If you have a huge list of users in your application and you frequently modify their details, you should consider storing the user details in a database for easy maintenance. Spring Security provides built-in support to query user details from the database.

In order to perform authentication against database, tables need to be created to store users and their roles details. Refer to `http://docs.spring.io/spring-security/site/docs/3.2.3.RELEASE/reference/htmlsingle/#user-schema` for more details on user schema.

The USER_AUTHENTICATION table is used to authenticate the user and contains the following columns.

The script is as follows:

```
CREATE TABLE USER_AUTHENTICATION (
    USERNAME VARCHAR(45) NOT NULL ,
    PASSWORD VARCHAR(45) NOT NULL ,
    ENABLED SMALLINT NOT NULL DEFAULT 1,
    PRIMARY KEY (USERNAME)
);
```

The table structure is as follows:

Username	Password	Enabled
admin	adminpassword	1
ravisoni	mypassword	1
user	mypassword	0

The USER_ AUTHORIZATION table is used to authorize the user and contains the following columns.

The script is as follows:

```
CREATE TABLE USER_ AUTHORIZATION (
    USERNAME VARCHAR(45) NOT NULL,
    AUTHORITY VARCHAR(45) NOT NULL,
    FOREIGN KEY (USERNAME) REFERENCES USERS
);
```

The table is as follows:

Username	Authority
admin	ROLE_ADMIN
ravisoni	ROLE_USER
user	ROLE_USER

Now, dataSource has to be declared in the Spring configuration file to allow Spring Security to access these tables, which will help in creating a connection to the database, as shown here:

```
<bean id="dataSource"
    class="org.springframework.jdbc.datasource.DriverManager
DataSource">
```

```
            <property name="driverClassName"
value="org.apache.derby.jdbc.ClientDriver" />
            <property name="url"
value="jdbc:derby://localhost:1527/test;create=true" />
            <property name="username" value="root" />
            <property name="password" value="password" />
    </bean>
```

Then, configure the authentication provider using the `<jdbc-user-service>` element that queries this database. Specify the query statement to get the user's information and authority in the `user-by-username-query` and `authorities-by-username-query` attributes, as follows:

```
<authentication-manager>
        <authentication-provider>
                <jdbc-user-service data-source-ref="dataSource"
                    user-by-username-query=
                    "select username, password, enabled from
user_authentication where username=?"
                    authorities-by-username-query=
                    "select username, authority from
user_authorization where username =?   "
                />
        </authentication-provider>
    </authentication-manager>
```

Encrypting passwords

Spring Security supports some hashing algorithms, such as MD5 (`Md5PasswordEncoder`), SHA (`ShaPasswordEncoder`), and BCrypt (`BCryptPasswordEncoder`) for password encryption.

To enable the password encoder, use the `<password-encoder/>` element and set the hash attribute, as follows:

```
    <authentication-manager>
     <authentication-provider>
        <password-encoder hash="md5" />
        <jdbc-user-service data-source-ref="dataSource"
        . . .
     </authentication-provider>
    </authentication-manager>
```

Method-level security

This is an alternative to securing URL access in the web layer. Sometimes, it is also required to secure method invocation in the service layer by enforcing fine-grained security control on methods. This is because, sometimes, it's easier to control it on particular methods than filtering by address, which can be called by typing. We can secure method invocation using Spring Security in a declarative way. We can annotate methods declaration in a bean interface or its implementation class with @Secured annotation and specify the access attributes as its value whose type is String[], and enable security for these annotated methods by adding <global-method-security> in Spring-Security.xml file. This can be done as follows:

```
<beans:beans
xmlns="http://www.springframework.org/schema/security"
xmlns:beans="http://www.springframework.org/schema/beans"
xmlns:xsi="http://www.w3.org/2001/XMLSchema-instance"
xsi:schemaLocation="http://www.springframework.org/schema/beans
http://www.springframework.org/schema/beans/spring-beans-3.1.xsd
http://www.springframework.org/schema/security
http://www.springframework.org/schema/security/spring-security-
3.1.xsd">

    <!-- To allow standards-based @Secured annotation, enable
secured-annotations -->
    <global-method-security secured-annotations="enabled" />

    <http
            . . .
            . . .

</beans>
```

The global-method-security namespace is configured along with its secured-annotations="enabled" attribute to enable annotation-based security. And annotate methods with @Secured annotation to allow method access for one or more than one role:

```
public interface EmployeeService {

@Secured("ROLE_USER", "ROLE_GUEST")
public List<employee> employeeList();

@Secured("ROLE_USER", "ROLE_ADMIN")
public Person employeeAdd(Employee employee);

@Secured("ROLE_ADMIN")
```

```
public Person employeeDelete(int employeeId);

}
```

Let's get down to business

In this section, we will develop an application using Spring MVC, Hibernate, and Spring Security. Here, we have a custom login page, logout page, employee page (to list employees), and add employee page (to add employees), which is secured by the Spring Framework. A user can log into the application using the custom login page and view the secured page based on the authentication and authorization. A user will be redirected to the custom login page on any authentication failure along with the error message, which describes the reason for failure. User will be logged out from the application on clicking on the logout link and redirected to the logout page.

Project structure

The overall project structure is as follows (refer to the *Spring MVC with Hibernate Integration* section from *Chapter 5*, *Spring Web MVC Framework*, to perform CRUD operations using Hibernate):

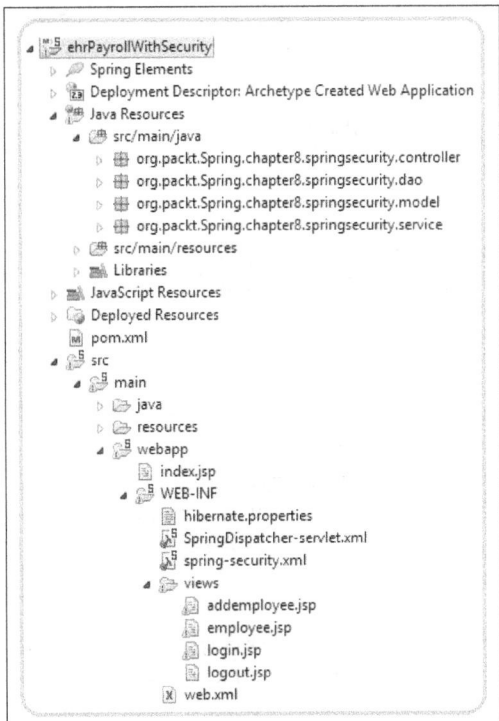

In the pom.xml file, you'll find the following code:

A list of all required dependencies are listed here in pom.xml. To get Spring Security features, you need to add spring-security-core, spring-security-web, and spring-security-config to the pom.xml file:

```xml
<project xmlns="http://maven.apache.org/POM/4.0.0"
xmlns:xsi="http://www.w3.org/2001/XMLSchema-instance"
    xsi:schemaLocation="http://maven.apache.org/POM/4.0.0
http://maven.apache.org/maven-v4_0_0.xsd">
    <modelVersion>4.0.0</modelVersion>
    <groupId>org.packt.Spring.chapter8.springsecurity</groupId>
    <artifactId>ehrPayrollWithSecurity</artifactId>
    <packaging>war</packaging>
    <version>0.0.1-SNAPSHOT</version>
    <name>ehrPayrollWithSecurity Maven Webapp</name>
    <url>http://maven.apache.org</url>
```

Here, the properties specify the versions used:

```xml
<properties>
        <spring.version>4.1.3.RELEASE</spring.version>
        <security.version>4.0.0.CI-SNAPSHOT</security.version>
        <hibernate.version>4.2.11.Final</hibernate.version>
        <org.aspectj-version>1.7.4</org.aspectj-version>
</properties>
```

Here are the dependencies for all the JARs:

```xml
<dependencies>
    <dependency>
        <groupId>junit</groupId>
        <artifactId>junit</artifactId>
        <version>4.11</version>
        <scope>test</scope>
    </dependency>
    <!-- Spring  -->
    <dependency>
        <groupId>org.springframework</groupId>
        <artifactId>spring-core</artifactId>
        <version>${spring.version}</version>
    </dependency>
    <dependency>
        <groupId>org.springframework</groupId>
        <artifactId>spring-web</artifactId>
```

```
        <version>${spring.version}</version>
    </dependency>
    <dependency>
        <groupId>org.springframework</groupId>
        <artifactId>spring-webmvc</artifactId>
        <version>${spring.version}</version>
    </dependency>
    <!-- Spring transaction -->
    <dependency>
        <groupId>org.springframework</groupId>
        <artifactId>spring-tx</artifactId>
        <version>${spring.version}</version>
    </dependency>
    <!-- Spring Security -->
    <dependency>
        <groupId>org.springframework.security</groupId>
        <artifactId>spring-security-core</artifactId>
        <version>${security.version}</version>
    </dependency>
    <dependency>
        <groupId>org.springframework.security</groupId>
        <artifactId>spring-security-web</artifactId>
        <version>${security.version}</version>
    </dependency>
    <dependency>
        <groupId>org.springframework.security</groupId>
        <artifactId>spring-security-config</artifactId>
        <version>${security.version}</version>
    </dependency>
    <!-- Spring ORM -->
    <dependency>
        <groupId>org.springframework</groupId>
        <artifactId>spring-orm</artifactId>
        <version>${spring.version}</version>
    </dependency>
    <!-- AspectJ -->
    <dependency>
        <groupId>org.aspectj</groupId>
        <artifactId>aspectjrt</artifactId>
        <version>${org.aspectj-version}</version>
    </dependency>
    <!-- Hibernate ORM framework dependencies -->
    <dependency>
        <groupId>org.hibernate</groupId>
```

```xml
        <artifactId>hibernate-core</artifactId>
        <version>${hibernate.version}</version>
    </dependency>
    <dependency>
        <groupId>org.hibernate</groupId>
        <artifactId>hibernate-entitymanager</artifactId>
        <version>${hibernate.version}</version>
    </dependency>
    <!-- Java Servlet and JSP dependencies (for compilation only) -
->
    <dependency>
        <groupId>javax.servlet</groupId>
        <artifactId>servlet-api</artifactId>
        <version>3.0.1</version>
        <scope>provided</scope>
    </dependency>
    <dependency>
        <groupId>javax.servlet.jsp</groupId>
        <artifactId>jsp-api</artifactId>
        <version>2.1</version>
        <scope>provided</scope>
    </dependency>
    <!-- JSTL dependency -->
    <dependency>
        <groupId>jstl</groupId>
        <artifactId>jstl</artifactId>
        <version>1.2</version>
    </dependency>
    <!-- Apache Commons DBCP dependency (for database connection
pooling) -->
    <dependency>
        <groupId>commons-dbcp</groupId>
        <artifactId>commons-dbcp</artifactId>
        <version>1.4</version>
    </dependency>
    <!-- postgresql Connector Java dependency (JDBC driver for
postgresql) -->
    <dependency>
        <groupId>postgresql</groupId>
        <artifactId>postgresql</artifactId>
        <version>9.0-801.jdbc4</version>
    </dependency>
    <!-- logging -->
    <dependency>
```

```
        <groupId>org.slf4j</groupId>
        <artifactId>slf4j-log4j12</artifactId>
        <version>1.4.2</version>
    </dependency>
    <dependency>
        <groupId>log4j</groupId>
        <artifactId>log4j</artifactId>
        <version>1.2.14</version>
    </dependency>
</dependencies>
<build>
    <finalName>ehrPayrollWithSecurity</finalName>
</build>
</project>
```

Adding filters to web.xml

Add filters to web.xml, where all incoming requests will be handled by Spring Security. The Spring Security JAR contains DelegatingFilterProxy, which delegates control to a filter chaining in the Spring Security internals. The bean name should be springSecurityFilterChain.

In the web.xml file, you'll find the following code:

```
<?xml version="1.0" encoding="UTF-8"?>
<web-app xmlns:xsi="http://www.w3.org/2001/XMLSchema-instance"
    xmlns="http://java.sun.com/xml/ns/javaee"
    xmlns:web="http://java.sun.com/xml/ns/javaee/web-app_2_5.xsd"
    xsi:schemaLocation="http://java.sun.com/xml/ns/javaee
    http://java.sun.com/xml/ns/javaee/web-app_3_0.xsd"
    id="WebApp_ID" version="3.0">
    <display-name>Archetype Created Web Application</display-name>
    <servlet>
        <servlet-name>SpringDispatcher</servlet-name>
        <servlet-class>
            org.springframework.web.servlet.DispatcherServlet
        </servlet-class>
        <load-on-startup>1</load-on-startup>
    </servlet>
    <servlet-mapping>
        <servlet-name>SpringDispatcher</servlet-name>
        <url-pattern>/</url-pattern>
    </servlet-mapping>
    <listener>
```

```
        <listener-class>org.springframework.web.context.
ContextLoaderListener</
listener-class>
    </listener>
    <context-param>
        <param-name>contextConfigLocation</param-name>
        <param-value>
            /WEB-INF/SpringDispatcher-servlet.xml,
            /WEB-INF/spring-security.xml
        </param-value>
    </context-param>
    <!-- Spring Security -->
    <filter>
        <filter-name>springSecurityFilterChain</filter-name>
        <filter-class>org.springframework.web.filter.
DelegatingFilterProxy</filter
-class>
    </filter>
    <filter-mapping>
        <filter-name>springSecurityFilterChain</filter-name>
        <url-pattern>/*</url-pattern>
    </filter-mapping>
</web-app>
```

Resolving your view

To resolve the view, view resolver has been added to the `SpringDispatcher-servlet.xml` configuration file. Also, `dataSource`, `sessionFactory`, and `transactionManager` have been defined here:

```xml
<?xml version="1.0" encoding="UTF-8"?>
<beans xmlns="http://www.springframework.org/schema/beans"
    xmlns:xsi="http://www.w3.org/2001/XMLSchema-instance"
xmlns:aop="http://www.springframework.org/schema/aop"
    xmlns:context="http://www.springframework.org/schema/context"
    xmlns:mvc="http://www.springframework.org/schema/mvc"
xmlns:tx="http://www.springframework.org/schema/tx"
    xsi:schemaLocation="http://www.springframework.org/schema/beans
http://www.springframework.org/schema/beans/spring-beans.xsd
    http://www.springframework.org/schema/aop
http://www.springframework.org/schema/aop/spring-aop-4.1.xsd
    http://www.springframework.org/schema/context
http://www.springframework.org/schema/context/spring-context-
4.1.xsd
```

```
      http://www.springframework.org/schema/mvc
 http://www.springframework.org/schema/mvc/spring-mvc-3.2.xsd
      http://www.springframework.org/schema/tx
 http://www.springframework.org/schema/tx/spring-tx-4.1.xsd">
    <context:component-scan base-
 package="org.packt.Spring.chapter8.springsecurity" />
    <context:property-placeholder location="/WEB-
 INF/hibernate.properties" />
    <bean id="dataSource"

 class="org.springframework.jdbc.datasource.DriverManagerDataSource
 ">
      <property name="driverClassName"
 value="${jdbc.driverClassName}" />
      <property name="url" value="${jdbc.url}" />
      <property name="username" value="${jdbc.username}" />
      <property name="password" value="${jdbc.password}" />
    </bean>
    <bean id="sessionFactory"
      class="org.springframework.orm.hibernate4.
 LocalSessionFactoryBean"
 >
      <property name="dataSource" ref="dataSource" />
      <property name="annotatedClasses"
        value="org.packt.Spring.chapter8.springsecurity.model.
 Employee" />
      <property name="hibernateProperties">
        <props>
          <prop key="hibernate.dialect">${hibernate.dialect}</prop>
          <prop key="hibernate.show_sql">${hibernate.show_sql}</
 prop>
        </props>
      </property>
    </bean>
    <bean id="transactionManager"
      class="org.springframework.orm.hibernate4.HibernateTransaction
 Manager">
      <property name="sessionFactory" ref="sessionFactory" />
    </bean>
    <tx:annotation-driven transaction-manager="transactionManager"
 />
    <bean
      class="org.springframework.web.servlet.view.InternalResource
 ViewResolver">
      <property name="prefix">
```

```
            <value>/WEB-INF/views/</value>
        </property>
        <property name="suffix">
            <value>.jsp</value>
        </property>
    </bean>
</beans>
```

Let's add a custom login

We have defined a role called ROLE_ADMIN. We have defined credentials for this role.
Also, we have mapped URLs with roles that will be handled by Spring Security.
To provide custom login form, add <form:login> in this file. When the user tries
to access a secured resource, a custom login page will be served.

In the security-config.xml file, you'll find the following code:

```xml
<?xml version="1.0" encoding="UTF-8"?>
<beans:beans xmlns:beans="http://www.springframework.org/schema/beans"
    xmlns:xsi="http://www.w3.org/2001/XMLSchema-instance"
xmlns="http://www.springframework.org/schema/security"
    xsi:schemaLocation="http://www.springframework.org/schema/beans
    http://www.springframework.org/schema/beans/spring-beans.xsd
    http://www.springframework.org/schema/security
    http://www.springframework.org/schema/security/spring-security-
3.1.xsd">
    <http auto-config="true">
        <intercept-url pattern="/employee/*" access="ROLE_ADMIN" />
        <form-login login-processing-url="/login" login-page="/
loginPage"
            username-parameter="username" password-
parameter="password"
            default-target-url="/employee/listemployee"
            authentication-failure-url="/loginPage?auth=fail" />
        <logout logout-url="/logout" logout-success-
url="/logoutPage" />
    </http>
    <authentication-manager>
        <authentication-provider>
            <user-service>
                <user name="ravi" password="ravi@123" authorities="ROLE_
ADMIN" />
            </user-service>
        </authentication-provider>
    </authentication-manager>
</beans:beans>
```

Mapping your login requests

The `LoginController` class contains two methods, namely `logoutPage` and `loginPage`, with request mapping. The `/loginPage` redirects the user to the login page and the `/logoutpage` redirects the user to the logout page:

```java
package org.packt.Spring.chapter8.springsecurity.controller;

import org.springframework.stereotype.Controller;
import org.springframework.web.bind.annotation.RequestMapping;
import org.springframework.web.bind.annotation.RequestMethod;

@Controller
public class LoginController {

    @RequestMapping(value = "/logoutPage", method =
RequestMethod.GET)
    public String logoutPage() {
        return "logout";
    }

    @RequestMapping(value = "/loginPage", method =
RequestMethod.GET)
    public String loginPage() {
        return "login";
    }
}
```

Obtaining the employee list

This controller class has the `listEmployee()`, `addEmployee()`, and `deleteEmployee()` methods. In the `EmployeeController.java` file, you'll find the following code:

```java
package org.packt.Spring.chapter8.springsecurity.controller;

import org.packt.Spring.chapter8.springsecurity.model.Employee;
import org.packt.Spring.chapter8.springsecurity.service.
EmployeeService;
import org.springframework.beans.factory.annotation.Autowired;
import org.springframework.stereotype.Controller;
import org.springframework.ui.ModelMap;
import org.springframework.web.bind.annotation.ModelAttribute;
```

```
import org.springframework.web.bind.annotation.PathVariable;
import org.springframework.web.bind.annotation.RequestMapping;
import org.springframework.web.bind.annotation.RequestMethod;
import org.springframework.web.servlet.ModelAndView;

@Controller
@RequestMapping("/employee")
public class EmployeeController {

    @Autowired
    private EmployeeService employeeService;

    @RequestMapping(value = "/listemployee", method =
RequestMethod.GET)
    public String listEmployees(ModelMap model) {
            model.addAttribute("employeesList",
employeeService.listEmployee());
            return "employee";
    }


    @RequestMapping(value = "/addemployee", method =
RequestMethod.GET)
    public ModelAndView addEmployee(ModelMap model) {
            return new ModelAndView("addemployee", "command", new
Employee());
    }


    @RequestMapping(value = "/updatemployee", method =
RequestMethod.POST)
    public String updateEmployee(
                @ModelAttribute("employeeForm") Employee employee,
ModelMap model) {
            this.employeeService.insertEmployee(employee);
            model.addAttribute("employeesList",
employeeService.listEmployee());
            return "employee";
    }


    @RequestMapping(value = "/delete/{empId}", method =
RequestMethod.GET)
    public String deleteEmployee(@PathVariable("empId") Integer
empId,
                ModelMap model) {
          this.employeeService.deleteEmployee(empId);
```

```
        model.addAttribute("employeesList",
employeeService.listEmployee());
        return "employee";
    }
}
```

Let's see some credentials

This login page provides an input box to accept credentials from the user. In the
`login.jsp` file, you'll find the following code:

```
<%@ taglib uri='http://java.sun.com/jsp/jstl/core' prefix='c'%>
<html>
<head>
<title>Login Page</title>
</head>
<body>
    <h2 style="color: orange">Login to eHR Payroll</h2>
    <c:if test="${'fail' eq param.auth}">
        <div style="color:red">
                Login Failed!!!<br />
                Reason : ${sessionScope["SPRING_SECURITY_LAST_
EXCEPTION"].message}
        </div>
    </c:if>
    <form action="${pageContext.request.contextPath}/login"
method="post">
        <table frame="box" cellpadding="0" cellspacing="6">
            <tr>
                <td>Username:</td>
                <td><input type='text' name='username' /></td>
            </tr>
            <tr>
                <td>Password:</td>
                <td><input type='password' name='password'></td>
            </tr>
            <tr>
                <td colspan='2'><input name="submit" type="submit"
value="Submit"></td>
            </tr>
        </table>
    </form>
</body>
</html>
```

Time to log out

This logout page reflects that the user has been logged out from the application.
In the `logout.jsp` file, you'll find the following code:

```html
<html>
<title>Logout Page</title>
<body>
    <h2>You have been successfully logged out.</h2>
    <a href="${pageContext.request.contextPath}/employee/
listemployee">
Login to eHR Payroll</a>
</body>
</html>
```

Running the application

Once you deploy the web application after starting the server, open the URL
`http://localhost:8080/ehrPayrollWithSecurity/loginPage` a custom
login page will appear:

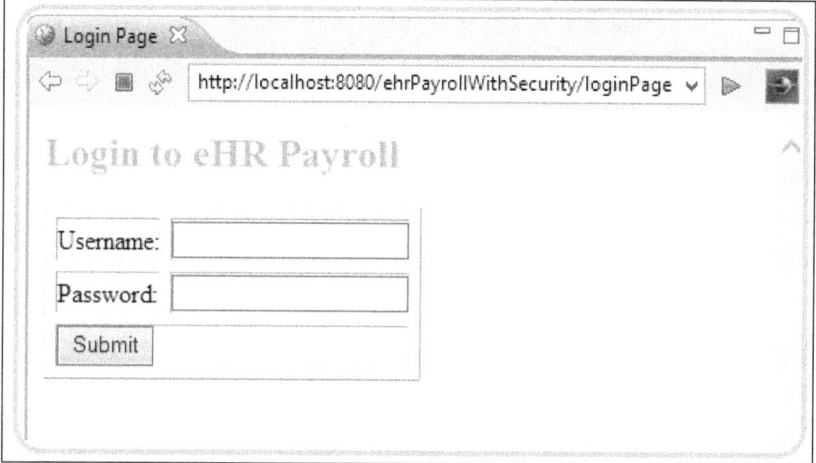

If you enter the wrong credentials, the following error will appear:

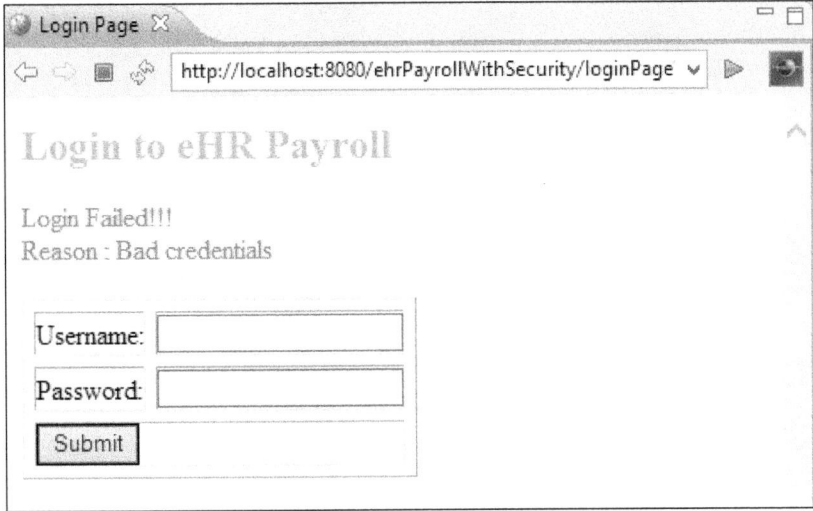

If you enter the correct credentials, you will be navigated to the listEmployee page:

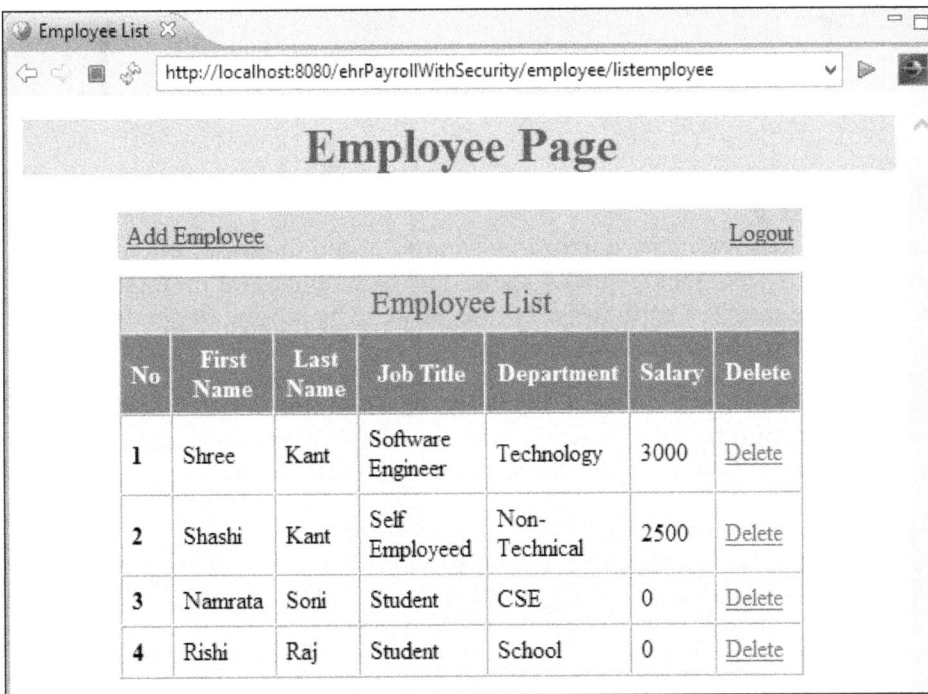

Clicking on **Logout** will navigate you to the logout page, as shown here:

Exercise

Q1. What is Spring Security?

Q2. What is authentication and authorization?

Q3. What are the different ways supported by Spring Security for users to log into a web application?

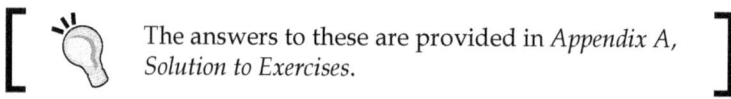

The answers to these are provided in *Appendix A, Solution to Exercises*.

Summary

In this chapter, you learned what Spring Security is and the major operations in Spring Security. We took a quick look at the Servlet filter and understood the security use case. We configured Spring Security by adding dependencies in pom.xml and also configured namespace.

We secured the web application's URL access by providing `DelegatingFilterProxy` as the filter class and the URL pattern. We created a separated Spring Security configuration file. We saw different ways of logging into the web application.

We authenticated users with in-memory definition and also against the database. We saw Spring Security supports for encrypt password. Lastly, we configured the method-level security in Spring Security.

In the next chapter, we will cover Spring testing. We will understand testing using JUnit4 and TestNG. We will also understand the Mockito framework (look into MockMVC).

7
Spring Testing

In software development, testing is a crucial part. Software development cannot be completed without testing. Testing is a process that ensures the performance and quality of software development, and verifies that the applications run smoothly and flawlessly. For this, unit testing is the easiest technique. It allows us to test each component of the application separately. Integration testing ensures that multiple components are working well in a system.

To avoid the mixing of the test code with the normal code, usually unit tests are created in a separate source folder or a separate project. Some developers, on the hot topic, "What should be tested", hold that every statement in the code should be tested.

Testing can be done either automatically or manually, and automated tests can be run continuously and repeatedly at different phases of the software development process. This is highly recommended for the Agile development process. Since the Spring Framework is an Agile framework, it supports these kinds of processes.

The Java platform supports many testing frameworks, in which JUnit and TestNG are the most popular frameworks. In this chapter, we will discuss a popular Java testing framework and the basic techniques of testing. We will also discuss the support provided by the Spring Framework for unit and integrating testing.

Here is the list of topics that will be covered in this chapter:

- Testing using JUnit 4
- Testing using TestNG
- Agile software testing
- Spring MVC test framework

Testing using JUnit 4

JUnit 4 is the most widely accepted unit testing framework on the Java platform. It allows you to annotate the methods that need to be tested by using the `@Test` annotation, and it is used to create automated tests for your Java application, which can be run repeatedly to ensure the correctness of your application. The website for JUnit is `http://junit.org/`.

A `Test` class contains the JUnit tests. These are methods and are only used for testing. A test method needs to be annotated with the `@org.junit.Test` annotation. In this test method, you use a method provided by the JUnit framework to check the actual result versus the expected result of the code execution.

JUnit 4 annotations

JUnit 4 uses annotations; a few of these are listed in the following table:

Annotation	Import	Description
@Test	org.junit.Test	The `@Test` annotation identifies the test cases. A public void method annotated with the `@org.junit.Test` annotation can be run as a test case.
@Before	org.junit.Before	A public void method annotated with the `@Before` annotation is executed before each `Test` method in that class execute. It may be used to set up an environment variable.
@After	org.junit.After	A public void method annotated with the `@After` annotation is executed after each `Test` method in that class execute. It may be used to release the external resource that was allocated in a `Before` method or clean up the test environment and save memory.
@BeforeClass	org.junit.BeforeClass	A public static void method annotated with the `@BeforeClass` annotation is executed once, before all the tests in that class are executed.

Annotation	Import	Description
@AfterClass	org.junit.AfterClass	A public static void method annotated with the @AfterClass annotation is executed once, after all the test methods in that class have been executed. It can be used to perform some clean-up activities, such as disconnect from the database.
@Ignore	org.junit.Ignore	A method annotated with the @Ignore annotation will not be executed.

Assert methods

JUnit provides the static assert methods declared in the org.junit.Assert class to test for certain conditions. An assert method starts with assert, and then compares the expected value with the actual value returned by a test. The Assert class provides a set of assertion methods of the return type void. These are useful for writing tests. A few of these are listed in the table shown here:

Method	Description
assertTrue(boolean expected, boolean actual)	This method checks whether the Boolean condition is true
assertFalse(boolean condition)	This method checks whether the Boolean condition is false
assertEquals(boolean expected, expected, actual)	This method compares the equality of any two objects using the equals() method
assertEquals(boolean expected, expected, actual, tolerance)	This method compares either the float or the double values and tolerance defines number of the decimal that must be the same
assertNull(Object object)	This method tests whether a single object is null
assertNotNull(Object object)	This method tests that a single object is not null
assertSame(Object object1, Object object2)	This method tests whether two objects refer to the same object, and it must be exactly the same object pointed to
assertNotSame(Object object1, Object object2)	This method tests if two objects do not refer to the same object

An example of JUnit 4

Suppose we are going to develop a simple calculator. We have to test it in order to ensure the system's quality. Let's consider a simple calculator whose interface is defined as follows:

```
package org.packt.Spring.chapter9.SpringTesting.Calculator;

public interface SimpleCalculator {

    public long add(int a, int b);

}
```

Now, we can implement this SimpleCalculator:

```
package org.packt.Spring.chapter9.SpringTesting.Calculator;

public class SimpleCalculatorImpl implements SimpleCalculator {

    public long add(int a, int b) {
            return a + b;
    }
}
```

Next, we will test this SimpleCalculator with JUnit 4. Most of the IDEs, such as Eclipse, STS, and NetBeans support the creation of the JUnit tests through wizards. Add JUnit 4 JAR to your CLASSPATH to compile and run the test cases created for JUnit 4, as shown here:

```
package org.packt.Spring.chapter9.SpringTesting.Calculator;

import static org.junit.Assert.*;

import org.junit.Before;
import org.junit.Test;

public class SimpleCalculatorJUnit4Tests {

    private SimpleCalculator simpleCalculator;

    @Before
    public void init() {
            simpleCalculator = new SimpleCalculatorImpl();
    }
```

```
    @Test
    public void verifyAdd() {
            long sum = simpleCalculator.add(3, 7);
             assertEquals(10, sum);
    }
}
```

Now we can run our test case by right-clicking on the test, and then choosing **Run As | JUnit** test, and we can verify the JUnit view as the test case should run successfully, as shown in the following two cases:

- It will display a green bar if the test case passes:

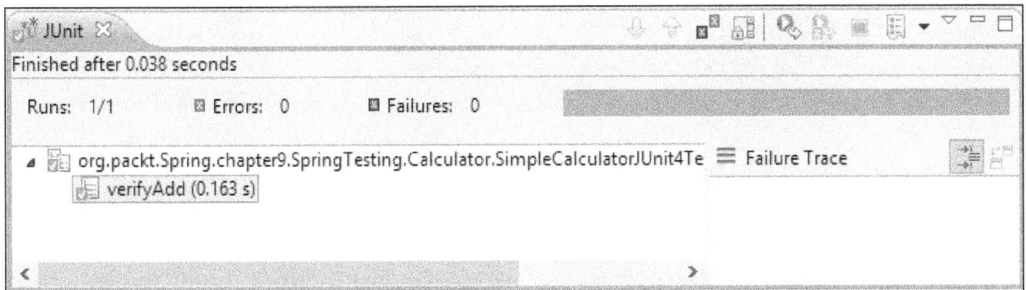

- It will display a red bar if the test case fails:

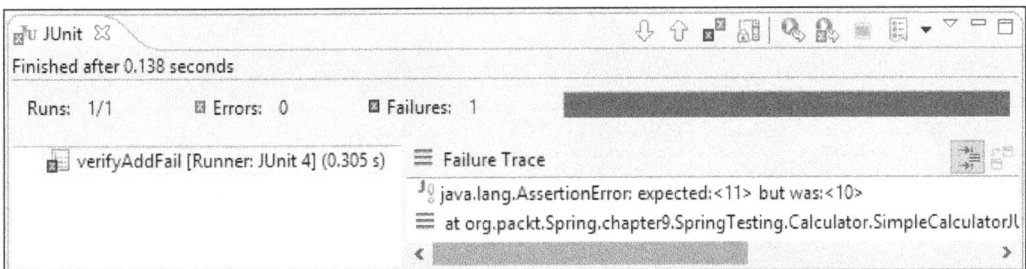

Here is the error code in the second case:

```
    @Test
    public void verifyAddFail() {
            long sum = simpleCalculator.add(3, 7);
            assertEquals(11, sum);
    }
```

Testing using TestNG

TestNG (Next Generation) is another testing framework that is similar to the JUnit 4 framework, but it has new functionalities such as grouping concept, and dependency testing. These have made testing easier and more powerful. It is designed to cover all the categories of tests, such as the unit test, the functional test, the integration test, and so on. TestNG also supports multi-threaded testing.

TestNG annotations

TestNG uses annotations; a few of them are listed in the following table:

Annotation	Import	Description
@Test	org.testng.annotations.Test	It marks the method as a test method
@BeforeMethod	org.testng.annotations.BeforeMethod	The annotated method will be executed before each @test annotated method
@AfterMethod	org.testng.annotations.AfterMethod	The annotated method will be executed after the execution of each and every @test annotated method
@BeforeClass	org.testng.annotations.BeforeClass	The annotated method will be executed only once before the first test method in the current class is invoked
@AfterClass	org.testng.annotations.AfterClass	The annotated method will be executed only once after the execution of all the @Test annotated methods of that class

Annotation	Import	Description
@BeforeTest	org.testng.annotations.BeforeTest	The annotated method will be executed before any @Test annotated method belonging to that class is executed
@AfterTest	org.testng.annotations.AfterTest	The annotated method will be executed after any @Test annotated method belonging to the classes is executed

Example of TestNG

Refer to the link http://testng.org/doc/download.html to set up TestNG for your IDEs. Add TestNG JAR to your CLASSPATH to compile and run the test cases created for TestNG, as shown here:

```
package org.packt.Spring.chapter9.SpringTesting.Calculator;

import org.testng.Assert;
import org.testng.annotations.BeforeMethod;
import org.testng.annotations.Test;

public class SimpleCalculatorTestNGTests {

    private SimpleCalculator simpleCalculator;

    @BeforeMethod
    public void beforeMethod() {
            simpleCalculator = new SimpleCalculatorImpl();
    }

    @Test
    public void verifyAdd() {
            long sum = simpleCalculator.add(3, 7);
            Assert.assertEquals(10, sum);
    }
}
```

You will see a progressive green bar if your test case passes:

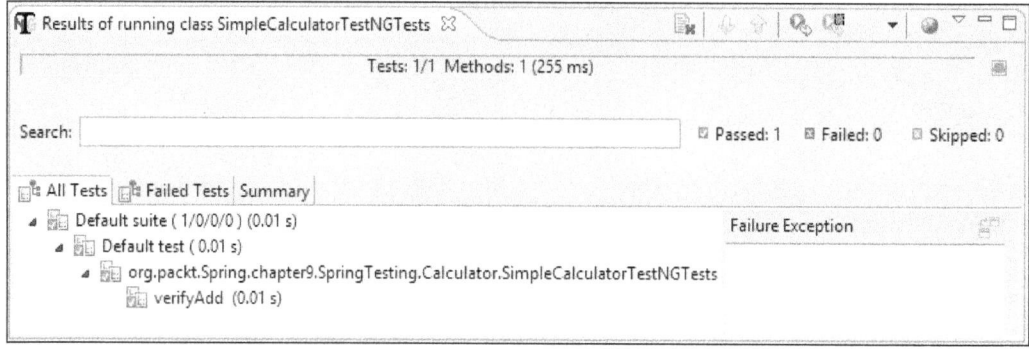

Agile software testing

The term Agile, in the world of software development, typically refers to an approach to project management that aims to unite teams around the principles of collaboration, simplicity, flexibility, and responsiveness throughout the process of developing a new program in an application.

An Agile software testing means the practice of testing software for any performance issues or bugs within the context of Agile workflow. The developers and testers, in the agile approach, are seen as the two sides of the same coin. The Agile software testing includes unit testing and integration testing. It helps with executing the tests as quickly as possible.

Let's understand the significance and the objectives of unit and integration testing.

Unit testing

Unit testing, as the name suggests, is the testing of every individual method of the code. It is the method of testing the fundamental pieces of your functionality. It is a piece of code written by the software developer to test a specific functionality of the code. Unit tests are used for improving the quality of the code and preventing bugs. They are not commonly used for finding them. They are automated testing frameworks.

Let's take an example of the EmployeeService class that needs the employeeDao object for loading the data from the database. This employeeDao is a real object. So, to test the EmployeeService class, it is required to provide the employeeDao object that has a valid connection to the database. We also have to insert the data needed for the test into the database.

Inserting the data into the database after setting up the connection and then testing on an actual database can be a lot of work. Instead, we can provide the EmployeeService instance with a fake EmployeeDao class, which will just return the data that we need to complete the test. This fake EmployeeDao class will not read any data from the database. This fake EmployeeDao class is a mock object that is a replacement for a real object, which makes it easier to test the EmployeeService class.

A common technique that can be applied while testing a unit that depends on other units is to simulate the unit's dependencies with stubs and mock objects, which help in reducing the complexity because of the dependencies in the unit test. Let's look at each of them in detail:

- **Stub**: A stub is a dummy object, which simulates real objects with the minimum number of methods required for a unit test. It can be configured to the return value by implementing the methods in a predetermined way along with the hardcoded data that suite the test.

- **Mock**: A mock object is a fake object or a substitute object that is added to the system, and it usually knows how its method is expected to be called for a test, and decides whether the unit test has passed or failed. The mock object tests whether the real object interacted as expected with the fake object. There may be one or more mock objects per test. A mock object is an object which mimics an actual object. In Java, there are several libraries, which are available for implementing mocking, including jMock, EasyMock, and *Mockito* (we are interested in this particular tool).

State verification is used to check whether the actual method returns the correct value. Behavior verification is used to check whether the correct method was called. Stub is used for state verification, whereas a mock object is used for behavior verification. A stub object cannot fail a unit test but a mock object can. This is because we know what and why we are implementing a stub object, whereas a mock is just a fake object that mimics a real object and if the business logic in the code is wrong, then the unit test fails even if we have passed a real object.

Unit testing for isolated classes

Unit testing is easy for the isolated class, which tests either the class or its method in isolation. Let's create unit tests for the isolated class, where the class under testing will not directly depend on any other class, as shown in the following diagram:

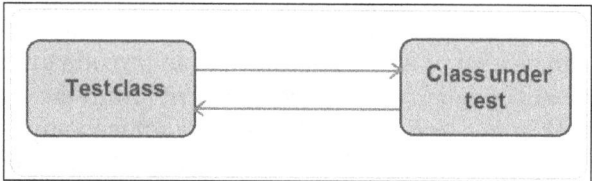

The core functions of the `HrPayroll` system should be designed around employee details. First, we need to create the `Employee` class and override the `equals()` method, as shown in the following code snippet:

```java
package org.packt.Spring.chapter9.SpringTesting.modle;

public class Employee {

    private String employeeId;
    private String firstName;
    private String lastName;
    private int salary;

    // constructor, Getters and setters

    @Override
    public boolean equals(Object obj) {

            if (!(obj instanceof Employee)) {
                    return false;
            }

            Employee employee = (Employee) obj;
            return employee.employeeId.equals(employeeId);
    }
}
```

Now, to persist the `employee` object to the `HrPayroll` system, we need to define the `EmployeeDao` interface:

```java
package org.packt.Spring.chapter9.SpringTesting.dao;

import org.packt.Spring.chapter9.SpringTesting.modle.Employee;
```

```
public interface EmployeeDao {

    public void createEmployee(Employee employee);

    public void updateEmployee(Employee employee);

    public void deleteEmployee(String employeeId);

    public Employee findEmployee(String employeeId);

}
```

Let's implement the `EmployeeDao` interface to demonstrate the unit testing for this isolated class:

```
package org.packt.Spring.chapter9.SpringTesting.dao;

import java.util.Collections;
import java.util.HashMap;
import java.util.Map;

import org.packt.Spring.chapter9.SpringTesting.modle.Employee;

public class InMemeoryEmployeeDaoImpl implements EmployeeDao {

    private Map<String, Employee> employees;

    public InMemeoryEmployeeDaoImpl() {
        employees = Collections
                    .synchronizedMap(new HashMap<String,
Employee>());
    }

    public boolean isOldEmployee(String employeeId) {
        return employees.containsKey(employeeId);
    }

    @Override
    public void createEmployee(Employee employee) {
        if (!isOldEmployee(employee.getEmployeeId())) {
            employees.put(employee.getEmployeeId(), employee);
        }
    }
```

```
@Override
public void updateEmployee(Employee employee) {
        if (isOldEmployee(employee.getEmployeeId())) {
                employees.put(employee.getEmployeeId(), employee);
        }
}

@Override
public void deleteEmployee(String employeeId) {
        if (isOldEmployee(employeeId)) {
                employees.remove(employeeId);
        }
}

@Override
public Employee findEmployee(String employeeId) {
        return employees.get(employeeId);
}
}
```

From the aforementioned code snippet, we can see that the
InMemeoryEmployeeDaoImpl class doesn't depend on any other class directly,
which makes it easier to test, because we don't need to be worried about setting
dependency and their working.

Here is an implementation of InMemeoryEmployeeDaoTest:

```
package org.packt.Spring.chapter9.SpringTesting.test;

import junit.framework.Assert;

import org.junit.Before;
import org.junit.Test;
import org.packt.Spring.chapter9.SpringTesting.dao.
InMemeoryEmployeeDao
Impl;
import org.packt.Spring.chapter9.SpringTesting.modle.Employee;

public class InMemeoryEmployeeDaoTest {

    private static final String OLD_EMPLOYEE_ID = "12121";
    private static final String NEW_EMPLOYEE_ID = "53535";

    private Employee oldEmployee;
    private Employee newEmployee;
    private InMemeoryEmployeeDaoImpl empDao;
```

The `setUp()` method is annotated with the `@Before` annotation, as shown in the code snippet here:

```
@Before
public void setUp() {
        oldEmployee = new Employee(OLD_EMPLOYEE_ID, "Ravi",
"Soni", 1001);
        newEmployee = new Employee(NEW_EMPLOYEE_ID, "Shashi",
"Soni", 3001);

        empDao = new InMemeoryEmployeeDaoImpl();
        empDao.createEmployee(oldEmployee);
}
```

The `isOldEmployeeTest()` method is annotated by the `@Test` annotation. This test method verifies the `employeeId`, as shown in the following code snippet:

```
@Test
public void isOldEmployeeTest() {

Assert.assertTrue(empDao.isOldEmployee(OLD_EMPLOYEE_ID));

Assert.assertFalse(empDao.isOldEmployee(NEW_EMPLOYEE_ID));
}
```

The `createNewEmployeeTest()` method is annotated by the `@Test` annotation. This test method creates a new employee and then verifies the new `employeeId`:

```
@Test
public void createNewEmployeeTest() {
        empDao.createEmployee(newEmployee);

Assert.assertTrue(empDao.isOldEmployee(NEW_EMPLOYEE_ID));
}
```

The `updateEmployeeTest()` method is annotated by the `@Test` annotation. This test method updates employee details and then verifies the employee's `firstName`, as shown here:

```
@Test
public void updateEmployeeTest() {
        String firstName = "Sharee";
        oldEmployee.setFirstName(firstName);
        empDao.updateEmployee(oldEmployee);
        Assert.assertEquals(firstName,
empDao.findEmployee(OLD_EMPLOYEE_ID)
                        .getFirstName());
}
```

The `deleteEmployeeTest()` method is annotated by the `@Test` annotation. This test method deletes employee details and then verifies the employee ID, as shown in the following code snippet:

```
@Test
public void deleteEmployeeTest() {
        empDao.deleteEmployee(OLD_EMPLOYEE_ID);
    Assert.assertFalse(empDao.isOldEmployee(OLD_EMPLOYEE_ID));
    }
}
```

The test results of the aforementioned test cases will be as shown here:

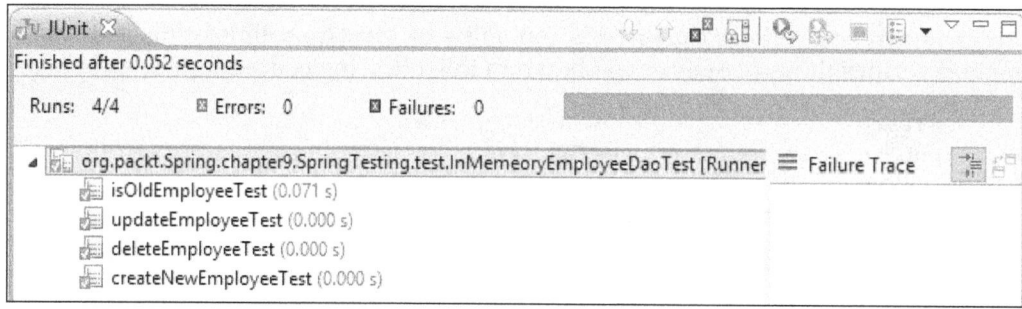

Unit testing for dependent class using mock objects

As we have seen in the previous section, testing either an isolated class or an independent class is easy. However, it would be a little more difficult to test a class that depends on another class, such as the `EmployeeService` class (that holds business logic), which depends on the `EmployeeDao` class (this class knows how to communicate with the database and get the information). Unit testing is harder and has dependencies, as shown here:

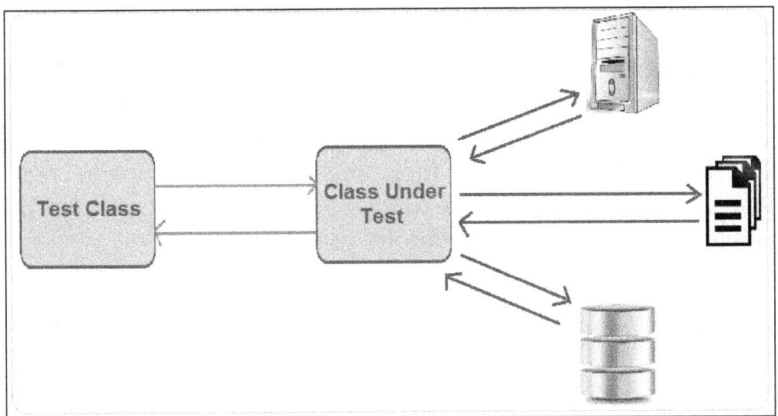

Class Under Test means that whenever we write a unit test, generally the term "unit" refers to a single class against which we have written the tests. It is the class that is being tested. So it's good to remove the dependencies, create a mock object and continue with the unit testing, as shown in the following diagram:

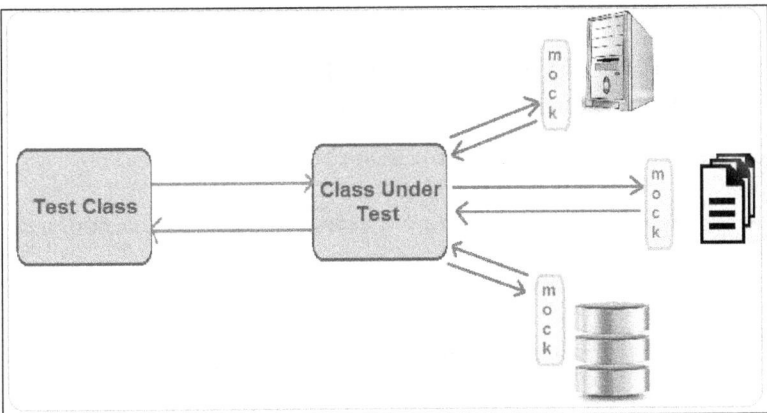

The concept behind removing the dependencies and creating a mock object is that by creating an object that can take the place of a real dependent object. If we are writing a unit test for our `EmployeeService` around business logic, then that particular unit test should not connect `EmployeeService` to the `EmployeeDao` intern, and then connect the `EmployeeDao` intern to the database and perform a crud operation, because we just want to perform the testing of the `EmployeeService` class, and so we need to create a mock `EmployeeDao`. The Mockito framework allows us to create the mock object.

The Mockito framework

The Mockito framework is an open source mock framework for unit testing; it was originally based on EasyMock, which can be downloaded from either http://mockito.org/ or https://code.google.com/p/mockito/. It can be used in conjunction with other testing tools, such as JUnit. It helps in creating and configuring mock objects. Add the Mockito JAR to your CLASSPATH along with JUnit. It uses the field-level annotations, as shown here:

- @Mock: This creates the mock object for an annotated field.

- @Spy: This creates spies for the objects or the files it annotates.

- @InjectMocks: The private field that is annotated by the @InjectMocks annotations is instantiated and Mockito injects the fields annotated with either the @Mock annotation or the @Spy annotation to it.

- @RunWith(MockitoJUnitRunner.class): If you use the aforementioned annotations, then it is must be done to annotate the test class with this annotation to use the MockitoJUnitRunner. When MockitoJUnitRunner executes the unit tests, it creates mock objects and spy objects for all the fields annotated by the @Mock annotation or the @Spy annotation.

Let's perform the unit testing using Mockito, where we create a mock object for a dependent object. Here is the code for the EmployeeService.java interface:

```
package org.packt.Spring.chapter9.SpringTesting.service;

import org.packt.Spring.chapter9.SpringTesting.modle.Employee;

public interface EmployeeService {

    public Employee findEmployee(String employeeId);

}
```

The following is an implementation of EmployeeService:

```
package org.packt.Spring.chapter9.SpringTesting.service;

import org.packt.Spring.chapter9.SpringTesting.dao.EmployeeDao;
import org.packt.Spring.chapter9.SpringTesting.modle.Employee;

public class EmployeeServiceImpl implements EmployeeService {

    private EmployeeDao employeeDao = null;
```

```
    public EmployeeServiceImpl(EmployeeDao employeeDao) {
           this.employeeDao = employeeDao;
    }

    @Override
    public Employee findEmployee(String employeeId) {
           return employeeDao.findEmployee(employeeId);
    }
}
```

And, here we have created our test class in the test folder, and created a
mock object by annotating EmployeeDao. We have annotated the class by the
@RunWith(MockitoJUnitRunner.class) annotation. We have created two test
methods by using the @Test annotation, where, in the first test case, we verify that
the findEmployee behavior happened once and in the second test case, we verify
that no interactions happened on employeeDao mocks:

```
package org.packt.Spring.chapter9.SpringTesting.service;

import static org.mockito.Mockito.verify;
import static org.mockito.Mockito.verifyNoMoreInteractions;
import static org.mockito.Mockito.verifyZeroInteractions;
import static org.mockito.Mockito.when;
import junit.framework.Assert;

import org.junit.Before;
import org.junit.Test;
import org.junit.runner.RunWith;
import org.mockito.Mock;
import org.mockito.runners.MockitoJUnitRunner;
import org.packt.Spring.chapter9.SpringTesting.dao.EmployeeDao;
import org.packt.Spring.chapter9.SpringTesting.modle.Employee;

@RunWith(MockitoJUnitRunner.class)
public class EmployeeServiceTest {

    private static final String OLD_EMPLOYEE_ID = "12121";
    private Employee oldEmployee;
    private EmployeeService employeeService;

    @Mock
    private EmployeeDao employeeDao;
```

```
    @Before
    public void setUp() {
            employeeService = new EmployeeServiceImpl(employeeDao);
            oldEmployee = new Employee(OLD_EMPLOYEE_ID, "Ravi",
"Soni", 1001);
    }


    @Test
    public void findEmployeeTest() {

    when(employeeDao.findEmployee(OLD_EMPLOYEE_ID)).
thenReturn(oldEmployee);
            Employee employee =
employeeService.findEmployee(OLD_EMPLOYEE_ID);
            Assert.assertEquals(oldEmployee, employee);


            // Verifies findEmployee behavior happened once
            verify(employeeDao).findEmployee(OLD_EMPLOYEE_ID);


            // asserts that during the test, there are no other
calls to the mock
            // object.
            verifyNoMoreInteractions(employeeDao);
    }


    @Test
    public void notFindEmployeeTest() {

    when(employeeDao.findEmployee(OLD_EMPLOYEE_ID)).thenReturn
(null);
            Employee employee =
employeeService.findEmployee(OLD_EMPLOYEE_ID);
            Assert.assertNotSame(oldEmployee, employee);


            verify(employeeDao).findEmployee(OLD_EMPLOYEE_ID);


            // Verifies that no interactions happened on employeeDao
mocks
            verifyZeroInteractions(employeeDao);
            verifyNoMoreInteractions(employeeDao);
    }
}
```

And, the result of running the test as JUnit is as follows:

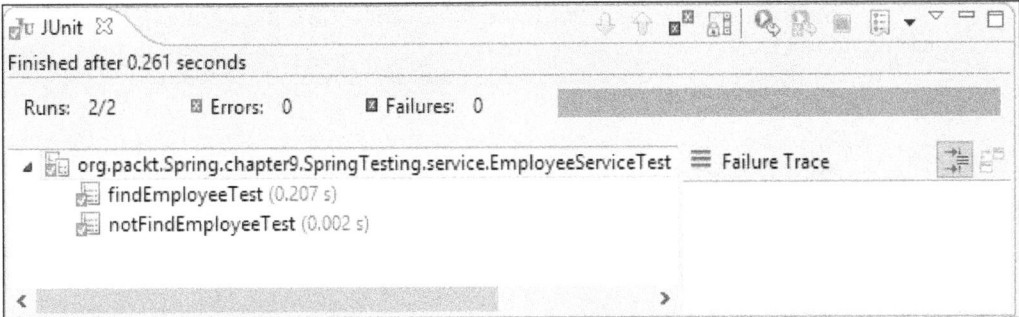

Integration testing

Integration testing is a phase of software testing in which individual software modules are combined and tested as a group to ensure that the required units are properly integrated and interact correctly with each other. The purpose of integration testing is to verify the functionality, performance, and reliability of the code. Integration testing is used for testing several units together.

Let's take an example. We can create an integration test to test `EmployeeServiceImpl` using `InMemeoryEmployeeDaoImpl` as a DAO implementation:

```
package org.packt.Spring.chapter9.SpringTesting.service;

import org.junit.Assert;
import org.junit.Before;
import org.junit.Test;
import org.packt.Spring.chapter9.SpringTesting.dao.EmployeeDao;
import org.packt.Spring.chapter9.SpringTesting.dao.
InMemeoryEmployeeDaoImpl;
import org.packt.Spring.chapter9.SpringTesting.modle.Employee;

public class EmployeeServiceIntegrationTest {

    private static final String OLD_EMPLOYEE_ID = "12121";
    private static final String NEW_EMPLOYEE_ID = "53535";

    private Employee oldEmployee;
    private Employee newEmployee;
    private EmployeeService employeeService;
```

```
    @Before
    public void setUp() {
            oldEmployee = new Employee(OLD_EMPLOYEE_ID, "Ravi",
"Soni", 1001);
            newEmployee = new Employee(NEW_EMPLOYEE_ID, "Shashi",
"Soni", 3001);

            employeeService = new EmployeeServiceImpl(
                        new InMemeoryEmployeeDaoImpl());
            employeeService.createEmployee(oldEmployee);
    }

    @Test
    public void isOldEmployeeTest() {

    Assert.assertTrue(employeeService.isOldEmployee
(OLD_EMPLOYEE_ID));

    Assert.assertFalse(employeeService.isOldEmployee
(NEW_EMPLOYEE_ID));
    }

    @Test
    public void createNewEmployeeTest() {
            employeeService.createEmployee(newEmployee);

    Assert.assertTrue(employeeService.isOldEmployee
(NEW_EMPLOYEE_ID));
    }

    @Test
    public void updateEmployeeTest() {
            String firstName = "Sharee";
            oldEmployee.setFirstName(firstName);
            employeeService.updateEmployee(oldEmployee);
            Assert.assertEquals(firstName,

    employeeService.findEmployee(OLD_EMPLOYEE_ID).getFirstName());
    }

    @Test
    public void deleteEmployeeTest() {
            employeeService.deleteEmployee(OLD_EMPLOYEE_ID);
```

```
      Assert.assertFalse(employeeService.isOldEmployee
   (OLD_EMPLOYEE_ID));
      }


   }
```

The result is shown here:

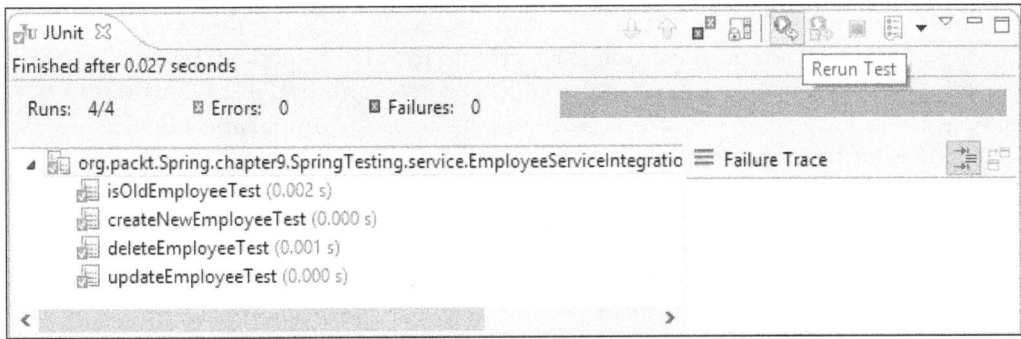

Create unit tests of the Spring MVC controller

We will take the example of the Spring MVC from this chapter as a target application to test and execute unit testing. We have the EmployeeController class as a target class to test.

You'll find the following code in EmployeeController.java:

```
package org.packt.Spring.chapter7.springmvc.controller;

import org.springframework.stereotype.Controller;
import org.springframework.ui.ModelMap;
import org.springframework.web.bind.annotation.RequestMapping;
import org.springframework.web.bind.annotation.RequestMethod;

@Controller
@RequestMapping("/employee")
public class EmployeeController {

    @RequestMapping(method = RequestMethod.GET)
    public String welcomeEmployee(ModelMap model) {
```

```
            model.addAttribute("name", "Hello World!");
            model.addAttribute("greetings",
                        "Welcome to Packt Publishing - Spring MVC
    !!!");
            return "hello";
        }
    }
```

In the aforementioned code snippet, the `welcomeEmployee()` method in the `EmployeeController` class gets mapped into the HTTP request. In the `welcomeEmployee()` method, the request is processed and bound to the model objects. Then, the `EmployeeController` class updates the model and the view state, and after this it returns to the logical view.

The main objective of the unit testing controller class is to verify that the methods of the controller class update the model and the view states properly and also return to the correct view. Since we perform the testing of the controller class's behavior, we should mock the service layer (if present) with the correct behavior.

For the `EmployeeController` class, we would like to develop the test cases for the `welcomeEmployee()` method. Here we will test the `welcomeEmployee()` method of the controller using JUnit 4.

It is important to note that the classes undergoing testing should be placed in the folder `/src/test/java` and the resources filed should be placed in the folder `/src/test/resources`.

You'll find this code in `EmployeeControllerTest.java`:

```
package org.packt.Spring.chapter7.springmvc.controller;

import org.junit.Assert;
import org.junit.Test; WelcomeEmployee
import org.packt.Spring.chapter7.springmvc.controller.
EmployeeController;
import org.springframework.ui.ExtendedModelMap;
import org.springframework.ui.ModelMap;

public class EmployeeControllerTest {

    @Test
    public void test () {

            EmployeeController controller = new EmployeeController();
```

```
        ModelMap modelMap = new ExtendedModelMap();

        String view = controller.welcomeEmployee(modelMap);

        // verify view page name
        Assert.assertNotNull(view);
        Assert.assertEquals("hello", view);

        // verify page title
        String titlename = modelMap.get("name").toString();
        Assert.assertEquals("Hello World!", titlename);

        // verify greeting message
        String greetings = modelMap.get("greetings").toString();
        Assert.assertEquals("Welcome to Packt Publishing - Spring
MVC !!!",
                    greetings);
    }
}
```

Even though the preceding code works, it has the following problems:

- The preceding test case tests the controller API strictly but disagrees on the request methods, such as GET, POST, PUT, or DELETE
- The preceding test case only tests the return value that is put in the ModelMap
- The preceding test case tests for the correct view name

It is always challenging to perform unit testing of web applications. A better solution for the aforementioned problem is provided by the Spring MVC test framework, which allows us to test the Spring MVC controller.

Spring MVC test framework

The Spring MVC test framework makes unit testing and integration testing of the Spring MVC controller more meaningful by offering first class JUnit support. It helps in testing all the aspects of the controller method that have not been tested before. It allows us to test these aspects in depth without starting a web container.

In order to perform a test on the Spring MVC framework, the Spring TestContext framework along with JUnit or TestNG makes it so simple by providing an annotation-driven unit and integration testing support. The Spring TestContext framework can be tested by annotations such as, @RunWith, @WebAppConfiguration, and @ContextConfiguration, to load the Spring configuration and inject the WebApplicationContext into the MockMvc for the unit and the integration test.

Required dependencies

We can configure the Spring `TestContext` framework by updating `pom.xml` with the required dependencies, such as `spring-test`, `junit`, and `mockito-all`. The following table explains them in detail:

Group ID	Artifact ID	Version	Description
`org.springframework`	`spring-test`	3.2.4 release	It supports unit and integration testing of the Spring components
`org.mockito`	`mockito-all`	1.9.5	The library of the Mockito mocking framework
JUnit	`junit`	4.10	The library of the JUnit framework

You'll find the following code at `pom.xml`:

```
<project xmlns="http://maven.apache.org/POM/4.0.0" xmlns:xsi="http://
www.w3.org/2001/XMLSchema-instance"
    xsi:schemaLocation="http://maven.apache.org/POM/4.0.0 http://maven.
apache.org/maven-v4_0_0.xsd">
    <modelVersion>4.0.0</modelVersion>
    <groupId>org.packt.Spring.chapter7.springmvc</groupId>
    <artifactId>SpringMVCPayrollSystem</artifactId>
    <packaging>war</packaging>
    <version>0.0.1-SNAPSHOT</version>
    <name>SpringMVCPayrollSystem Maven Webapp</name>
    <url>http://maven.apache.org</url>
    <properties>
        <spring.version>3.2.0.RELEASE</spring.version>
    </properties>
    <dependencies>
        <dependency>
            <groupId>org.springframework</groupId>
            <artifactId>spring-core</artifactId>
            <version>${spring.version}</version>
        </dependency>
        <dependency>
            <groupId>org.springframework</groupId>
            <artifactId>spring-webmvc</artifactId>
            <version>${spring.version}</version>
```

```xml
    </dependency>
    <!-- Servlet -->
    <dependency>
        <groupId>javax.servlet</groupId>
        <artifactId>servlet-api</artifactId>
        <version>2.5</version>
        <scope>provided</scope>
    </dependency>
    <!-- Test -->
    <dependency>
        <groupId>org.springframework</groupId>
        <artifactId>spring-test</artifactId>
        <version>3.2.4.RELEASE</version>
        <scope>test</scope>
    </dependency>
    <dependency>
        <groupId>org.mockito</groupId>
        <artifactId>mockito-all</artifactId>
        <version>1.9.5</version>
    </dependency>
    <dependency>
        <groupId>junit</groupId>
        <artifactId>junit</artifactId>
        <version>4.10</version>
        <scope>test</scope>
    </dependency>
</dependencies>
<build>
    <finalName>SpringMVCPayrollSystem</finalName>
</build>
</project>
```

Annotations in Spring testing

The Spring Framework provides the annotations that can be used to perform unit and integration testing with the TestContext framework. Here, we will discuss the two important annotations: @ContextConfiguration and @WebAppConfiguration.

The @ContextConfiguration annotation

This annotation is used to set `ApplicationContext` for the test classes by taking the actual configuration file with the file path. In the following code, we have given the file, so it will take the relative path as the root package. We can also give the exact path by specifying the file: `prefix`. Also, we can pass more than one configuration file using a comma separator, as shown here:

```
@ContextConfiguration ({"classpath*: SpringDispatcher-
servlet.xml"})
public class EmployeeControllerTestWithMockMvc {
    // class body
}
```

The `@ContextConfiguration` annotation caches the `ApplicationContext` for us and puts it in the static memory for the entire duration of the test or the test suite. And the entire test executes it in the same JVM because `ApplicationContext` is stored in the static memory. If the second JVM is there, it will not have access to the static context, and it will result in a second `ApplicationContext` being created.

The @WebAppConfiguration annotation

It is a class-level annotation used to create a web version of the application context in the Spring Framework. It is used to denote that the `ApplicationContext`, which is loaded for an integration test and used by that class, is an instance of `WebApplicationContext`. It is important to note that the `@WebAppConfiguration` annotation must be used with the `@ContextConfiguration` annotation:

```
@WebAppConfiguration
@ContextConfiguration ({"classpath*: SpringDispatcher-
servlet.xml"})
public class EmployeeControllerTestWithMockMvc {
    // class body
}
```

MockMvc

The MockMvc is a key part of the Spring MVC Test framework, which can be used to write the tests for the applications developed using the Spring MVC. It is the entry point for Spring MVC testing. The `MockMvc` mock the entire Spring MVC infrastructure and is created using the implementations of the `MockMvcBuilder` interface. In order to use the Spring MVC testing, the first step is to create an instance of MockMvc. There are four static methods in the `MockMvcBuilders` class.

They are as follows:

- `ContextMockMvcBuilder annotationConfigSetup(Class...  configClasses)`: Use this method when you need to configure the application context using Java configuration.

- `ContextMockMvcBuilder xmlConfigSetup(String... configLocations)`: Use this method when you need to configure the application context by using the XML configuration files.

- `StandaloneMockMvcBuilder standaloneSetup(Object... controllers)`: You can use this method when you need to configure the test controller manually, and when you want to run the individual components for testing. We don't need to configure the entire application context; instead we only need to configure and execute the associated controller component files.

- `InitializedContextMockMvcBuilder webApplicationContextSetup(Web ApplicationContext context)`: This method must be used when you have already fully initialized the `WebApplicationContext` object.

Here, we have created the MockMvc instance using `MockMvcBuilders` and calling the `standaloneSetup()` method after passing an instance of the controller class as a parameter and then building it by calling the `build()` method, as shown in the following code snippet:

```
private MockMvc mockMvc;

@Before
public void setup() {
        this.mockMvc = MockMvcBuilders.standaloneSetup
        (employeeController).build();
}
```

Once we have an instance of MockMvc, we can perform the testing using MockMvc. We can send the HTTP request after specifying all the details, such as the HTTP method, the content type, and so on. And then, we can verify the results.

Assertion

To perform the assertion, first we use the instance of MockMvc and then we call the `perform()` method to pass a relative path to run the test case. And then, we can verify the different components inside the controller using `andExpect`. The `andExpect(status().isOk())` is used to check for a 200 status. Similarly, we can perform the `contentType` validation, the `xpath` validation, validate data in the model, URL validation, and the view name validation.

The sample code for this is as shown here:

```
this.mockMvc
                        .perform(get("/employee"))
                        .andExpect(status().isOk())
                        .andExpect(view().name("hello"))
                        .andExpect(model().attribute("name", "Hello
World!"))
                        .andExpect(
                                model().attribute("greetings",
                                        "Welcome to Packt
Publishing - Spring MVC !!!"));
```

@RunWith(SpringJUnit4ClassRunner.class)

This is a JUnit annotation. It executes the tests in a class annotated by the `@RunWith` annotation, or extends a class annotated by the `@RunWith` annotation by invoking the class passed as a parameter, which means that the tests in the annotated class are not executed by the in-built API in the JUnit framework, the runner class used to execute the test case. In order to use the Spring's JUnit class runner for running the test cases within the Spring's `ApplicationContext` environment, passed spring's `SpringJUnit4ClassRunner` class as parameter.

So now, we have the complete code to perform the testing of the `EmployeeController` controller using the Spring MVC test framework. We will use the MockMvc that will mock the entire Spring MVC infrastructure. We will create a MockMvc instance in the method annotated by the `@Before` annotation, so that it will be available before the test starts.

You'll find this code in `EmployeeControllerTestWithMockMvc.java`:

```
package org.packt.Spring.chapter7.springmvc.controller;

import static org.springframework.test.web.servlet.request.
MockMvcRequestBuilder
s.get;
import static org.springframework.test.web.servlet.result.
MockMvcResultMatchers.
status;
import static org.springframework.test.web.servlet.result.
MockMvcResultMatchers.
view;
import static org.springframework.test.web.servlet.result.
MockMvcResultMatchers.
model;
```

```
import org.junit.Before;
import org.junit.Test;
import org.junit.runner.RunWith;
import org.mockito.InjectMocks;
import org.mockito.MockitoAnnotations;
import org.packt.Spring.chapter7.springmvc.controller.
EmployeeController;
import org.springframework.test.context.ContextConfiguration;
import org.springframework.test.context.junit4.
SpringJUnit4ClassRunner;
import org.springframework.test.context.web.WebAppConfiguration;
import org.springframework.test.web.servlet.MockMvc;
import org.springframework.test.web.servlet.setup.MockMvcBuilders;

@RunWith(SpringJUnit4ClassRunner.class)
@WebAppConfiguration
@ContextConfiguration({ "classpath*:SpringDispatcher-servlet.xml"
})
public class EmployeeControllerTestWithMockMvc {

    @InjectMocks
    private EmployeeController employeeController;

    private MockMvc mockMvc;

    @Before
    public void setup() {
            MockitoAnnotations.initMocks(this);
            this.mockMvc =
MockMvcBuilders.standaloneSetup(employeeController).build();
    }

    @Test
    public void testHome() throws Exception {

            this.mockMvc
                        .perform(get("/employee"))
                        .andExpect(status().isOk())
                        .andExpect(view().name("hello"))
                        .andExpect(model().attribute("name", "Hello
World!"))
                        .andExpect(
                                    model().attribute("greetings",
                                            "Welcome to Packt
Publishing - Spring MVC !!!"));
    }
}
```

Now, we can run the test case by right-clicking on the test and then choosing **Run As | JUnit Test**. We can verify in the JUnit view as the test case should run successfully, as shown here:

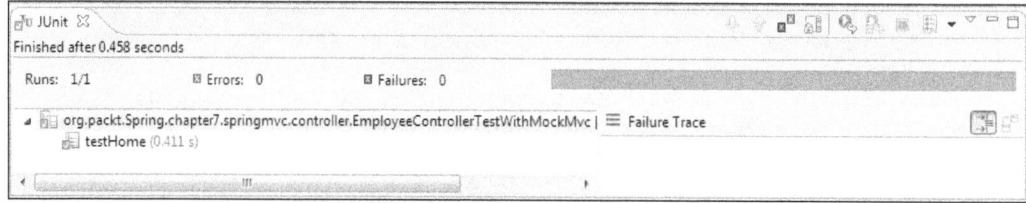

Exercise

Q1. What is the difference between JUnit 4 and TestNG?

Q2. What is the difference between unit testing and integration testing?

Q3. Explain the Spring MVC test framework.

Q4. Explain `@ContextConfiguration` and `@WebAppConfiguration`.

Q5. Explain MockMvc and `@RunWith(SpringJUnit4ClassRunner.class)`.

 The answers to these are provided in *Appendix A, Solution to Exercises*.

Summary

In this chapter, you learned about the Spring test. We understood testing using JUnit 4, its annotations, it's assert statements, and demonstrated all this with an example. Then, we moved on to testing using TestNG and its annotations. We also demonstrated this with an example. We understood Agile software testing, which includes unit testing and integration testing. And then, we went through unit testing for the isolated classes and then we went through the Mockito framework for the dependent class. We also looked into integration testing with the help of an example. Then, we created a unit test for the Spring MVC controller using JUnit. And finally, we discussed the topic of the Spring MVC test framework, where we saw the dependencies required to use the Spring MVC test and the annotations provided by them. And then, we looked into MockMvc and their assertion method.

In the next chapter, we will go through the e-mail support in Spring to develop an e-mail application. We will then look at the JavaMail API and the Spring API to write e-mails. You will also learn to develop a simple Spring e-mail application.

8
Integrating JavaMail and JMS with Spring

In this chapter, first, we will go through the e-mail support in Spring to develop an e-mail application. We will then look into the JavaMail API and the Spring API for e-mails. Later in this chapter, you will learn to develop a simple Spring e-mail application.

In an e-mail application, an e-mail composed by a client is sent to a server and then delivered to the destination and then sends back a response to the client. Here, the communication between the client and the server is completely synchronous, which can be enriched by making this communication asynchronous. The Java messaging system is the standard **application programming interface (API)** to perform asynchronous communication.

Secondly, we will cover JMS and what message and messaging is. Then, we will look into the JMS application and its components. We will also cover MOM Service Provider and the configuration of ActiveMQ as Message Queue. Then, we will configure a Spring bean in the Spring configuration file, and using Spring JMS template, we will create a `MessageSender` class and run an application to perform a functionality related to JMS.

The list of the topics covered in this chapter is as follows:

- E-mail support in Spring
- Spring Java Messaging Service

E-mail support in Spring

Electronic mail (e-mail) plays an important role in all day-to-day activities in this era of global networks. Suppose you want to get periodic updates of a particular feature on a website, by just subscribing to that feature, you will start receiving e-mails regarding these updates. E-mails also allow you to send notifications, business orders, or any periodic reports of a producer.

Oracle provides a simple yet powerful API known as a JavaMail API for creating an application with an e-mail support. The JavaMail API provides a set of classes and interfaces for creating an e-mail application. This API is used to programmatically send and receive e-mails, which can be scaled up to work with different protocols associated with the mailing system. Although it is a powerful API, it is very complex, and using the JavaMail API directly in our application is a slightly tedious task as it involves writing a lot of code.

The Spring Framework provides a simplified API and plugging for a full e-mail support, which minimizes the effect of the underlying mailing system specifications. The Spring e-mail support provides an abstract, easy, and implementation-independent API for sending e-mails. In this chapter, we will get an overview on the JavaMail API and learn how to send e-mail using the JavaMail API in Spring.

Introducing the JavaMail API

The JavaMail API provides a protocol-independent and platform-independent framework to provide e-mail support for a Java application. The JavaMail API is a collection of classes and interfaces that comprise an e-mail system. The steps involved in sending a simple e-mail using the JavaMail API are as follows:

1. Connect to an e-mail server by specifying the username and password; let's say for example, if you want to send an e-mail from abc@xyz.com, then you need to connect to the e-mail server of xyz.com.

2. Create a message by specifying the recipient's addresses that can include Cc and Bcc addresses as well.

3. Add attachments to the message if any.

4. Transport the message to the e-mail server.

Sending a simple e-mail requires the use of a number of classes and interfaces that are present in the `javax.mail` and `javax.mail.internet` packages. The important classes and interfaces in the JavaMail API are listed in the following table:

Class/interface	Description
Session	The `javax.mail.Session` is the key class of the JavaMail API. It represents an e-mail session. Typically, we create a `Session` object, set the properties, and send a message.
Message	The `javax.mail.Message` is an abstract class of the JavaMail API that models an e-mail message. It represents the e-mail sent.
Transport	The `javax.mail.Transport` is an abstract class of the JavaMail API that represents the protocol used to send and receive e-mails. The `Transport` object is used for sending an e-mail message.
Authenticator	The `javax.mail.Authenticator` is an abstract class of the JavaMail API that represents an authentication for the e-mail provider.
PasswordAuthentication	The `PasswordAuthentication` holds the username and password by the `Authenticator` object.
MimeMessage	The `javax.mail.internet.MimeMessage` is an abstract class that represents a **Multipurpose Internet Mail Extension (MIME)** message. `MimeMessage` is an e-mail message, which will understand the MIME types and headers.
InternetAddress	The `javax.mail.internet.InternetAddress` represents an Internet e-mail address such as To, Bcc, and Cc.

The JavaMail application uses the JavaMail API to exchange e-mails, as shown in the following figure:

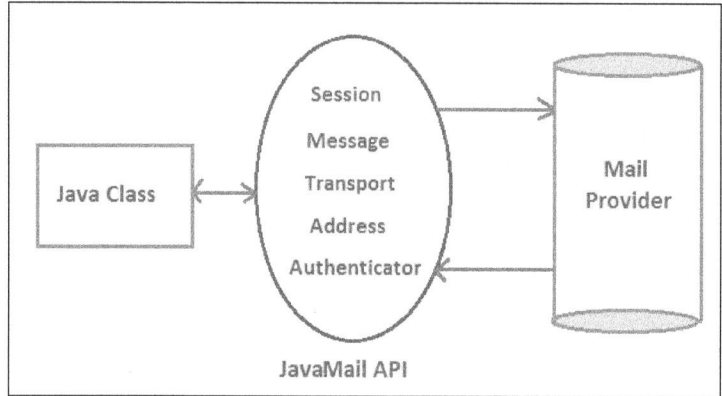

Using the JavaMail API

The JavaMail API can be used to create a class to send an e-mail using the `MailHelper` class. This `MailHelper` class contains a constructor, which can be used to initialize the host, username, and password. This `MailHelper` class also contains the `sendMail()` method.

The following code snippet shows the `MailHelper.java` class:

```
public class MailHelper {

    private Properties props;
    private String host;
    private String userName;
    private String password;

    public MailHelper(String host, String username, String
password){
            this.userName = username;
            this.password = password;
            props = new Properties();
            // put host information
            props.put("mail.stmp.host", host);
            // put true for authentication mechanism
```

```
            props.put("mail.smtp.auth", "true");
    }


    public void sendMail(String from, String to, String subject,
String body){
            Session session = Session.getDefaultInstance(props, new
PasswordAuthenticator());
            try{
                Message message = new MimeMessage(session);
                message.setFrom(new InternetAddress(from));
                InternetAddress toAddress = new
InternetAddress(to);
                message.addRecipient(RecipientType.TO, toAddress);
                message.setSub(subject);
                message.setText(body);
                Transport transport =
session.getTransport("smtp");
                transport.connect();
                transport.sendMessage(message,
message.getAllRecipients());
                transport.close();
            } catch(NoSuchProviderException ex){
                ex.printStackTrace();
            } catch(MessagingException ex){
                ex.printStackTrace();
            }
    }


    private class PasswordAuthenticator extend Authenticator{
            protected PasswordAuthentication
getPasswordAuthentication(){
                return new PasswordAuthentication(userName,
password);
            }
    }
}
```

In the preceding code snippet, the `MailHelper` class has instance variables and a constructor. The `props` variable, of the `Properties` collection type, used to specify the common properties to connect to the e-mail provider host.

Simple Mail Transfer Protocol (SMTP) is a protocol that is used to send e-mails. The SMTP server performs this job. The `props.put("mail.stmp.host", host)` code inside the constructor is used to specify the host information, where we connect to the SMTP server of our host. The `props.put("mail.smtp.auth", "true")` code inside the constructor specifies the use of an authentication mechanism to connect to the SMTP server.

The `sendMail` method of the `MailHelper` class creates a `Session` object using the host information and the username-password credentials. The `from-address` and the `to-address` are added to the instance of the `MimeMessage` class. The subject and the body of the e-mail are also added to this `MimeMessage` object. Finally, the message is sent using an instance of the `Transport` class.

The `PasswordAuthenticator` class is an inner class that has been used by a `Session` object to hold the username and the password.

From the preceding code, the following problems can be encountered:

- Lots of initialization and creation work involved in sending a simple e-mail
- Exceptions need to be taken care of while using the JavaMail API; this results in some extra lines of code
- Some extra classes are needed if required to perform the attachment operation while sending an e-mail using the JavaMail API
- A solution to the preceding problem is provided by the Spring Framework that simplifies the use of the JavaMail API to send e-mails

Let's understand the use of the Spring API for the JavaMail API and rewrite the `MailHelper` class.

The Spring API for JavaMail

The Spring Framework provides an API to simplify the use of the JavaMail API. The classes handle the initialization, clean-up operations, and exceptions. The packages for the JavaMail API provided by the Spring Framework are listed in the following table:

Package	Description
`org.springframework.mail`	This defines the basic set of classes and interfaces for sending e-mails
`org.springframework.mail.java`	This defines JavaMail API-specific classes and interfaces for sending e-mails

In the Spring mail API hierarchy, the `org.springframework.mail` package is the root-level package for the Spring Framework's e-mail support, as shown here:

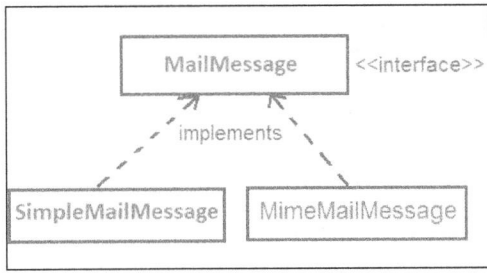

The important classes and interfaces in the `org.springframework.mail` package are listed in the following table:

Class/interface	Description
MailMessage	Refers to a common interface for all types of messages that can be sent. It doesn't support complex MIME messages. It is used for sending simple plain-text e-mails.
MailSender	Refers to an interface that defines methods for sending simple e-mails. It supports only the plain-text e-mails.
MailException	Refers to a base class for all the exceptions thrown by the mailing system.
SimpleMailMessage	Refers to the class that defines the representation of a simple message that can be sent.

The important classes and interfaces in the `org.springframework.mail.java` package are listed in the following table:

Class/interface	Description
JavaMailSenderImpl	Refers to the implementation of the JavaMailSender interface. It is a core class that is used to send simple as well as MIME messages. It extends the MailSender interface and provides the methods for constructing and sending a MIME message.
MimeMailMessage	Implements the MailMessage interface. It is based on the JavaMail MIME message.
MimeMessageHelper	Acts as a wrapper for a MIME message. It is used to populate a MIME message and is used by the JavaMailSenderImpl class.

The Java application can use Spring to access the JavaMail API for sending e-mails, as shown in the following figure:

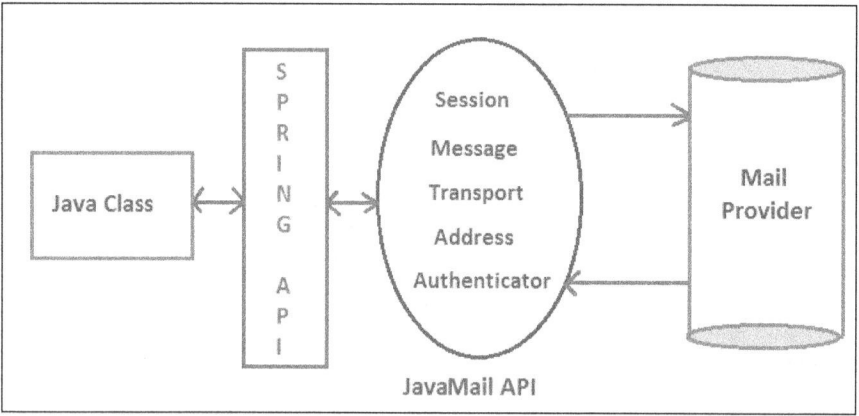

In the preceding figure, the Java classes use the Spring API, which indirectly uses the JavaMail API to send e-mails.

Developing a Spring Mail Application

Let's create a JavaMail API with the Spring application for sending e-mails via the Gmail SMTP server using the Spring mail API. Here, we develop a basic e-mail application that creates simple e-mails containing text only.

Configuration file – Spring.xml

Let's now create the configuration file, `Spring.xml`, and configure the `mailSender` bean of the `JavaMailSenderImpl` class and define its properties:

- `host`
- `port`
- `username`
- `password`

Also, configure the bean for the `EmailService` class with the `mailSender` property:

```
<!-- SET default mail properties -->
<bean id="mailSender" class="org.springframework.mail.javamail.
JavaMailSenderImpl">
    <property name="host" value="smtp.gmail.com" />
    <property name="port" value="25" />
```

```
        <property name="username" value="username" />
        <property name="password" value="password" />

        <property name="javaMailProperties">
            <props>
                    <prop key="mail.smtp.auth">true</prop>
                    <prop key="mail.smtp.starttls.enable">true</prop>
                </props>
        </property>
    </bean>

    <bean id="emailService" class="org.packt.Spring.chapter10.mail">
        <property name="mailSender" ref="mailSender" />
    </bean>
```

The preceding configuration file sets the host as `"smtp.gmail.com"` and the port as `"25."` The `username` and the `password` properties need to be set with reader's username and password of their Gmail account. The username is used as the sender of the e-mail.

Spring's e-mail sender

It is the e-mail API-specific Java file. It provides the definition of the `sendEmail()` method, which is used to send the actual e-mail to the recipient:

```java
package org.packt.Spring.chapter10.mail;

import org.springframework.mail.MailSender;
import org.springframework.mail.SimpleMailMessage;

public class EmailService
{

    @Autowired
    private MailSender mailSender;

    public void sendEmail(String to, String subject, String msg) {

            // creates a simple e-mail object
            SimpleMailMessage email = new SimpleMailMessage();

            email.setTo(to);
            email.setSubject(subject);
            email.setText(msg);
```

```
            // sends the e-mail
            mailSender.send(email);
    }
}
```

Here, we have autowired `MailSender` and called the `send()` method that will send the e-mails.

The MailerTest class

The `MailerTest` class has the `main()` method that will call the `sendEmail()` method of the `EmailService` class and send an e-mail:

```java
package org.packt.Spring.chapter10.mail;

import org.springframework.context.ApplicationContext;
import org.springframework.context.support.ClassPathXml
ApplicationContext;

public class MailerTest
{
    public static void main( String[] args )
    {
        //Create the application context
        ApplicationContext context =
            new ClassPathXmlApplicationContext("Spring.xml");

      //Get the mailer instance
       EmailService emailService =
(EmailService)context.getBean("emailService ");

        //Send a composed mail
        emailService.sendEmail("****@gmail.com",
                  "Email Test Subject",
                  "Email Testing body");

    }
}
```

The output of this application can be confirmed by opening the inbox.

We have developed an application using Spring e-mails. Let's now understand the Spring Java Messaging Service.

Spring Java Messaging Service

In this section, first, we will go through the basics of Java Messaging Service and will see the differences between JMS and e-mail. Then, we will look into the JMS application and its different components that create the complete JMS application. We will also look through other things such as the JMS provider and the messaging model. We will dig into the API programming model. Then, we will see the messaging consumption types. Then, we will jump into the Spring JMS integration and we will see some code samples. And then, we will look into the details of the code content.

Let's now discuss the message and messaging.

What is a message and messaging?

A message is nothing but just bytes of data or information exchanged between two parties. By taking different specifications, a message can be described in various ways. However, it is nothing but an entity of communication. A message can be used to transfer a piece of information from one application to another application, which may or may not run in the same platform.

Messaging is the communication between different applications (in a distributed environment) or system components, which are loosely coupled unlike its peers such as TCP sockets, **Remote Method Invocation (RMI)**, or CORBA, which is tightly coupled. The advantage of Java messaging includes the ability to integrate different platforms, increase the scalability and reliability of message delivery, and reduce the system bottlenecks. Using messaging, we can increase the systems and clients who are consuming and producing the message as much as we want.

We have quite a lot of ways in which we communicate right from the instance messenger, to the stock taker, to the mobile-based messaging, to the age-old messaging system; they are all part of messaging. We understand that a message is a piece of data transferred from one system to another and it can be between humans as well, but it is mainly between systems rather than human beings when we talk about the messaging using JMS.

What is JMS?

The **Java Message Service (JMS)** is a **Java Message Oriented Middleware (MOM)** API for sending messages between two or more clients. JMS is a part of the Java Enterprise edition. JMS is a broker like a postman who acts like a mediator between the message sender and receiver.

JMS is a specification that describes a common way for Java programs to create, send, and read distributed enterprise messages. It advocates the loosely coupled communication without caring about the sender and the receiver. It provides asynchronous messaging, which means that it doesn't matter whether the sender and the receiver are present at the same time or not. The two systems that are sending or receiving messages need not be up at the same time.

The JMS application

Let's look into the sample JMS application pictorial as shown in the following figure:

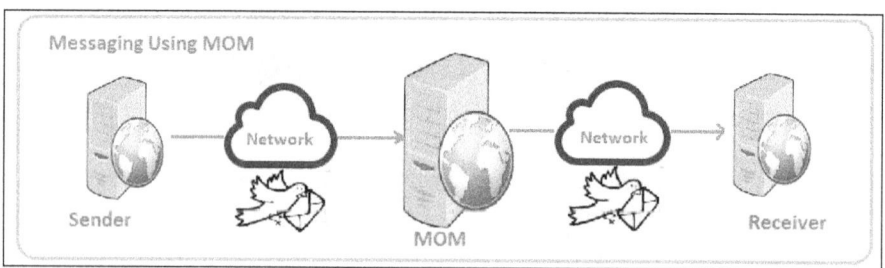

We have a **Sender** and a **Receiver**. The **Sender** sends a message while the **Receiver** receives one. We need a broker that is **MOM** between the **Sender** and the **Receiver** who takes the sender's message and passes it to the network to the receiver. **MOM** is basically an MQ application such as ActiveMQ or IBM-MQ, which are two different message providers. The **Sender** promises the loose coupling and it can be a .NET or mainframe-based application. The **Receiver** can be a Java or Spring-based application, and it sends back the message to the **Sender** as well. This is a two-way communication that is loosely coupled.

JMS components

Let's move on the JMS components listed in the following table:

Component	Description
JMS provider	The JMS provider is the messaging system (that is, MOM) and acts as a message broker or agent as like a post office or postman. It implements JMS in addition to other administrative and control functionalities required of a full-featured messaging product (Active MQ or IBM MQ). It is an agent or message broker that takes the messages and sends them across. It is like a post office or postman that takes your e-mail and delivers it to the recipient.

Component	Description
JMS client	The JMS client is a Java application that receives or produces messages. The JMS client is a Java application. It is the one who is producing or receiving the messages. Let's say that you are sending a postcard to your friend; then, you and your friend are the JMS client.
JMS producer/publisher	The JMS producer and publisher are two types of JMS client that creates and sends messages.
JMS consumer/subscriber	The JMS consumer and subscriber are two types of JMS clients that receive messages.
JMS application	The JMS application is the system composed of typically one JMS provider and many JMS clients.

Here is the pictorial representation:

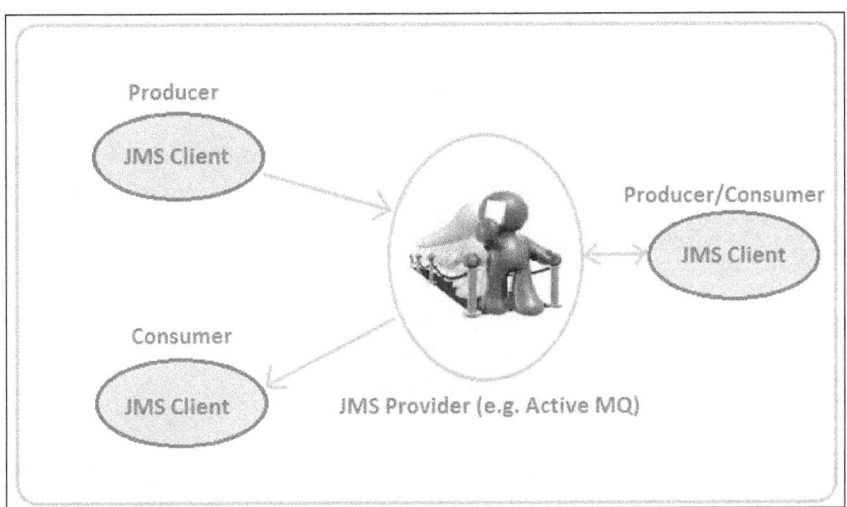

There are three JMS clients in the preceding figure. The **Producer** can be assumed as it's you who is going to send a message to your friend. The **Consumer** can be assumed to be your friend who will receive a message. The **Producer/Consumer** could be someone else who will receive as well as send a message. The **JMS Provider** can be assumed as the post office or postman via which the whole delivery things happen and which guarantee that the sure delivery happens only once.

MOM Service Provider

There are various MOM Service Provider products; some of them are listed in the following table:

Product	Company
WebLogic	Oracle
MQ Series	IBM
JBOSSMQ	JBOSS
SoniqMQ	Progress
ActiveMQ	Apache

We will mainly look into the ActiveMQ message queue. The Active MQ is from Apache, and it's free.

Configuring ActiveMQ – message queue

We need to follow the given steps to configure ActiveMQ to our system:

1. While configuring ActiveMQ to our system, we need to download the ZIP distribution from the official link `http://activemq.apache.org/download.html`, as shown in the following screenshot:

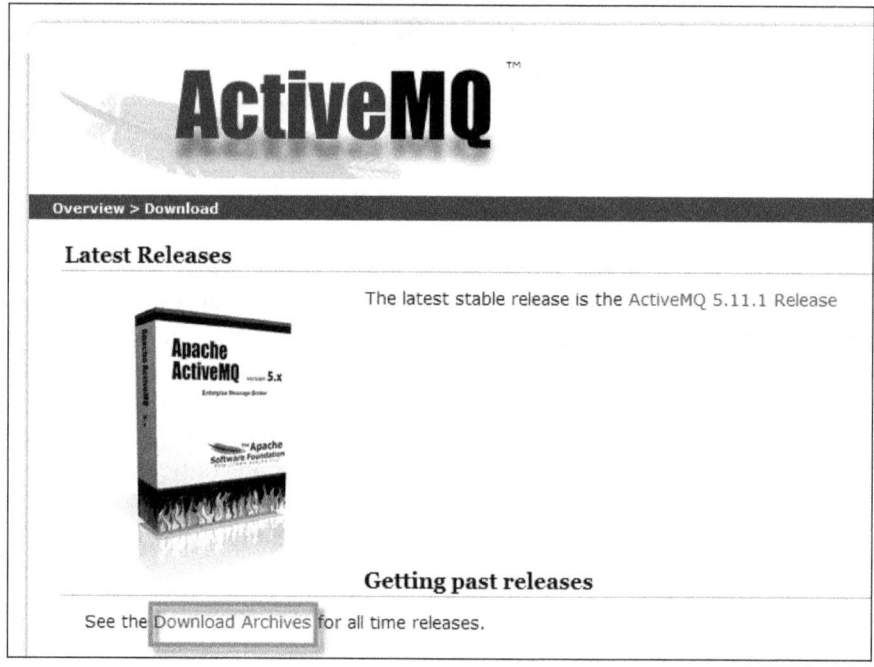

2. Then, extract the ZIP distribution to a folder.

3. Navigate to the `activemq-5.10.0\bin` folder, inside which you will find the following folders:

   ° `activemq-5.10.0\bin for 64 bit`

   ° `activemq-5.10.0\bin for 32 bit`

These folders can be seen in the following screenshot:

Name	Date modified	Type	Size
win32	2/25/2015 4:54 PM	File folder	
win64	2/25/2015 4:54 PM	File folder	
activemq	6/5/2014 3:35 PM	File	22 KB
activemq.bat	6/5/2014 3:35 PM	Windows Batch File	5 KB
activemq.jar	6/5/2014 3:17 PM	Executable Jar File	16 KB
activemq-admin	6/5/2014 3:35 PM	File	6 KB
activemq-admin.bat	6/5/2014 3:35 PM	Windows Batch File	5 KB
wrapper.jar	6/5/2014 2:48 PM	Executable Jar File	82 KB

4. Navigate to the `win32` or `win64` folder based on your machine, and open Command Prompt at this location and then run `activemq`, as shown here:

```
rsoni\Desktop\ravi-book\apache-activemq-5.10.0\bin\win64\..\..\data\kahadb]
jvm 1    | INFO | Apache ActiveMQ 5.10.0 (localhost, ID:HCLWRAVISO01-56084-1424
863503840-0:1) is starting
jvm 1    | INFO | Listening for connections at: tcp://HCLWRAVISO01:61616?maximu
mConnections=1000&wireFormat.maxFrameSize=104857600
jvm 1    | INFO | Connector openwire started
jvm 1    | INFO | Listening for connections at: amqp://HCLWRAVISO01:5672?maximu
mConnections=1000&wireFormat.maxFrameSize=104857600
jvm 1    | INFO | Connector amqp started
jvm 1    | INFO | Listening for connections at: stomp://HCLWRAVISO01:61613?maxi
mumConnections=1000&wireFormat.maxFrameSize=104857600
jvm 1    | INFO | Connector stomp started
jvm 1    | INFO | Listening for connections at: mqtt://HCLWRAVISO01:1883?maximu
mConnections=1000&wireFormat.maxFrameSize=104857600
jvm 1    | INFO | Connector mqtt started
jvm 1    | INFO | Listening for connections at ws://HCLWRAVISO01:61614?maximumC
onnections=1000&wireFormat.maxFrameSize=104857600
jvm 1    | INFO | Connector ws started
jvm 1    | INFO | Apache ActiveMQ 5.10.0 (localhost, ID:HCLWRAVISO01-56084-1424
863503840-0:1) started
jvm 1    | INFO | For help or more information please see: http://activemq.apac
he.org
jvm 1    | INFO | ActiveMQ WebConsole available at http://0.0.0.0:8161/
jvm 1    | INFO | Initializing Spring FrameworkServlet 'dispatcher'
jvm 1    | INFO | jolokia-agent: No access restrictor found at classpath:/jolok
ia-access.xml, access to all MBeans is allowed
```

We can see in the preceding screenshot, that `activemq` is run and has provided some information on the console. This MQ can be listed at `tcp://localhost:61616` URL. The admin page URL `http://localhost:8161/admin` provides access to the admin page (username: `admin`, password: `admin`):

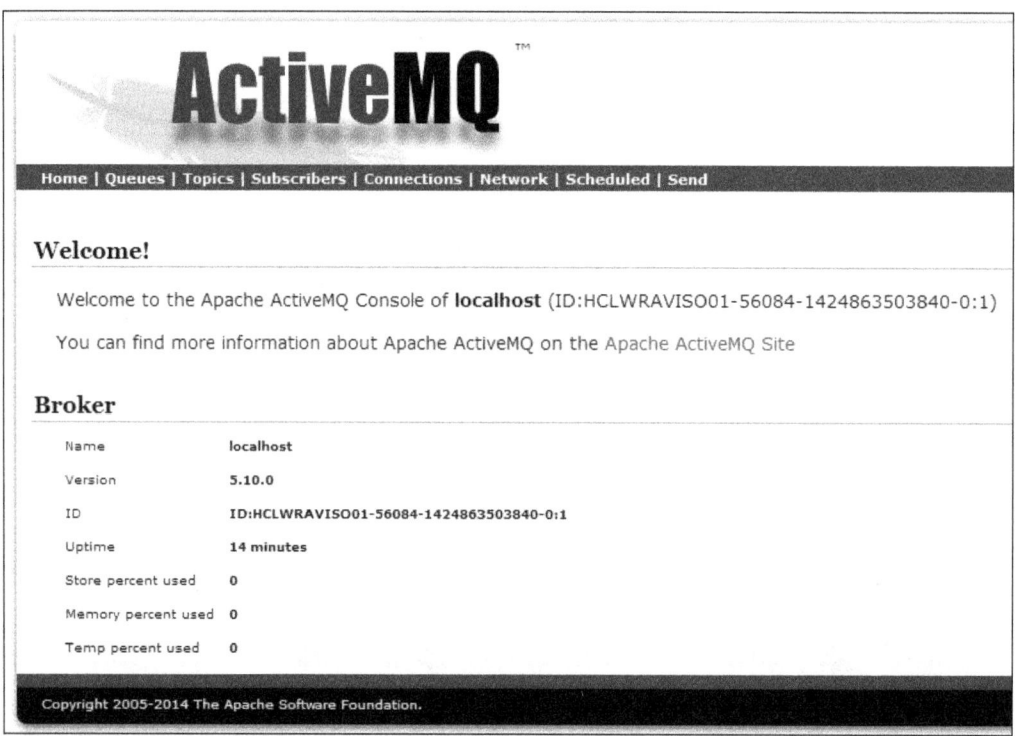

The Spring bean configuration (Spring.xml)

Create the configuration file `Spring.xml` and define the respective bean definitions such as ActiveMQ ConnectionFactory, ActiveMQ queue destination, and JMS template as follows:

```xml
<?xml version="1.0" encoding="UTF-8"?>
<beans xmlns="http://www.springframework.org/schema/beans"
    xmlns:xsi="http://www.w3.org/2001/XMLSchema-instance"
xmlns:context="http://www.springframework.org/schema/context"
    xmlns:jms="http://www.springframework.org/schema/jms"
    xsi:schemaLocation="http://www.springframework.org/schema/beans
                        http://www.springframework.org/schema/
beans/spring-beans.xsd
```

```
                              http://www.springframework.org/schema/
context
                              http://www.springframework.org/schema/
context/spring-context.xsd
                              http://www.springframework.org/schema/jms
                              http://www.springframework.org/schema/jms/
spring-jms.xsd
                              http://activemq.apache.org/schema/core
                              http://activemq.apache.org/schema/core/
activemq-core.xsd">

    <context:component-scan base-package="org.packt.Spring.chapter10.
JMS" />

    <bean id="jmsTemplate"
class="org.springframework.jms.core.JmsTemplate">
          <property name="connectionFactory"
ref="connectionFactory" />
          <property name="defaultDestination" ref="destination" />
    </bean>

    <bean id="connectionFactory" class="org.apache.activemq.
ActiveMQConnectionFactory">
          <property name="brokerURL">
                <value>tcp://localhost:61616</value>
          </property>
    </bean>

    <bean id="destination"
class="org.apache.activemq.command.ActiveMQQueue">
          <constructor-arg value="myMessageQueue" />
    </bean>

</beans>
```

The Spring Framework supports JMS with the help of the following classes:

- `ActiveMQConnectionFactory`: This will create a JMS ConnectionFactory for ActiveMQ that connects to a remote broker on a specific host name and port

- `ActiveMQQueue`: This will configure the ActiveMQ queue name as in our case `myMessageQueue`

- `JmsTemplate`: This is a handy abstraction supported by Spring, and it allows us to hide some of the lower-level JMS details while sending a message

MessageSender.java – Spring JMS Template

The MessageSender class is responsible for sending a message to the JMS queue:

```
package org.packt.Spring.chapter10.JMS.Message;

import org.springframework.beans.factory.annotation.Autowired;
import org.springframework.jms.core.JmsTemplate;
import org.springframework.stereotype.Component;

@Component
public class MessageSender {

    @Autowired
    private JmsTemplate jmsTemplate;

    public void send(final Object Object) {
            jmsTemplate.convertAndSend(Object);
    }
}
```

App.java

The App class contains the main method, which calls the send() method to send a message, as shown in the following code snippet:

```
package org.packt.Spring.chapter10.JMS.Main;

import java.util.HashMap;
import java.util.Map;

import org.packt.Spring.chapter10.JMS.Message.MessageSender;
import org.springframework.context.ApplicationContext;
import org.springframework.context.support.
ClassPathXmlApplicationContext
;

public class App {
```

```
    public static void main(String[] args) {

            ApplicationContext context = new
ClassPathXmlApplicationContext(
                        "Spring.xml");

            MessageSender messageSender = (MessageSender) context
                        .getBean("messageSender");

            Map<String, String> message = new HashMap<String,
String>();
            message.put("Hello", "World");
            message.put("city", "Sasaram");
            message.put("state", "Bihar");
            message.put("country", "India");

            messageSender.send(message);

            System.out.println("Message Sent to JMS Queue: " +
message);
    }
}
```

Start ActiveMQ

Before you run App.java, you need to start ActiveMQ, which allows us to run a broker; it will run ActiveMQ Broker using the out-of-the-box configuration.

Output

Run App.java and get the output on the console as follows:

```
Message Sent to JMS Queue: {state=Bihar, Hello=World,
country=India, city=Sasaram}
```

Monitoring the broker

We can monitor ActiveMQ Broker using the web console by pointing the browser to `http://localhost:8161/admin`. Once `app.java` gets executed, a message will be sent to the JMS queue, as shown in the following screenshot:

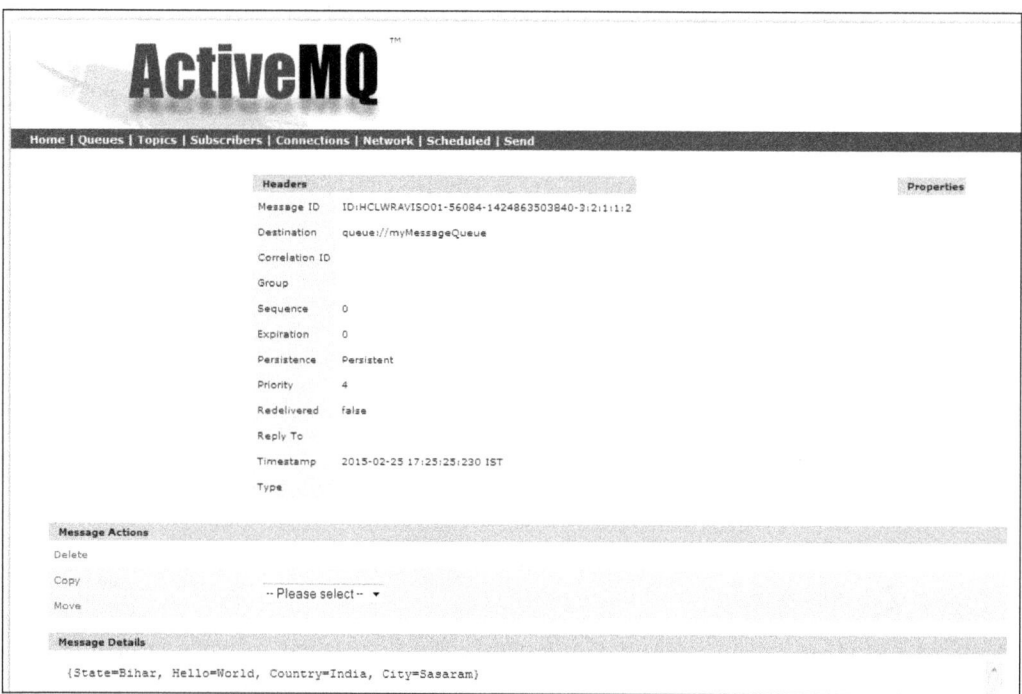

Exception on running App.java

There are chances of getting the error `Could not connect to broker URL exception: tcp://localhost:61616. Reason: Java.net.ConnectException: Connection refused: connect`. This exception will come if the message broker service is not up, so make sure that ActiveMQ is running, as shown here:

```
Exception in thread "main"
org.springframework.jms.UncategorizedJmsException: Uncategorized
exception occurred during JMS processing; nested exception is
javax.jms.JMSException: Could not connect to broker URL:
tcp://localhost:61616. Reason: java.net.ConnectException:
Connection refused: connect
    at
org.springframework.jms.support.JmsUtils.convertJmsAccessException
(JmsUtils.java:316)
```

Exercise

Q1. What is a JavaMail API?

Q2. What is message and messaging?

Q3. What is JMS?

 The answers to these are provided in *Appendix A, Solution to Exercises*.

Summary

In this chapter, we discussed the e-mail support in Spring and JMS in Spring. We took a look at the JavaMail API and Spring API for JavaMail. Then, we developed a Spring Mail Application. We discussed Spring Java Message Service and understood message, messaging, and JMS components. We took a look at the MOM Service Provider and configured ActiveMQ. We also developed an application to perform messaging using a Spring JMS Template. Then, we discussed the exception on running the application.

In the next chapter, we will go through the solutions of all the exercises given thus far.

Online chapters

Chapter 9, Inversion of Control in Spring – Using Annotation, configures Spring beans and Dependency Injection using annotation. It covers annotation-based Dependency Injection and life cycle annotation. It explains how to reference beans using Spring Expression Language (SpEL), invoke methods using SpEL, and work with operators in SpEL. It also covers the text messages and internationalization provided by Spring, which we will learn to implement in our application. This is an online chapter available at `https://www.packtpub.com/sites/default/files/downloads/7368OS_Chapter9.pdf`.

Chapter 10, Aspect-oriented Programming with Spring, introduces you to aspect-oriented programming. It shows you how and where to apply your aspects in your application using Spring's powerful pointcut mechanism and discusses proxies in the Spring AOP. This is an online chapter available at `https://www.packtpub.com/sites/default/files/downloads/7368OS_Chapter10.pdf`.

Appendix C, Spring Form Tag Library, shows the Spring form tag library provided by the Spring Web MVC framework. The Spring form tag library is a set of tags in the form of a tag library, which is used to construct views (web pages). This is an online appendix available at `https://www.packtpub.com/sites/default/files/downloads/7368OS_AppendixC.pdf`.

A

Solutions to Exercises

Chapter 1, Introducing the Spring Framework

Q1. What is Spring?

Spring is an open-source framework created by Rod Johnson. He addressed the complexity of enterprise application development, and described a simpler, alternative approach in his book *Expert One-on-One J2EE Design and Development*, *Wrox*. Spring is a lightweight inversion of control and aspect-oriented container framework. Any Java EE application can benefit from the Spring Framework, in terms of simplicity, loose coupling, and testability.

Spring is modular, allowing you to use only those parts that you need without having to bring in extra complexity. The Spring Framework can be used either for all layer implementations or for the development of particular layer of an application.

Q2. List some of the features of Spring?

The Spring Framework contains following features:

- **Lightweight**: Spring is described as a lightweight framework when it comes to size and transparency.

- **Non-intrusive**: Non-intrusive means that your domain logic code has no dependencies on the framework itself. The Spring Framework is designed to be non-intrusive.

- **Container**: Spring's container is a light-weight container that contains and manages the life cycle and configuration of application objects.

- **Inversion of Control**: IoC is an architectural pattern that describes the Dependency Injection that needs to be done by an external entity, rather than creating the dependencies by the component itself.

- **Aspect-oriented programming**: AOP refers to the programming paradigm that isolates supporting functions from the main program's business logic.

- **JDBC exception handling**: The JDBC abstraction layer of the Spring Framework provides an exception hierarchy.

- **Spring Web MVC framework**: This helps in building robust and maintainable web applications. The Spring Web MVC framework also offers utility classes to handle some of the most common tasks in the web application development.

- **Spring Security**: This provides a declarative security mechanism for Spring-based applications, which is a critical aspect of many applications.

Q3. Explain different modules in the Spring Framework.

The Spring Framework contains following modules:

- Spring Core Module
- Spring AOP Module
- Spring DAO(JDBC) Module
- Spring ORM Module
- Spring Web Module
- Spring Test Module

Chapter 2, Inversion of Control in Spring

Q1. What are Inversion of Control (IoC) and Dependency Injection (DI)?

IoC is a more general concept, and DI is a concrete design pattern. In software engineering, IoC is a programming technique where the assembler object compels object coupling at runtime using static analysis. DI reduces the coupling between objects. DI is a design pattern on which the dependency of object is injected by the framework, rather than created by the object itself.

IoC makes your code more portable, more testable, and more manageable and keeps component configuration, dependencies, and life cycle events outside of the components.

Q2. What are the different types of Dependency Injection in Spring?

In the Spring Framework, DI is used to satisfy the dependencies between objects. It exits in two major types:

- **Constructor Injection**: Constructor-based DI can be accomplished by invoking parameterized constructor. These constructor arguments will be injected during the instantiation of the instance.

- **Setter Injection**: Setter-based DI is the preferred method of Dependency Injection in Spring that can be accomplished by calling setter methods on your bean after invoking a no-argument static factory method or no-argument constructor to instantiate this bean.

Q3. Explain autowiring in Spring. What are the different modes of autowiring.

A Spring container can use five modes of autowiring as follows:

- no: By default, Spring bean autowiring is turned off which means that no autowiring is to be performed, and you should use explicit bean reference ref for wiring.

- byName: This property name is used for this type of autowiring. If the bean property is same as other bean name, autowire it. The setter method is used for this type of autowiring to inject dependency.

- byType: This data type is used for this type of autowiring. If the data type bean property is compatible with data type of other bean, autowire it. For this type, only one bean should be configured in configuration file else a fatal exception will be thrown.

- constructor: This is similar to autowire byType, but here constructor is used for injecting dependency.

- autodetect: Autowiring by autodetect in Spring is deprecated, and it first tries to autowire by constructor, and if it does not work, then autowire by type.

Q4. Explain different Spring bean scope.

The following list gives the Spring bean scope:

- **Singleton**: Singleton in Spring represents in a particular Spring Container and there is only one instance of bean created in that container that is used across different references.

- **Prototype**: This is a new bean created with every request or reference. For every getBean() call, Spring has to do initialization so instead of doing default initialization while a context is being created, it waits for getBean() call.

- **Request**: A new bean is created per Servlet request. Spring will be aware of when a new request is happening because it ties well with Servlet APIs and depending on request, Spring creates a new bean.

- **Session**: A new bean is created per session. As long as there is one user accessing in a single session, on each call to getBean() will return same instance of bean.

- **Global-session**: This is applicable in portlet context. There will be a global session in an individual portlet session, and a bean can be tied with global session. Here, a new bean is created per global HTTP session.

Chapter 3, DAO and JDBC in Spring

Q1. Explain Spring JDBC packages.

To handle different aspects of JDBC, Spring JDBC is divided into packages, as shown in following table:

Spring JDBC packages	Description
org.springframework.jdbc.core	In the Spring Framework, this package contains the foundations of JDBC classes, which includes Core JDBC Class and JdbcTemplate. It simplifies the database operation using JDBC.
org.springframework.jdbc.datasource	This package contains DataSource implementations and helper classes, which can be used to run the JDBC code outside JEE container.
org.springframework.jdbc.object	In the Spring Framework, this package contains classes that helps in converting the data returned from the database into plain java objects.
org.springframework.jdbc.support	SQLExceptionTranslator is the most important class in this package of the Spring Framework. Spring recognizes the error code used by database using this class, and map error code to higher-level exception.
org.springframework.jdbc.config	This package contains classes that supports JDBC configuration within ApplicationContext of the Spring Framework.

Q2. What is `JdbcTemplate`?

The `JdbcTemplate` class instances are thread-safe once configured. A single `JdbcTemplate` can be configured and injected in multiple DAOs. We can use `JdbcTemplate` to execute different types of SQL statements. **Data Manipulation Language (DML)** is used to insert, retrieve, update, and delete data in database. The `SELECT`, `INSERT`, or `UPDATE` statements are examples of DML. **Data Definition Language (DDL)** is used to either create or modify the structure of database objects in database. The `CREATE`, `ALTER`, and `DROP` statements are examples of DDL.

Q3. Explain the JDBC operation in Spring.

The single executable unit for performing multiple operations is known as a batch. The batch update operation allows submitting multiple of SQL queries `DataSource` for processing at once. Submitting multiple SQL queries together, instead of individually improves the performance. The `JdbcTemplate` includes a support for executing the batch of statements through a JDBC Statement and PreparedStatement. The `JdbcTemplate` includes two overloaded `batchUpdate()` methods in support of this feature:

- One for executing a batch of SQL statements using JDBC Statement like:

  ```
  public int[] batchUpdate(String[] sql) throws
  DataAccessException
  ```

- The other for executing the SQL Statement for multiple times with different parameters using `PreparedStatement` such as:

  ```
  public int[] batchUpdate(String sql,
  BatchPreparedStatementSetter bPSS) throws
  DataAccessException
  ```

Chapter 4, Hibernate with Spring
Q1. What is ORM?

ORM is the process of persisting objects in a relational database such as RDBMS. ORM bridges the gap between object and relational schemas, allowing object-oriented application to persist objects directly without having the need for converting object to and from a relational format.

ORM is about mapping object representations to JDBC Statement parameters, and in turn mapping JDBC query results back to object representations. The database columns are mapped to instance fields of domain objects or JavaBeans' properties.

Q2. Explain the basics elements of Hibernate architecture.

The basics elements of Hibernate architecture are described in the following sections:

- `Configuration`: The `org.hibernate.cfg.Configuration` class is the basic element of the Hibernate API that allows us to build `SessionFactory`. Configuration can be referred as factory class that can produce `SessionFactory`.

- `SessionFactory`: The `SessionFactory` is created during the startup of the application, and is kept for later use in the application. The `org.hibernate.SessionFactory` interface serves as factory, provides an abstraction to obtain the Hibernate session object. The `SessionFactory` initialization process includes various operations that consume huge resource and extra time, so it is recommended to use single `SessionFactory` per JVM instance.

- `Session`: The `org.hibernate.Session` is an interface between Hibernate system and the application. It is used to get the connection with a database. It is light weight, and is initiated each time an interaction is needed with the database. After we complete the use of `Session`, it has to be closed to release all the resources, such as cached entity objects and JDBC connection.

- `Transaction`: Transactional interface is an optional interface that represents a unit of work with the database, and supported by most of RDBMS. In Hibernate, `Transaction` is handled by the underlying transaction manager.

- `Query`: The `org.hibernate.Query` interface provides an abstraction to execute the Hibernate query and to retrieve the results. The `Query` object represents Hibernate query built using Hibernate Query Language.

- `Criteria`: The `org.hibernate.Criteria` is an interface for using Criterion API and is used to create and execute object oriented criteria queries, alternative to HQL or SQL.

- `Persistent`: These classes are the entity classes in an application. Persistent objects are objects that are managed to be in persistent state. Persistent objects are associated with exactly one `org.hibernate.Session`. Once the `org.hibernate.Session` is closed, these objects will be detached and will be free to use in any layer of application.

Q3. What is HQL?

Hibernate Query Language (HQL) is an object-oriented query language that works on the `Persistence` object and their properties, instead of operating on tables and columns. Hibernate will translate the HQL queries into conventional SQL queries during the interaction of database. In HQL, the keywords such as SELECT, FROM, WHERE, and GROUP BY, and so on is not case sensitive.

Chapter 5, Spring Web MVC Framework

Q1. What is Spring Web MVC framework?

The Spring Web **Model View Controller (MVC)** framework is flexible, robust, and well-designed and is used for developing web applications. It is designed in such a way that development of a web application is highly configurable into model, view, and controller. The Spring Web MVC framework is implemented using Java technologies such as Java, Servlet, and JSP, which allows us to host Spring MVC project on any Java enterprise web server just by including Spring JARS into `lib` of web application/project.

The Spring MVC module in the Spring Framework, provides comprehensive support for the MVC design support, with support for features such as i18n, theming, validation, and so on, to ease the implementation of the presentation layer. The Spring MVC framework is designed around a `DispatcherServlet`. The `DispatcherServlet` dispatches the HTTP request to handler which is a very simple controller interface.

Q2. What is `DispatcherServlet` in Spring MVC framework?

The `DispatcherServlet` of Spring MVC framework is an implementation of Front Controller and is a Java Servlet component for Spring MVC applications. `DispatcherServlet` of Spring MVC framework is a front controller class that receives all incoming HTTP client request for the Spring MVC application. It is also responsible for initializing the framework components which will be used to process the request at various stages.

The `DispatcherServlet` is fully configured with the IoC container that allows us to use various Spring features such as Spring context, Spring **Object Relational Mapping (ORM)**, Spring **Data Access Object (DAO)**, and so on. `DispatcherServlet` is a Servlet that handles HTTP request and is inherited from `HTTPServlet` base class. A Spring MVC application can have any number of `DispatcherServlet`, and each `DispatcherServlet` will have its own `WebApplicationContext`.

Q3. What is controller in Spring MVC?

`DispatcherServlet` delegates the incoming HTTP client request to the controllers to execute the functionality specific to it. Controller interprets the user input and transforms this input into a specific model, which will be represented by the view to the user. The `@Controller` annotation is used to define a class as controller class without inheriting any interface or class.

Q4. What is `ViewResolver` in Spring MVC?

The controller class handler methods return different values that denote the logical view names. The views can represent **Java Server Pages (JSP)**, FreeMarker, **Portable Document Format (PDF)**, Excel, and **Extensible Stylesheet Language (XSL)** pages. The control will be delegated to view template from `DispatcherServlet`. The view name returned by the method is resolved to the actual physical source by the view resolver beans declared in the context of web application. Spring provides a number of view resolver classes that are configured in the `.xml` files. The `ViewResolver` interface maps the view names with the implementations of the `org.springframework.web.servlet.ViewResolver` interface.

Chapter 6, Spring Security

Q1. What is Spring Security?

The Spring Security framework is the de-facto standards for securing Spring-based applications. Spring Security framework provides security services for enterprise Java software application by handling authentication and authorization. Spring Security handles authentication and authorization at both; the web request level and at method invocation level. Spring Security is a highly customizable and powerful authentication and can access control framework.

Q2. What is authentication and authorization?

Authentication is the process of assuring that a user is the one what user claim to be. Authentication is a combination of identification and verification. The identification can be performed in a number of different ways; for example, as username and password, which can be stored in a database, or LDAP, or CAS (single sign-on protocol) and so on.

Authorization provides access control to the authenticated user. Authorization is the process of ensuring that the authenticated user is allowed to access only those resources which he/she is authorized to use.

Q3. What are the different ways supported by Spring Security for users to log into a web application?

There are multiple ways to be supported by Spring Security for users to log into a web application as follows:

- **HTTP basic authentication**: HTTP basic authentication is supported by Spring Security by processing the basic credentials presented in the header of HTTP request. HTTP basic authentication is generally used with stateless clients who on each request pass their credential.

- **Form-based login Service**: Spring Security supports form-based login service, by providing default login form page for users, to log into the web application.

- **Anonymous login**: An anonymous login service is provided by Spring Security that grants authorities to an anonymous user like the normal user.

- **Remember Me support**: Remember Me login is also supported by Spring Security by remembering the user's identity across multiple browser sessions.

Chapter 7, Spring Testing

Q1. What is the difference between JUnit4 and TestNG?

JUnit and TestNG, both are unit testing frameworks, which look very similar in functionality. Both provide functionalities such as annotation supports, exception test, timeout test, ignore test, and suite test. Whereas, a group test and dependency test is only supported by TestNG. TestNG has the ability to dynamically generate the test data for parameterized test, whereas JUnit cannot. The following is a list of few annotations supported by TestNG and JUnit4:

Feature	TestNG	JUnit4
Test annotation	@Test	@Test
Before the first test method in the current class	@BeforeClass	@BeforeClass
After all the test methods in the current class	@AfterClass	@AfterClass
Before each test method	@BeforeMethod	@Before
After each test method	@AfterMethod	@After
Before all tests in this suite run	@BeforeSuite	-
After all tests in this suite run	@AfterSuite	-
Run before the test	@BeforeTest	-
Run after the test	@AfterTest	-

Q2. What is the difference between unit testing and integration testing?

Unit testing, as the name suggests, is testing of every individual method of the code. It is the method of testing fundamental pieces of your functionality. It is a piece of code written by a software developer to test a specific functionality in the code. Unit tests are more about improving quality and preventing bugs, less about finding them, and are automated using testing frameworks.

Integration testing is the phase of software testing in which individual software modules are combined and tested as a group to ensure that required units are properly integrated and interacted with each other correctly. The purpose of integration testing is to verify functional, performance, and reliability of the code. The integration testing is used to test several units altogether.

Q3. Explain the Spring MVC test Framework.

Spring MVC test framework makes unit testing and integration testing of Spring MVC controller more meaningful by offering first class JUnit support. It helps in testing all aspects of controller method, which has not tested before. It allows us to perform testing in depth without starting a web container.

In order to perform a test of Spring MVC, the Spring `TestContext` framework, along with JUnit or TestNG, make it simple by providing annotation driven unit and integration testing support. The Spring `TestContext` framework can be used using `@RunWith`, `@WebAppConfiguration`, and `@ContextConfiguration` annotation to load Spring configuration, and inject the `WebApplicationContext` to the MockMvc for unit and integration test.

Q4. Explain `@ContextConfiguration` and `@WebAppConfiguration`.

The `@ContextConfiguration` annotation is used to set the `ApplicationContext` for test classes, by taking the actual configuration file with the file path. In the following code, we have given the file, so it will take relative path as the root package. We can also give the exact path by specifying the file: prefix. The `@ContextConfiguration` caches the `ApplicationContext` for us, and puts it in a static memory for the entire duration of the test or the test suite. The entire tests executes in the same JVM because of `ApplicationContext` stored in the static memory. If the second JVM is there, it will not have access to the static context, and will result in second `ApplicationContext` to be created.

The `@WebAppConfiguration` annotation is a class-level annotation used to create a web version of the application context in Spring. It is used to denote that the `ApplicationContext`, which is loaded for an integration test and used by that class, is an instance a `WebApplicationContext`. It is important to note that the `@WebAppConfiguration` annotation must be used together with `@ContextConfiguration`.

Q5. Explain MockMvc and `@RunWith(SpringJUnit4ClassRunner.class)`.

The MockMvc is a key part of Spring MVC Test framework, which can be used to write tests for applications developed using Spring MVC. It is the entry point for Spring MVC Testing. The MockMvc mock the entire Spring MVC infrastructure and is created by using the implementations of the `MockMvcBuilder` interface. In order to use Spring MVC testing, the first step is to create an instance of MockMvc.

The `@RunWith` annotation is a JUnit annotation. It executes the tests in a class annotated with the `@RunWith` annotation, or extends a class annotated with the `@RunWith` annotation by invoking the class passed as the parameter, which means that the tests in annotated class are not executed by the in-built API in the JUnit framework, the runner class used to execute the test case. In order to use Spring's JUnit class runner for running test cases within Spring's `ApplicationContext` environment passed Spring's `SpringJUnit4ClassRunner` class as a parameter.

Chapter 8, Integrating JavaMail and JMS with Spring

Q1. What is a JavaMail API?

A JavaMail API provides a protocol and platform independent framework to provide e-mail support for a Java application. The JavaMail API is a collection of classes and interfaces that comprise an e-mail system. These steps are involved in sending a simple email, using the JavaMail API. They are as follows:

1. Connect to a e-mail server by specifying the username and password, let's say an example; if you want to send an email from abc@xyz.com, then you need to connect to the e-mail server of xyz.com.

2. Create a message by specifying the recipient's addresses that can include Cc and Bcc addresses as well.

3. Add attachments to the message if any.

4. Transport the message to the e-mail server.

Q2. What is message and messaging?

Message is nothing but bytes of data or information, which are being exchanged between two parties. By taking different specifications; a message can be described in various ways. However, it is nothing but an entity of communication. A message can be used to transfer a piece of information from one application to another application, which may or may not run in the same platform.

Messaging is communication between different applications (in a distributed environment), or system components which are loosely coupled unlike its peers, like TCP sockets, **Remote Method Invocation (RMI)** or CORBA, which is tightly coupled. The advantage of Java messaging includes the ability to integrate different platforms, increase the scalability and reliability of message delivery and reduces the system bottlenecks. Using messaging, we can increase the systems and clients who are consuming and producing the message as much as we want.

Q3. What is JMS?

The JMS, that is, Java Message Service is a Java **Message Oriented Middleware (MOM)** API for sending messages between two or more clients. JMS is a part of Java Enterprise edition. JMS is a broker like a postman, who acts like a mediator between the message sender and receiver.

JMS is a specification that describes a common way for Java programs to create, send, and read distributed enterprise messages. It advocates the loosely coupled communication without caring about sender and receiver. It provides asynchronous messaging, that means it doesn't matter whether the sender and the receiver are present at the same time or not. The two systems that are sending or receiving messages need not be up at same time.

Chapter 9, Inversion of Control in Spring – Using Annotation

Q1. What are Stereotype annotations?

The `@Component` annotation which is a parent stereotype annotation can be used to define all beans. However, the Spring Framework supports different stereotype annotations to divide components by layer as listed here:

- `@Component`: It is a generic stereotype annotation, which defines a class as bean. It is required to import `org.springframework.stereotype`, in order to use this annotation.

- `@Repository`: Annotate all your repository classes with `@Repository` annotation, which is a marker for a class. A repository class serves in the persistence layer of the application as a **Data Access Objects (DAO)** that contains all your database access logic. It is required to import, `org.springframework.stereotype.Repository` to use `@Repository` annotation.

- @Service: Annotate all your service classes with @Service annotation, which contains all your business logic. It is required to import org. springframework.stereotype.Service, in order to use @Service.

- @Controller: The @Controller indicates that the annotated class is a Spring component of type "controller". It is a class-level annotation that indicates that an annotated class serves the role of a controller in Spring MVC. It is required to import org.springframework.stereotype. Controller, in order to use @Controller.

Q2. Explain different components of event handling.

Event handling is an important feature provided by ApplicationContext. Event handling consists of three core components as follows:

- ApplicationListener: This interface has to be implemented by a class that listens to an event. If any bean implements the ApplicationListener interface, then that bean is notified every time an ApplicationEvent gets published to the ApplicationContext.

- ApplicationEventPublisher: This interface has to be implemented by a class that publishes an event. Any bean can publish an event by calling an application event publisher's publishEvent() method.

- ApplicationEvent: This class is used when you are writing your own custom event, adding additional functionality, and additional metadata about the event.

Q3. What is Spring Expression Language (SpEL)?

In Spring, SpEL is a powerful expression language that supports the features to query and manipulate the object graph at runtime. SpEL can be used to dynamically evaluate property and use it as a value configured in IoC controller. SpEL supports operators such as mathematical operators, logical operators, and relational operators. SpEL also supports regular expressions using the matches operator.

SpEL provides dynamic bean wiring at runtime. SpEL picks the right bean or value to Dependency Inject at runtime. SpEL can also be used to inject a bean, or a bean property, or a bean method in another bean.

The features of SpEL are as follows:

- To reference beans using beans ID
- To inject methods and Properties on beans
- To perform mathematical, logical, and relational operations on values
- To match regular expression
- To manipulate collections

Chapter 10, Aspect-oriented Programming with Spring

Q1. What is **Aspect-oriented Programming (AOP)**?

AOP is a promising technology to separate crosscutting concerns, which is sometimes hard to perform in object-oriented programming, that is, OOP. AOP refers to the programming paradigm that isolates main business logic from other supporting functions. AOP in the Spring Framework provides declarative enterprise services. Here, in AOP, application objects perform the business logic and are not responsible for other system concerns such as, logging, auditing, locking, or an event handling. AOP is a methodology of applying middleware services such as security service, transaction management service, and so on Spring application.

Q2. What are concern, advice, aspect, join-point and point cut in Spring?

Concern refers to a part of system divided on the basis of the functionality. It can be either core or crosscutting. Core concern represents a specific functionality for primary requirements. Crosscutting concern is also known as system-wide concern; represent functionality for secondary requirement, such as logging, security, and so on.

- `Advice`: This represents code that is executed at joinpoint. It includes API invocation to the system-wide concern.

- `Aspect`: The combination of pointcut and advice is referred to as aspect, which is a cross-cutting functionality that should be included in the application.

- `Joinpoint`: This refers to a point in the execution flow of your application, such as class initialization, object instantiation, method invocation, field access, or throwing an exception. Aspect code can be inserted at joinpoint to add new behavior into your application. Crosscutting concern is automatically added before/after joinpoint by AOP.

- `Pointcut`: This represents a collection of joinpoint specifying where an advice needs to be applied.

Q3. What are the different types of advice?

There are different types of advices as follows:

- **Before advice**: This executes before joinpoint. Using it, we can execute the advisor code before the method is invoked.

- **After-returning advice**: This is used to apply advice after the method successfully finishes its execution.

- **Throws advice**: This can be applied when a method throws an exception during its execution.
- **After (finally) advice**: As the name suggests, this advice gets executed after the join point method execution got finished, either normally, or by throwing some exceptions.
- **Around Advice**: This can be applied before and after the method execution.

Q4. What is weaving in Spring?

Weaving is the process of inserting aspects to the application at the appropriate point. The weaving can take place at different stages in the target class's lifetime:

- **Compile time**: To inject the byte code of the advice at the joint point during the compile time is called as compile time weaving.
- **Classload time**: Classload time is injecting the byte code at the class loading time. During this, the byte code will be injected to the loaded class to have the advice code at the joint point.
- **Runtime – Spring way**: The target object will be shielded with the Proxy bean, which is created by the Spring Framework. Whenever the caller calls the method on the target bean, the Spring Framework invokes the proxy and applies advices to target method. Once the method execution is over, again Spring apply advices to the target method if required, and the response will return back to caller.

Spring uses this kind of weaving. Runtime weaving is an effective way as it keeps the code clean.

B

Setting up the Application Database – Apache Derby

To set up some kind of database running on your development environment, we use Apache Derby database. Apache Derby is a light weight in memory database, which is easy to setup and takes less resources, and is also perfect for testing out new concepts and trying out things that we are doing right now.

To download Apache Derby, hit over the Apache Derby website at `http://db.apache.org/derby/derby_downloads.html`, and download the latest release. Once the downloaded ZIP file is extracted, we will have some important folder named `bin` and `lib` folder as shown:

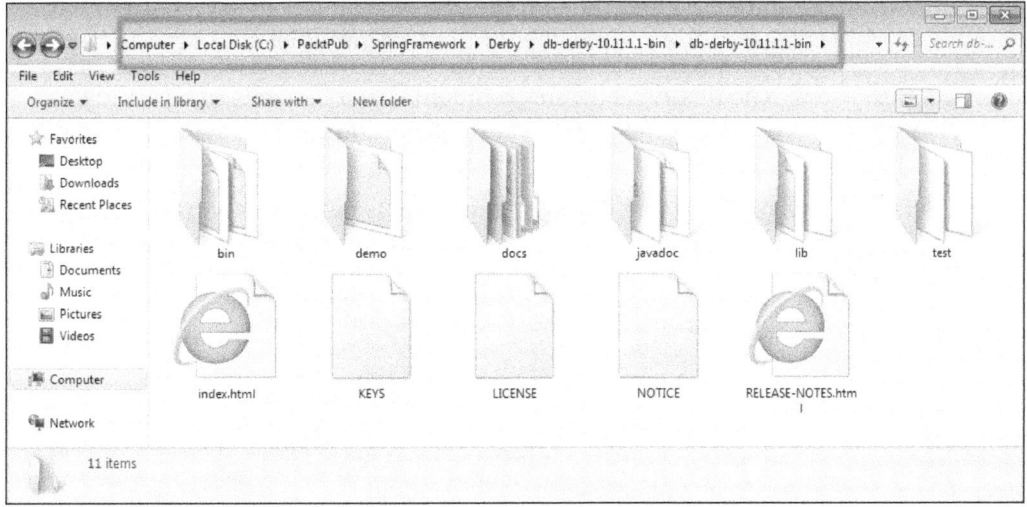

The lib folder contains the jar that needs to be included in our program when we connect to the Derby database. The bin contains programs like startNetworkServer.bat and stopNetworkServer.bat for database as follows:

```
C:\PacktPub\SpringFramework\Chapter-5\Derby\db-derby-10.11.1.1-bin\db-derby-10.1
1.1.1-bin\bin>dir
 Volume in drive C is Local Disk
 Volume Serial Number is 9265-383D

 Directory of C:\PacktPub\SpringFramework\Chapter-5\Derby\db-derby-10.11.1.1-bin
\db-derby-10.11.1.1-bin\bin

16/09/2014  07:37 PM    <DIR>          .
16/09/2014  07:37 PM    <DIR>          ..
16/09/2014  07:37 PM             5,740 dblook
16/09/2014  07:37 PM             1,387 dblook.bat
16/09/2014  07:37 PM             2,426 derby_common.bat
16/09/2014  07:37 PM             5,876 ij
16/09/2014  07:37 PM             1,379 ij.bat
16/09/2014  07:37 PM             5,801 NetworkServerControl
16/09/2014  07:37 PM             1,413 NetworkServerControl.bat
16/09/2014  07:37 PM             1,073 setEmbeddedCP
16/09/2014  07:37 PM             1,278 setEmbeddedCP.bat
16/09/2014  07:37 PM             1,079 setNetworkClientCP
16/09/2014  07:37 PM             1,284 setNetworkClientCP.bat
16/09/2014  07:37 PM             1,075 setNetworkServerCP
16/09/2014  07:37 PM             1,273 setNetworkServerCP.bat
16/09/2014  07:37 PM             5,807 startNetworkServer
16/09/2014  07:37 PM             1,397 startNetworkServer.bat
16/09/2014  07:37 PM             5,810 stopNetworkServer
16/09/2014  07:37 PM             1,403 stopNetworkServer.bat
16/09/2014  07:37 PM             5,789 sysinfo
16/09/2014  07:37 PM             1,389 sysinfo.bat
              19 File(s)         52,679 bytes
```

After downloading and extracting the JAR file, the next step is to set environment variable. Derby recommends a couple of environment variables that need to be set.

- DERBY_HOME: The DERBY_HOME environment variable needs to be set to the location where we have extracted our distribution containing the bin and lib folder.

- Path: The second variable that we need to set is path environment variable. We need to set DERBY_HOME/bin to path environment variable:

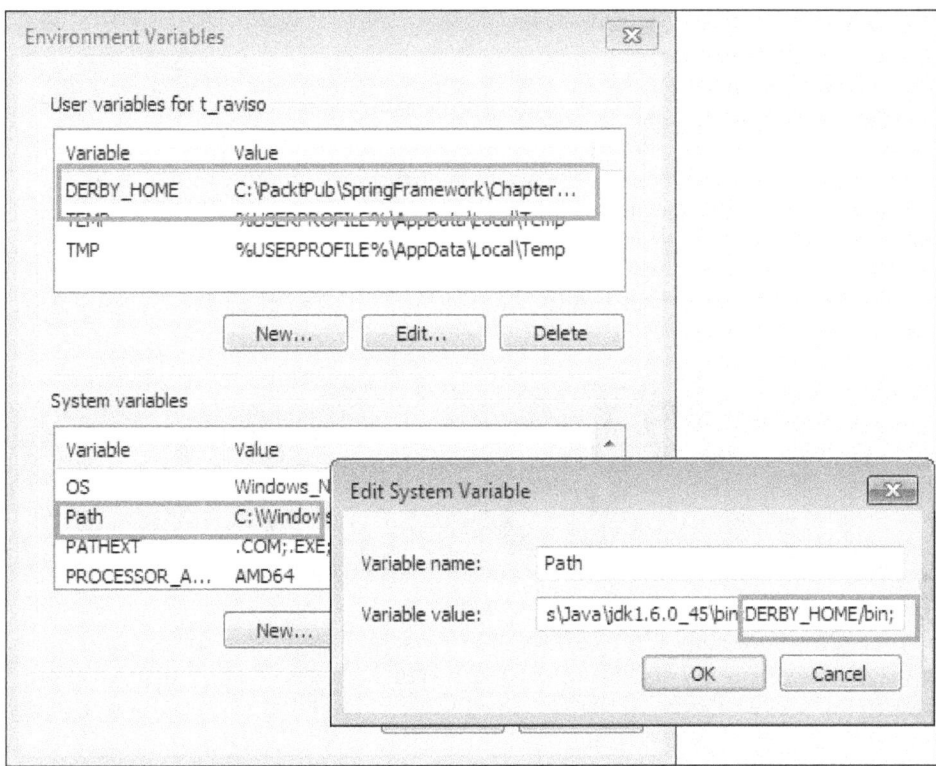

Now, open a command prompt, and hit over to location where we have Apache Derby as follows:

```
C:\Windows\system32\cmd.exe
Microsoft Windows [Version 6.1.7601]
Copyright (c) 2009 Microsoft Corporation.  All rights reserved.

C:\Users\t_raviso>cd c:\PacktPub\SpringFramework\Chapter-5\Derby\db-derby-10.11.
1.1-bin\db-derby-10.11.1.1-bin

c:\PacktPub\SpringFramework\Chapter-5\Derby\db-derby-10.11.1.1-bin\db-derby-10.1
1.1.1-bin>_
```

Here in the preceding screenshot, we have changed the directory to the `bin` directory in Apache Derby, which contains batch files and script files. For Windows OS, we need these batch files while running.

Apache Derby operates in two modes:

- The Network-Server mode
- The Embedded mode

First, we need to start derby as Network Server mode which is similar to all the databases on one machine, and the other machine on the network that can connect to it. Embedded mode is something specific to derby.

To start derby Network Server mode, we need to run `startNetworkServer.bat` as follows:

```
C:\Windows\system32\cmd.exe - startNetworkServer.bat

C:\PacktPub\SpringFramework\Chapter-5\Derby\db-derby-10.11.1.1-bin\db-derby-10.1
1.1.1-bin\bin>startNetworkServer.bat
Tue Sep 16 19:50:53 IST 2014 : Security manager installed using the Basic server
 security policy.
Tue Sep 16 19:50:53 IST 2014 : Apache Derby Network Server - 10.11.1.1 - (161654
6) started and ready to accept connections on port 1527
```

In the preceding screenshot, we can see that Apache Derby Network-Server started and ready to accept connection on port `1527`, which we can test by using a client to connect to the server. Derby actually comes with a client called `ij.bat`, which can be used to connect to the server to execute queries.

So, we need to have a second command line prompt, which hits same `bin` directory, and run `ij.bat` to client, and executes the query to connect to the server `connect jdbc:derby://localhost:1527/db;create=true';` as follows:

```
C:\Windows\system32\cmd.exe - ij.bat

Microsoft Windows [Version 6.1.7601]
Copyright (c) 2009 Microsoft Corporation.  All rights reserved.

C:\Users\t_raviso>cd c:\PacktPub\SpringFramework\Chapter-5\Derby\db-derby-10.11.
1.1-bin\db-derby-10.11.1.1-bin\bin

c:\PacktPub\SpringFramework\Chapter-5\Derby\db-derby-10.11.1.1-bin\db-derby-10.1
1.1.1-bin\bin>ij.bat
ij version 10.11
ij> connect 'jdbc:derby://localhost:1527/db;create=true';
ij>
```

We can create a table using create query for table employee (as shown in the following screenshot with two column as ID and NAME), and insert values using insert query, and also print data to console using select query, as follows:

```
ij> create table employee (id integer, name char(30));
0 rows inserted/updated/deleted
ij> insert into employee values (03, 'Ravi');
1 row inserted/updated/deleted
ij> select * from employee
> ;
ID          |NAME
------------------------------------------------
3           |Ravi

1 row selected
ij>
```

Index

Symbols

Spring MVC form 238
View page 236
front controller design pattern 170, 171

G

Google Web Toolkit (GWT) 167

H

Hibernate
about 87, 127
architecture 128
integrating, with Spring Framework 131
Spring MVC, integrating with 204
references 132, 135
Hibernate architecture
configuration 129
elements 338
org.hibernate.Criteria interface 130
org.hibernate.Query interface 130
Persistent objects 130
SessionFactory 129
Session interface 130
Transaction interface 130
Hibernate Criteria Query Language (HCQL)
about 157
Criteria interface 157
Hibernate, integrating with Spring Framework
about 131
annotated domain model class 138-141
application, directory structure 146
application, running 146
Hibernate SessionFactory, configuring 134, 135
JARs requisites 133
persistence layer 142
sample data model 131, 132
service layer 144
Session interface 141
steps 132
Hibernate Query Language (HQL)
about 127, 150, 338
Query interface 150
used, for performing database operation 150

Hibernate SessionFactory configuration
about 134
hibernate.dialect property 135
hibernate.jdbc.fetch_size property 135
hibernate.max_fetch_depth property 135
hibernate.properties 137
hibernate.show_sql property 135
XML Spring configuration 135-137
Hyper Text Transfer Protocol (HTTP) 170

I

iBATIS 87
initialization callbacks, Spring bean lifecycle
about 80
init-method, using in XML configuration 82
org.springframework.beans.factory.
InitializingBean interface,
implementing 81, 82
integration testing 297-299, 342
internationalization (i18n), Spring MVC
application, running 231, 232
configuration 229
hello.jsp page 231
LocaleChangeInterceptor 230
properties file 229
ReloadableResourceBundleMessage
Source 229
SessionLocaleResolver 230
using 229
Inversion of Control (IoC)
about 32, 33, 87, 142, 189, 334
container 33
issues 32
Spring Container 34

J

JAR files
URL 17
Java Database Connectivity (JDBC)
about 90, 128
APIs 90
JavaMail API
about 343
Spring API 316, 317

used, for sending e-mail 312, 343
using 314-316
Java Message Oriented Middleware (MOM) 13, 321
Java Naming and Directory Interface (JNDI) 128
Java Persistence API (JPA) 127
Java Server Faces (JSF) 167
Java Server Pages (JSP) 167, 201, 340
Java Transaction API (JTA) 128
JDBC batch operation
about 113, 114
directory structure 115
JDBC module 13
JdbcTemplate class
about 105, 106
used, for querying database 108, 109
JdbcTemplateExample application
directory structure 110
JdbcTemplate object
configuring, as Spring bean 106
Spring.xml file 107
JDBC, without Spring
about 90, 91
JdbcHrPayrollSystem 91
JDBC, with Spring
about 99
DataSource 100, 101
DataSource, in DAO class 101
JMS
about 13, 322, 344
application 322
JMS components
JMS application 323
JMS client 323
JMS consumer/subscriber 323
JMS producer/publisher 323
JMS provider 322
JPA annotation
@Column 139
@Entity 138
@GeneratedValue 139
@Id 138
@Table 138
JUnit
URL 280

JUnit 4
annotations 280
differentiating, with TestNG 341, 342
examples 282
used, for testing 280

L

life cycle, Spring bean
about 78
activation 80
destruction 80
destruction callbacks 83
initialization 79
initialization callbacks 80

M

major operations, Spring Security
about 246
authentication 246
authorization 246, 247
message 343
Message Oriented Middleware (MOM) 344
method-level security 264
method parameters, @RequestMapping annotation
@ModelAttribute 200
@PathVariable 199
@RequestBody 200
@RequestHeader 200
@RequestParam 200, 201
Errors/BindingResult 200
HttpSession 199
java.util.Local 199
Map 200
Model 200
ModelMap 200
ServletRequest/HttpServletRequest 199
Session Status 200
Mockito framework
about 294-297
field-level annotations 294
URL 294
MockMvc
about 304, 305, 343
assertion, performing 305

Thank you for buying
Learning Spring Application Development

About Packt Publishing

Packt, pronounced 'packed', published its first book, *Mastering phpMyAdmin for Effective MySQL Management*, in April 2004, and subsequently continued to specialize in publishing highly focused books on specific technologies and solutions.

Our books and publications share the experiences of your fellow IT professionals in adapting and customizing today's systems, applications, and frameworks. Our solution-based books give you the knowledge and power to customize the software and technologies you're using to get the job done. Packt books are more specific and less general than the IT books you have seen in the past. Our unique business model allows us to bring you more focused information, giving you more of what you need to know, and less of what you don't.

Packt is a modern yet unique publishing company that focuses on producing quality, cutting-edge books for communities of developers, administrators, and newbies alike. For more information, please visit our website at www.packtpub.com.

About Packt Open Source

In 2010, Packt launched two new brands, Packt Open Source and Packt Enterprise, in order to continue its focus on specialization. This book is part of the Packt Open Source brand, home to books published on software built around open source licenses, and offering information to anybody from advanced developers to budding web designers. The Open Source brand also runs Packt's Open Source Royalty Scheme, by which Packt gives a royalty to each open source project about whose software a book is sold.

Writing for Packt

We welcome all inquiries from people who are interested in authoring. Book proposals should be sent to author@packtpub.com. If your book idea is still at an early stage and you would like to discuss it first before writing a formal book proposal, then please contact us; one of our commissioning editors will get in touch with you.

We're not just looking for published authors; if you have strong technical skills but no writing experience, our experienced editors can help you develop a writing career, or simply get some additional reward for your expertise.

Spring MVC Beginner's Guide

ISBN: 978-1-78328-487-0   Paperback: 304 pages

Your ultimate guide to building a complete web application using all the capabilities of Spring MVC

1. Carefully crafted exercises, with detailed explanations for each step, to help you understand the concepts with ease.

2. You will gain a clear understanding of the end to end request/response life cycle, and each logical component's responsibility.

3. Packed with tips and tricks that will demonstrate the industry best practices on developing a Spring-MVC-based application.

Web Application Development with Yii 2 and PHP

ISBN: 978-1-78398-188-5   Paperback: 406 pages

Fast-track your web application development using the new generation Yii PHP framework

1. Implement real-world web application features efficiently using the Yii development framework.

2. Each chapter provides micro-examples that build upon each other to create the final macro-example, a basic CRM application.

3. Filled with useful tasks to improve the maintainability of your applications.

Please check **www.PacktPub.com** for information on our titles

open source
community experience distilled

Mockito for Spring

ISBN: 978-1-78398-378-0   Paperback: 178 pages

Learn all you need to know about the Spring Framework and how to unit test your projects with Mockito

1. Learn about the Spring testing framework, stubbing, mocking, and spying dependencies using the Mockito framework and explore its advanced features.

2. Create an automated JUnit safety net for building a reliable, maintainable, and testable software.

3. Step-by-step tutorial stuffed with real-world examples.

Spring Security [Video]

ISBN: 978-1-78216-865-2   Duration: 02:10 hours

An empirical approach to securing your web applications

1. Fully secure your web application with Spring Security.

2. Implement authentication and registration with the database as well as with LDAP.

3. Utilize authorization examples that help guide you through the authentication of users step-by-step.

Please check **www.PacktPub.com** for information on our titles

CPSIA information can be obtained
at www.ICGtesting.com
Printed in the USA
LVHW102019260721
693753LV00004B/16